DO-IT-YOURSELF DIRECT MARKETING

Secrets for Small Business

Mark S. Bacon

JOHN WILEY & SONS, INC.

New York / Chichester / Brisbane / Toronto / Singapore

This text is printed on acid-free paper.

Library of Congress Cataloging in Publication Data

Bacon, Mark S.
    Do-it-yourself direct marketing : secrets for small business / Mark S. Bacon.
      p. cm.
    Includes index.
    ISBN 0-471-53241-X (cloth) ISBN 0-471-00876-1 (paper)
    1. Direct marketing.   2. Small business.   I. Title.
HF5415.126.B33   1992
    658.8'4—dc20   91-13820

Printed in the United States of America

10 9 8 7 6 5 4 3 2

CONTENTS

• •

ACKNOWLEDGMENTS

· ·

The steady assistance of two friends was particularly valuable and helpful in the creation of this book. New Mexico copywriter Jane Gorby edited each chapter as I wrote it. She not only helped to make this more readable, but she contributed many direct marketing ideas. Mark Charlet, marketing manager for Griswold Controls, also reviewed my progress, made suggestions along the way, and cautioned me to explain all my jargon. Mark is in part responsible for this book's hands-on, step-by-step approach.

Adman Don Markofski taught me many of the design principles I've used over the years and now take for granted. His advice was invaluable in planning and writing the chapters on graphic design and print production.

My support team at John Wiley and Sons was headed by Associate Publisher Karl Weber. He was enthusiastic about the project from the beginning, and he made important suggestions as we went along. Editor Neal Maillet guided this project from manuscript to the book you're holding and helped me fill in gaps here and there. Linda Indig and Jacob Conrad also helped in the production stages of this project.

Dozens of professionals in the advertising and direct marketing business helped with this book, and I want to thank everyone who answered questions for me, provided an ad or mailer I could use, faxed me the name of a source, or contributed in some other way. Thanks to Pamela Mora, Ascent Marketing, for her expert help with list strategies and testing. In addition, I want to thank Tim Moroney, HDM Worldwide Direct; Linda Tamburo, Galusha and Associates; Howard Oberstein, The Marketing Place; Jeff Goldberg, R.L. Polk & Co. Inc.; Haley Chernoff, Response Communications, Inc.; Julie Marquardt, Carnegie Marketing Associates; Craig Walker and Nancy Zimmerman, Krupp/Taylor; David Stachovitz, Bruce McClure, and Lucille Lowe, United States Postal Service; Stacey Griffin, Greg Smith and Partners; Kim Stevens, The Blue Chip Marketing Group; and Nancy Fredsall, Cristal Radio.

Special recognition is also due the behind-the-scenes people at Publication Services, including production coordinator Greg Martel. Many thanks to editors Jerome Colburn and Al Davis, who provided grammatical changes that otherwise might not have been made.

Finally, thanks to my wife Anne for her love, friendship, and encouragement.

—M.S.B.

FOREWORD

• •

You may wonder why the foreword to a book intended specifically for small businesses is being written by an executive of a large, far-reaching organization as MasterCard International, Inc. The logic is simple: MasterCard was not always a large organization.

Direct marketing strategies and the use of direct mail played pivotal roles in MasterCard's tremendous growth. When MasterCard entered the financial scene in 1966, interbank cards were a relatively new concept and had to be promoted not only to issuing financial institutions and consumers but to merchants as well.

In one way or another, MasterCard has built its business with the principles of direct marketing covered in this book, from targeting markets and managing lists through the creative process and maintaining customer satisfaction. As MasterCard grew in popularity and acceptance, for example, so did the importance of maintaining accurate data bases. Today, with more than 160 million cardholders and nine million merchants worldwide, MasterCard processes more than a million transactions each day. Imagine keeping track of data on all these customers and merchants without a well-maintained data base.

Thousands of financial institutions use direct marketing to promote MasterCard throughout the world. The MasterCard in your wallet right now probably got there as a result of direct marketing. In addition, MasterCard plays a significant role in mail order by providing millions of customers a convenient way to pay for the products and services they buy.

I don't promise that, if you follow all the advice set forth in this book, your business is guaranteed to be as large and successful as MasterCard. But you definitely will have at your disposal the same fundamental marketing strategies and direct mail secrets employed not just by MasterCard, but by hundreds of major corporations today.

Direct marketing dynamics are suitable for a mega-bucks corporation, a mini-money mom-and-pop shop, and every budget in between. The objectives are the same: You want your advertising to trigger immediate, direct responses—either orders or requests for information. This is advertising you can measure, advertising you can count on. Direct marketing gets results.

Piece of cake, you say! All you have to do is establish an offer, identify your audience, and communicate in language that will persuade people to buy. But how do you do it? Do you use selective mailings, blanket your neighborhood, or buy ads? What's the best format? What makes some direct mail exceedingly successful while other mail advertising is routinely tossed in the wastebasket?

Do-It-Yourself Direct Marketing shows the way. The book assumes nothing and explains everything; it's easy to read and use. Each chapter explains terminology and builds on the foundation of previous chapters. Mixing numerous actual small business examples and samples of national direct response advertising you'll recognize, *Do-It-Yourself Direct Marketing* shows you how to put big-company ideas to work on a limited budget. An uncertain economy and rising postal rates make this book particularly timely.

The focus of the book is unique in that it speaks directly to you, a small business owner or manager who may or may not have any previous experience in direct marketing, and addresses every step of waging a successful direct marketing campaign. Not only do you have in one book information it would take you weeks to researching to uncover—if you could find it at all—but you also have a guide to economical, as well as effective, direct marketing.

There's another reason for my writing this foreword: I've known Mark Bacon for years and have seen the results of his work. In this book you can see the creative energy he uses when he tackles a project, whether it's a challenging marketing assignment or a book. He shares this energy with you, showing you how to release your own creativity to develop the advertising strategies and ideas you need to make your business profitable. He shows you how to use the psychological keys to persuasion when you write your advertising, and he carefully explains how to use words to reach your customers with just the right message.

Direct marketing requires bringing together a number of different disciplines to build successful campaigns, and Mark has the experience to show you how to make it all work. He even includes a chapter filled with production checklists so that you won't miss a thing.

Mark has written a practical book that focuses on the real-life marketing challenges of small business people...and he has done it with an uncluttered writing style that keeps you focused on the direct marketing techniques that will make money for you.

You can put this information into practice immediately. So what are you waiting for?

I wish you much success with your next and all succeeding direct marketing campaigns.

Heidi Goff
Senior Vice President
MasterCard International
New York, NY

INTRODUCTION
•
Murky Myths of Direct Marketing

Direct marketing is made for your small business. In the pages that follow you'll learn how direct marketing and its most popular expression, direct mail, provide a small organization with a multiplicity of advantages and opportunities. Direct mail is the workhorse of advertising. It can effectively accomplish several objectives, some at the same time.

This book is a do-it-yourself guide to direct marketing; it starts at the beginning and takes you step-by-step from direct marketing philosophy to implementing and evaluating campaigns. You don't need any prior knowledge of direct marketing; terms and concepts are explained along the way. This book provides you with the background and the basics you need to do it all yourself or to work with selected outside specialists.

Saving money is a theme throughout. You'll learn how to use cost-saving production techniques, how to save money at the post office, and how to get the most from each ad and mailing.

WHO THIS IS DESIGNED FOR

Do-It-Yourself Direct Marketing is not a mere primer, but a handbook designed specifically for owners and marketing managers of small businesses, self-employed business persons and professionals, and others in small organizations.

Whether you refer to the people you serve as customers, clients, members, patients, or something else, this book will show you how to reach them via direct marketing. This book is written for small business people who:

- Are planning to start a business or practice and want to know how to promote it by direct marketing;
- Have done some marketing or advertising, possibly some direct marketing, but need a guide to getting organized and getting maximum, professional results;
- Are managers who need to know something about direct marketing, even though someone else in the company will be primarily responsible for marketing;
- Have never done any direct marketing but want to get started right away.

I've been involved in direct marketing for more than a dozen years, and my advertising experience goes back to the mid-1970s. I've been both an in-house and an ad agency copywriter, and I was marketing director for Orange

County Federal, a large credit union in southern California. Several years ago I started my own business, which includes communications training and conducting direct marketing programs for financial institutions and other clients. Many of the examples in this book are drawn from my experiences, but I've also drawn on the experience of experts in specific areas of direct marketing to make this book as complete and up-to-date as possible. I make liberal use of real-life examples to explain each technique and idea.

One of the keys to success for small businesses today is that they can act swiftly to take advantage of changing conditions and consumer trends. They can often move more quickly than their giant competitors. This book shows you how to use direct mail, and other direct marketing techniques, to establish a new business quickly or revitalize the marketing of an established organization.

Direct marketing continues to be one of the fastest-growing segments of advertising. You need only look in your mailbox at home or your "in" basket at work to see that more and more small business people are venturing into direct mail and direct marketing. Unfortunately, much direct response advertising by small business is ineffective and wasteful. From one-third to one-half of all small business direct mail is seriously flawed. Many small enterprises, lacking the direct marketing basics, seem to mail indiscriminately, often with disappointing results.

Direct marketing contains contradictions. It combines simple concepts with complex execution. Despite its remarkable advantages and multi-billion-dollar successes, direct marketing is often misunderstood. Myths are common. These persistent myths can influence marketing decisions at companies large and small, making direct marketing seem inappropriate.

To take advantage of the many possibilities that direct marketing holds for your small business, you should approach it with an open mind and be aware of its scope, functions, and advantages, as well as its limitations. Let's review a few of the common misunderstandings about direct marketing and see the corresponding realities.

Myth 1. Direct mail is junk mail. It's surprising that people object to receiving direct mail (DM), even in its trashier forms. It's not as intrusive as a phone call, or even a TV commercial. If the marketer hasn't tempted you to read it, all you have to do is throw it away.

In spite of its uneven image, only a few people publicly complain about receiving direct mail, and I wonder how the average DM opponent would face a mailbox that had become a receptacle solely for bills, paid-subscription publications, and the rare personal letter. Believe it or not, the majority of direct mail is at least opened and scanned. The more precisely mail is targeted, the more people will open it. Some direct mail gets opened by 90 percent of its recipients.

Another negative connotation of direct marketing or perhaps mail-order selling can best be described by the word *schlock*, the Yiddish term meaning meaning cheap or of low quality. If you think *schlock* is a synonym for direct marketing, you're in need of a serious attitude adjustment before you embark on a marketing campaign. Remember, there are good companies and poor companies in every business. Direct marketing is no different. Many firms closely identified with direct marketing, however, are the antithesis of schlock. Mail order clothing merchants such as Land's End and L.L. Bean, for example, have some of the most loyal customers anywhere because they provide value and service unmatched by many retail stores.

One of the main causes of direct mail's junk reputation is poor targeting. If you receive mail offering you a product that you have no interest in or use for, that's junk. If you're a handyman and you get a tool catalog in the mail, that's *not* junk, but something valuable you may spend half an hour or more reading.

Myth 2. ***Direct mail is good only for mass marketers and mail-order firms.*** Sales and marketing executives, influenced by the number of mailings they see for magazine subscriptions and mail-order firms, may conclude that direct marketing is unsuited for their business. This attitude may be reinforced by an unproductive attempt at direct mail. If your organization has had an unsuccessful experience with DM, you may be doubly skeptical. Erroneous reasons for not using direct marketing include:

"We're not in the mail-order business."

"We tried it and it didn't work."

"We don't need direct marketing because we have an outside sales force."

"Direct marketing doesn't work in our business."

One form of this myth is that direct mail may be suitable for many industries, but not yours.

Mail order is only one purpose for direct marketing. Many firms spend millions on direct mail/marketing and rarely sell anything through the mail. Chapters 1 and 2 introduce you to the many purposes and capabilities of direct marketing.

Myth 3. ***Direct marketing is not appropriate for big-ticket items.*** Although it's a challenge to sell an expensive item strictly by mail order, direct marketing can play an important part in generating leads and in supporting the efforts of salespeople. Direct marketing has been used to help sell diamond jewelry, sports cars, expensive travel, real estate, yachts, antiques and collectibles, mutual funds, and just about every other product you can think of. With a little creativity it can take on the challenge to sell just about anything.

Myth 4. ***It's unsuitable for professionals or business consultants.*** Some people think that advertising itself is unseemly and that professionals such as accountants, dentists, chiropractors, consultants, and others who use the medium are unprofessional. If you have any doubts at all about the appropriateness of advertising in your profession, try direct mail. Not only can you target your potential clients/patients accurately, you have complete control over your message and its context.

Through your message and the design of your mailing, you can build in all the quality and professionalism you think is necessary. You can design a multicolor brochure listing all your services, or you can choose a personal letter on heavy, watermarked paper with engraved letterhead. In short, you have complete control over your image.

Myth 5. Response rates are low. I once conducted a campaign for a small organization that generated better than a 15 percent response. Considering the objectives of the mailing, the response was exceptionally high. Rather than being pleased, however, the company's general manager wanted to know what happened to the 85 percent who didn't respond.

Expected reply rates are probably responsible for more direct mail misconceptions than any other aspect of the business. People who might recognize 15 percent as being a good reponse might also say that a 1 percent response rate is the industry average. In fact, there is no such thing as an average DM response rate; there can't be. Differences are so great among products and services advertised through direct mail that no single average could apply. In general, compared to many other forms of advertising, direct mail response rates are much higher. Chapter 2 explores the factors that contribute to response rates.

Ultimately, whether you call a 1 percent—or a 15 percent—response high or low is unimportant. The sole benchmark of your success should be your profits. If direct marketing is profitable for you, your response rate compared to a mythical industry average is meaningless.

Myth 6. Direct marketing has no part in retailing. Is this myth prevalent because so few retailers take advantage of the valuable opportunities direct mail and direct marketing offer them, or do so few retailers use direct marketing because they believe the myth? Perhaps the term *direct mail* makes retailers think only of the competition they receive from mail order companies and not the possibilities open to them.

When was the last time you got a letter from your favorite retailer telling you the store was having a sale on the particular type of merchandise you have bought before? You have probably never received such a letter, but if you had, would you have responded?

Far from being unsuitable for retailing, direct marketing can be an exceptionally effective tool. By collecting data on your customers and segmenting them according to various criteria, you can design special sales events and mail promotions geared specifically to customers' buying habits and needs.

Myth 7. Let's send out a catalog sheet to a hundred people and see what happens. You're not convinced direct mail is the way, but you're willing to give it a try. You'll send out a hundred or so pieces and see what happens.

There's nothing like a half-hearted, unplanned direct mail effort to convince a skeptic that DM doesn't work. Even though direct mail is more flexible than any other medium, you can't just throw a catalog sheet in an envelope, send it off to a hundred names culled from somewhere, and expect an avalanche of new business. DM is based on percentages and on carefully constructed and targeted messages. Many good DM advertisements might not generate a single response if mailed to only 100 potential customers. If you hope for a two, three, or five percent response, the first 100 mailers might not yield a single reply, but the *next* 100 names might generate 10 responses. As your mailing quantity increases, there is a better chance that the percentages will even out.

Just because you *can* mail anything doesn't mean you should. Catalog sheets are written to give product specifications. Direct mail materials need to be written and designed as direct mail from the ground up. In addition, people respond in different ways to ads in a newspaper than they do to a message inside an envelope addressed specifically to them.

As you can see, direct marketing is a unique and complex form of communication. It's related to traditional advertising, yet it breaks some of the rules. These diverse characteristics can make direct marketing an enigma, but its idiosyncrasies also make it work.

When small business people approach direct marketing for the first time, they are sometimes skeptical. That skepticism quickly turns to interest (and sometimes to greed!) when they see what direct marketing can do for them. *Do-It-Yourself Direct Marketing* is your guide to this powerful form of marketing.

1 WHAT IS DIRECT MARKETING?

Billion Dollar Secrets for Small Business

What would be the ideal way to market your product or service? Imagine for a moment that you have an advertising budget as big as GM's. You can do anything you like.

Where would you start? First, you'd probably want to identify your top prospects and existing customers. While you were at it, you'd probably want to add some other people who would be likely to want your product or service.

In this ideal situation, you would want to meet with all these people individually. To prepare for your meetings, you would want to create the sales presentation of your life. Or, if you're not the sales/marketing expert in your organization, you'd want your top salesperson or most persuasive employee to handle the message. Perhaps you'd hire someone special.

Of course, no ideal sales presentation would be complete without asking for the order as convincingly as possible, giving customers the chance to buy your product or service at that golden moment when they are most interested in you.

Sound like an ideal way to make your business flourish? It is, and it doesn't take a General Motors–size budget to do it, either. This hypothetical example contains the basic ingredients and principles of direct marketing, principles that anyone can master and use, even on a small budget. The concept is simple: Identify your customers and best potential customers, and reach them with a personal message that (1) shows the benefits of doing business with you and (2) shows them how to respond.

In its simplest form, direct marketing is marketing that seeks an immediate response. That response may be to place an order, ask for more information, send in an application, make a phone call, or visit a store or office. Through the response, a person is identified to the marketer as a customer or potential customer who should be contacted again. As a result of this focus—almost an obsession—on generating action, direct marketing is also called *direct response*. Direct marketing executive, innovator, and author Bob Stone says, "Underlying all direct marketing success is the ability to trigger a direct action, a measurable action, at the right cost."[1]

Measurement is another key difference between conventional advertising or marketing and direct marketing. Conventional advertising wants to make a favorable impression on customers so that when they are about to make a buying decision they will remember a particular product or service. The effectiveness of this image advertising is difficult to measure. Often, large advertisers don't know whether credit for increased sales belongs to their television or radio commercials, their billboards, their ads in magazines and newspapers, or some other factor. Advertisers can determine how many people *see* their messages in the various media, but the link between advertising and sales is not as strong as it is in direct marketing.

As an example, if your direct mail goal is to get potential customers to call your 800 number to ask for more information about a new service, you simply count the number of calls (or sales that follow) to determine your success. Of course, direct response messages, like conventional advertising, can have cumulative effects that may contribute to later sales, but the main emphasis is on immediate and more easily measurable responses. With measurability come opportunities to modify your plans to capitalize quickly on your successes and eliminate spending that does not yield results.

DEFINING DIRECT MARKETING

Direct marketing is accountable. It's advertising you can justify and track. It's ideally suited for small business. Not only is direct marketing measurable, but it can be adapted to fit your budget and your changing business goals. Originally direct marketing referred to a direct sale, as in mail order, but today it's used to accomplish many marketing goals. It can be used by retailers to add a separate mail-order profit center, for example, or its many variations can be used to support a diversity of marketing and promotional activities such as increasing traffic or inquiries. It also can be used to change the way customers use your services. For example, you could use direct mail to encourage customers to make phone orders in order to alleviate crowding in your store or vice versa.

Further, direct marketing is efficient. Rather than showcasing its message for the whole world, such as on a billboard, much direct marketing aims at small target groups made up of the most likely or most interested customers.

Let's define direct marketing rather broadly, then, to include not only all the activities that generate responses, but also the fulfillment, customer service, and subsequent selling that follow. This follow-up is an essential element of direct marketing (specifically *data base* marketing) and one on which we'll spend considerable time. Fulfilling orders or providing requested services promptly, maintaining good customer relations, and selling the same customers again and again will determine your margin of success. Learning the skills to generate initial responses is just the first half of direct marketing.

Direct mail and **direct marketing** are sometimes mistakenly used interchangeably. Direct marketing may take many forms and use most media; it is not limited to the mail although mail is the most popular medium. We'll concentrate on how to use direct mail, but I'll also show ways to use the other forms of direct marketing.

Direct marketing encompasses organization, planning, pricing, strategy, list selection and purchasing, and many other details, as well as the work of creating the advertising. The terms **direct marketing** and **direct response** are somewhat synonymous, and I use them interchangeably. Since the term **direct mail** is used more frequently than others, it's abbreviated **DM**.

Direct marketing gives you many options beyond sending self-contained mailers, and it includes most, if not all, advertising media.

Magazines and newspapers can often be effective media for direct marketing. You can distinguish a direct response ad from a general image ad in a magazine in several ways; one way is to look for a coupon or the prominent use of an 800 telephone number. Direct response ads solicit direct results, just like direct mail. You can't have a coupon on a television or radio commercial, but 800 or 900 phone numbers make electronic media effective for direct response too. Television and radio are usually thought to be out of reach for small business, but we'll explore some possibilities.

Telemarketing has been called the medium marketers love to hate, but it's effective and widely used. Its one-on-one communication gives it immediacy but also makes it expensive. The trade term for the type of telephone sales calls you're probably familiar with is *outbound* telemarketing. The way companies respond to incoming calls from customers and potential customers is also an important form of telemarketing, called *inbound* telemarketing.

Free-standing inserts (FSIs) are another direct response medium you may be familiar with. These are printed flyers, booklets, or brochures that are inserted or nested loosely into newspapers and magazines. Sunday papers are often thick with FSIs. Advertisers can also choose **package inserts,** which are direct response ads in various formats inserted into packages sent to mail-order buyers. For example, customers who receive merchandise from a catalog company may find several direct response inserts from other companies in the package. Another form of direct marketing is created when advertisers share the cost of a mailing and include offers for their respective products in one envelope or other carrier. This is called a *co-op.* Technically, coupon mailings, package inserts, and other multiple-offer, multiple-company direct response advertisements are cooperative. Billing inserts and statement stuffers are other examples of direct marketing.

Of all forms of direct marketing, direct mail is the most versatile. Mail has almost all the advantages and lacks some of the disadvantages of other direct response media. The way to make DM successful for you today, however, especially in light of rising postal rates and improved computer capabilities, is to target your prospects assiduously through **data base marketing.**

A data base is a collection of information on customers and prospective customers, including their names, addresses, titles, companies, buying histories, and other facts. When a data base is established, customers and prospective customers can be segmented into groups based on common characteristics such as income, buying patterns, or lifestyles. The data base is used to fit products and services to customers and to aim precisely written advertising at special groups, or *market segments.*

Successful salespeople know that the more they know about their customers and prospects, the better they will be able to serve and sell to them. The same is true in direct marketing, and your data base is the key resource. In the years to come, the use of a data base will separate successful direct marketers from marginal ones, and data base marketing will become a greater factor in the success of large corporations such as package goods manufacturers and others whom you don't usually associate with direct marketing.

Data bases can be maintained by manual systems, but personal computers make storing and manipulating data easier. Special direct marketing/data base software is available to help you (see Chapter 6). Data processing (DP) service bureaus are also available to manage larger data bases.

A final thought on definitions: Direct marketing focuses on satisfying customers' *needs* and *wants*. This will be important to remember when you start to create your advertising. You're in the business of providing benefits for your customers and satisfying your customers' needs. We'll explore all the ways small business people can use direct marketing to satisfy customer needs and thus realize the profits of a successful enterprise.

GROWTH OF DIRECT MARKETING

Direct response may be the oldest form of advertising. Hundreds of years ago, before anyone started thinking about corporate images, spokesmodels, or new names for breakfast cereal, they wanted sales. They wanted people to buy their products, so they experimented with ways to get people to respond. Direct marketing in North America is older than the United States. In 1771, for example, the Prince Nursery in Flushing, New York, sent out its first garden catalog. It was not the first direct marketer in the colonies, but it was a leading mail-order merchant for nearly a century.

In 1913, Mr. Leon Leonwood Bean of Freeport, Maine, mailed his first single-sheet flyer advertising his Maine hunting shoes. His mailing list was made up of people who held hunting licenses. The orders he got back helped him start L.L. Bean, Inc., one of the largest direct mail/mail-order firms in the United States today. In 1926, copywriter John Caples wrote one of the most famous ads of all time, a direct response ad for correspondence school piano lessons. His headline, "They Laughed When I Sat Down at the Piano . . . But When I Started to Play!—" is an advertising classic.

Despite these and other successes, other types of mass advertising predominated for the first 70 years of this century. Direct marketing was considered the stepchild of the advertising industry. Few executives at even the largest advertising agencies saw the advantages of direct response. Direct marketing, most people thought, was reserved for record clubs and the Sears, Roebuck catalog. Much direct marketing was conducted either by in-house advertising departments or by specialized direct marketing agencies with names such as Wunderman Ricotta and Cline, certainly not household names, even among advertising people.

Then in the mid-1970s, in response to changing social patterns and as a result of the efforts of some astute practitioners, direct response, which had been growing slowly but steadily, started to leap forward. More families had two working spouses, so people had less time to shop; direct mail and mail order became a way to save time. Traffic congestion in cities made retail shopping more time-consuming and aggravating. Vast expansion of consumer credit through major credit cards gave direct mail shoppers a convenient way to pay for things they ordered through the mail or over the phone.

Advances in data processing also helped direct marketers become increasingly sophisticated in maintaining and using lists and, later, data bases to target their campaigns precisely. Technological developments in the computer industry also helped to expand the use of effective, personalized mail.

As the success of direct mail and direct marketing grew, people began to see many ways direct marketing could be used to sell more effectively. Direct marketing's flexibility made it an increasingly popular tool with both consumer and business-to-business marketers. Rather than competing with retail operations — or, in the case of business-to-business, the field sales force — direct mail could be used to enhance overall advertising response.

As advertisers saw the many advantages of direct response, they demanded more accountability from their advertising. They used direct marketing and particularly direct mail as integral parts of their marketing plans. Direct response became as important to many advertisers as general advertising on television or in newspapers. Over the last 15 years, in response to the success of direct marketing, major international advertising agencies have either started their own direct response divisions or bought existing direct marketing agencies. Corporate marketing and communications departments are using direct marketing in new ways every day.

Mail order, just one aspect of direct marketing, is responsible for about $200 billion in U.S. annual sales and contributions to charities. A 1993 study showed that about 50 U.S. companies each made a half billion dollars or more solely through mail-order sales. It's difficult to determine the volume of sales that *all* direct marketing is responsible for, in part because of varying definitions of direct response advertising. A conservative guess might be that between one-quarter and one-third of all U.S. consumer goods and services receive some sort of direct response advertising. Considering that the U.S. Department of Commerce places total personal consumption expenditures in the United States at about $3.7 trillion,[2] the consumer segment of direct marketing covers roughly one trillion dollars.

Through innovation and repetition, direct marketing has spread throughout business and industry:

The San Francisco Music Box Company recently mailed a sound catalog that played music on a tiny integrated circuit chip. In addition, interested buyers can call the firm's Dial-A-Tune service and hear dozens of recorded tunes over the phone.

A recent issue of American Airlines' in-flight magazine, American Way, *contained 27 ads with direct response coupons or stitched-in business reply postcards. Seventy-eight percent of the advertisers in the magazine either used coupons or highlighted their toll-free 800 phone numbers to generate direct inquiries or orders.*

Spiegel Inc., one of the most successful direct marketers in the United States, celebrated its 125th anniversary in 1990, and executives predicted that sales would rise to $5 billion within five years. The sales projection included $3.5 billion from catalog sales and $1.5 billion from retail.

HOW DIRECT MAIL
WILL BENEFIT YOUR BUSINESS

Benefits drive direct mail. Direct marketing focuses on providing benefits for buyers, and the chapters on constructing creative mailers and campaigns focus on the power of benefits. If you don't already think about your marketing in terms of benefits, now is a good time to start.

Look at direct marketing in terms of the benefits it has for you. Here are 10 ways that direct marketing, and especially direct mail, can help your small business, no matter what business you're in. These are the basics, some of the guiding principles of direct marketing, and they are expanded upon in following chapters.

1. You have control. Direct mail is like no other form of advertising in that you control the medium *and* the message. When you buy an ad in a magazine or newspaper or a commercial on the radio, you're buying only a portion of the medium. With direct mail your message is alone.

You control everything, from the size, texture, and color of the paper you use to the number of pages and the way you address your potential clients or customers. You can mail just about anything that postal regulations, your budget, and your conscience will permit. Do you need three inserts? Five? Ten? Want to include a color brochure, a map, a snapshot, a return envelope, a photo, or a coin? You can do it. Sunglasses, stuffed gorillas, and size-60 boxer shorts have all been used as direct mail inserts to demonstrate a point or attract attention. Further, direct mail, more than other media, allows you to involve your reader physically as well as mentally. You can get your reader involved in writing down answers to a quiz, peeling off stickers to see what's underneath, or opening an envelope sealed within an outer envelope. Just the act of opening your outer envelope starts to involve a recipient in your message.

In addition to controlling your message, you control who receives it and when. You can send one message to your existing customers and another to potential ones, or in the case of business mailings, to people in a specific industry or profession. And except for some uncertainties with mail delivery, you control when your message will be seen, regardless of deadlines for periodicals and lead times for reserving ad space.

The flexibility of direct mail should help you broaden your thinking. How can you put all this versatility to work? This book is filled with suggestions, but you should start thinking of ways to use this new marketing freedom. Your own ideas will help you implement the professional techniques.

2. You usually don't compete with other messages in the mailbox. The control direct mail gives you also means you rarely compete side by side with rival advertising messages. Your ad is not going to fight an ad on the opposite page. Your message is not sandwiched between two other commercials.

Yes, your readers may find your message in their mail boxes or "in" baskets next to other direct mail, and you may or may not reach your customers or potential customers on the same day as a competitor does. Even so, people will handle your message by itself, and if you are successful in attracting their interest, they'll open it.

3. *Precise targeting lets you search for specific prospects.* The more precise or accurate your targeted market, the less money you'll spend advertising to people who are not interested in or qualified to use your product or service. You can mail to every household within a certain distance from your location, or you can mail only to doctors in your area. You can send your advertising messages to people in your state who have bought fruitcake through the mail, or you can target a certain type of business.

With business-to-business direct mail you can reach more than one person in the same company. Some small firms simultaneously sell their services to many people and departments within one large corporation. Business mailers frequently know the job functions, number of employees, sales volumes, and other attributes of their customers and prospects. They can choose to mail only to corporate headquarters, or they can target branch managers/officers who may be more likely customers. The level of sophistication in business mailing, like consumer mailing, is limited only by the depth of the information—the data base—you have available.

In addition, print advertising provides opportunities to select publications that reach specific, unique groups of readers. (*Print* advertising refers to ads in magazines, newspapers, and other publications.)

4. *Direct mail is an equalizer for small business.* Giant corporations can afford to spend thousands of dollars for color ads in dozens of magazines, $50,000 per second for commercials on the Super Bowl, and millions of dollars for celebrity endorsements. You can't.

You can, however, spend hundreds or thousands of dollars sending out letters and brochures to prospective customers. You can look and sound every bit as prosperous and reliable as anyone or any company in the world. Your larger competitors can perhaps outspend you on direct mail and reach more people, but they won't necessarily look any better than you do. Some of your larger competitors may have salespeople combing territories. They're looking for prime prospects, the same prospects you can reach far more cheaply, and often more accurately, with direct mail.

A word of caution: Since direct mail is so accessible, it is just as easy, if not easier, for a small company to look much worse than its larger competitors if it jumps into DM using the "Let's see what happens" myth. You wouldn't (and couldn't) create your own TV commercials without studying the techniques of television production. Don't plunge into DM without becoming familiar with its requirements and, even more important, don't start marketing without developing long- and short-range business goals. It's the thinking and planning behind your direct mail that will make it successful.

5. *Direct marketing is immediate and personal.* Short of talking to someone, what is more immediate and personal than a letter? Print and even broadcast media lack the one-on-one urgency of a well-written letter addressed to the customer. Although repetition is important in advertising, the freshness of a letter just pulled out of an envelope is hard to beat in persuasive punch. Developing mailers that take full advantage of the personal aspects of direct mail advertising is a creative challenge addressed in Chapters 7 to 11.

Telemarketing can be even more immediate and personal than direct mail if properly executed. As with direct mail, there is wasted effort in using the telephone for marketing today, but handled properly and mixed with other forms of advertising, telemarketing can be a tremendous boost to your business.

Other forms of direct response advertising require different techniques to emphasize the urgency of an offer and persuasively communicate product/service benefits to prospects.

6. *You can accomplish several goals.*   The ability to make advertising work as hard as possible is especially important for small enterprises with limited budgets. Instead of just buying awareness with your advertising or just asking for the order, you can do both! More and more companies are learning that the simple addition of a toll-free 800 phone number in an ad can generate direct responses to their advertising while they are establishing recognition or an identity.

Gaining exposure and prompting orders are not the only things direct marketing can do for you. Customer service, a broad area that includes everything from responding to comments and surveying customers to improving customer satisfaction, can be accomplished effectively with direct marketing techniques. If you have a limited staff, direct mail methods can help you maintain good, profitable relations with customers. The ability of DM and telemarketing to supplement retail and field sales efforts is another plus.

7. *Direct marketing is the most testable form of advertising.*   Since direct response is accountable, it's also the most testable form of advertising. Every mailing and every direct response advertisement you run is an opportunity for you to test something and gain information that can help improve your marketing in the future.

With direct mail you always have the option of testing one list against another or one offer against another. (An *offer* is a selling proposition to your customers and is defined in detail in Chapter 2.) When testing is not feasible, you can at least track carefully the results of every direct response ad and mailer you use. The ability to track, test, and evaluate your responses and act accordingly is a prime benefit of direct marketing.

8. *Direct mail lets you manipulate your response rates.*   Not only does direct mail have higher response rates than general advertising, it also allows you to manipulate the number of responses you will get. Don't you always want the maximum number of responses? Not necessarily. You don't want to receive more inquiries or orders than you can effectively process promptly. It's often easier to spread out your responses over time.

Obviously, varying the number of mailings you send out will have an effect on your number of responses, but other factors affect response rates, too, such as prices and the type of products or services you offer. You can boost your response rate when you're looking for leads by not asking the potential customers to obligate themselves. Your job then is to convert as many responses as possible into sales. Conversely, you can have direct mail do more of the selling, thus identifying only the most serious prospects. Decisions that affect the size (and quality) of your responses constitute an element of your business planning and marketing strategies.

A key benefit of direct mail is your ability to plan your budget and know the return on your investment of advertising dollars. Budgeting for general advertising is an iffy proposition. Measurable direct response results give you more information upon which to base your budgeting.

9. You can use direct marketing to build a data base. Building a data base through direct marketing is a self-sustaining activity. When a customer orders, you get a sale and information you can add to your data base. Many large and small companies use direct response print ads offering free information as one way of building a data base.

The better you are able to build, organize, and use a data base, the better your direct marketing will be. And improved direct marketing will yield additional information on existing customers and new information on prospects.

Don't ignore the value of data base marketing if you're in retailing. Recently, the A&P supermarket chain won a national direct marketing award for its use of direct mail to generate traffic for a new upscale FutureStore location in suburban Atlanta. Rather than relying on pages of newspaper ads as most supermarket chains do, A&P sent out DM letters to residents along with store coupons and bar-coded FutureCards. The direct mail campaign was responsible for 48 percent of the store traffic the first week. In addition, after having their FutureCards scanned to see what prizes they had won (everyone won something), customers filled out an information panel on the card providing the store with names, addresses, and demographic information. Customers dropped their cards in a grand prize drawing box. Later, the store entered the data from the cards into a computer to start a data base of customers.[3]

10. You can resell your customers again and again. The reason for maintaining a data base is to continue selling your existing customers over and over. One of the first axioms to learn about direct marketing and marketing in general is that it's far easier and cheaper to resell your existing clients or customers than it is to get new customers. In many direct marketing efforts, especially in mail order, companies do not show a profit on the first sale to a customer, but rely on follow-up sales to make money. In the banking industry it costs about five times more to get a new customer than it does to keep an existing one, and other retailers report a similar cost ratio for new versus old customers.

Although this sales rule is right out of Marketing 101, even seasoned direct marketing professionals sometimes forget it. They may choose to concentrate on "expanding their business" by trying to generate more new customers, forgetting that they can also expand their businesses by simply selling more (with less effort) to existing customers.

These 10 concepts or benefits represent powerful methods you can use to build your business. Perhaps the greatest advantage of the direct marketing approach lies in one fundamental principle. The principle that separates direct marketing from all other marketing, advertising, and publicity is that *it includes a call to action.*

David Ogilvy, possibly the most famous U.S. adman alive, compared general advertising people to direct marketers in a speech in Paris a few years ago: "When you generalists write an advertisement or a commercial, you want everybody to congratulate you on your 'creativity.' When we write an advertisement or direct-mail package, we want people to order the product."[4] Ogilvy founded the Ogilvy and Mather advertising agency and has created some of the most memorable ads of the past few decades. In one of his books he calls direct response his first love and secret weapon. "We sell—or else," he says of direct marketers.

THE BUSINESS PLAN

Whether you're a self-employed professional or head of a growing company with a number of employees, the way you use direct marketing will not differ substantially except perhaps in scope. The principles outlined here will help you get action, no matter what it is you want your audience to do. The big difference in outcome among companies, even those of the same size in the same industry, lies in their specific corporate goals. Direct mail and direct marketing will take you where you want to go, but you have to provide the destination. Direct marketing can't help you if you haven't determined your specific objectives, and for that you need a comprehensive business plan.

Direct marketing's results are almost immediate, so it's easy to get caught up in day-to-day objectives and lose sight of the overall goals of your organization. Many companies falter even after initial marketing successes because they fail to make plans beyond their current direct mail campaigns. With direct marketing's unique flexibility you can tailor campaigns to help accomplish your company's short- *and* long-term goals, but you have to know what those goals are. I've learned from my experience, and from the experiences of others, the necessity of having a carefully conceived business plan. If you're not the person responsible for the plan, you should be intimately familiar with it before you start a marketing campaign.

If you do not have a business plan, *Do-It-Yourself Direct Marketing* will help you work on the marketing aspects of it. You will develop an understanding of the requirements of direct response and what kind of results you should be aiming for. We'll go through the steps necessary to chart effective direct marketing strategies, but the business plan is the guiding influence. Direct marketing is not your plan; it is simply one means of reaching your company objectives.

Start-up companies tend to omit the planning stage. Entrepreneurs seem especially liable to (1) get excited about a new idea or product; (2) receive enthusiastic, yet unrepresentative, support for the idea from friends and associates; and (3) start marketing their products or services (and spending money) with little thought of a plan. Even if your company has been around for a while, it can still benefit from a business plan. If you're planning a large, new marketing effort, a plan becomes even more important. Many large companies maintain a business plan, revising it regularly.

The more specific the marketing segment of your business plan, the better. Recommendations to "do some marketing" or even "prospect for new customers" are useless. Specific goals give you something to shoot for. Once you get a little experience with direct marketing, you will be able to adjust your goals periodically according to your budget, expected responses, expenses, market share, and other factors.

According to experts, here are some of the ingredients your business plan should include:

1. Statement of your business goals
2. Description of the products and services you offer
3. Summary of your operational plan detailing how your products or services will be created
4. Marketing strategy
5. Outline of company management and management philosophy, if relevant
6. Financial plan
7. Sources of financing

If you're a sole proprietor and are not seeking a business loan, you're probably tempted to skip the business plan. You don't have to tell yourself why you're in business, do you? Maybe you do. The act of reducing your goals and operational and marketing plans to paper will help you focus on what is important. As the day-to-day exigencies of business pull you in different directions, it's imperative to have a plan as your guide.

POSTSCRIPTS....
Swipe Ideas

Where's the best place to look for good direct mail ideas and suggestions? Try your mailbox. Every day you receive samples of ideas. Collect them. Make one special separate file just for your competitors' mailings. Most direct marketing agencies, direct response writers, and designers keep files of direct mail they receive. These "swipe" files are used for brainstorming and keeping track of what others are doing.

What should you look for? Watch for ideas for headlines, effective designs, attention-getting inserts, and persuasively written copy. In following chapters you'll learn about many DM creative variables. A large collection of samples will help when you want to find examples of an individual technique.

Sort your samples by those aimed at businesses and those directed to consumers. Look for ways to save money, too. Notice that not everyone uses full color, for example. Read magazine and newspaper ads as well. See if you can spot those ads designed to create action.

Remember that not all direct marketing is effective and that there are many pitfalls to avoid. By the time you finish with this book, you should be able to review your sample files and distinguish the good from the bad.

Save Money by Being Precise

To be effective in direct mail, it's not necessary to mail to every breathing human being, just to those people who are your most likely customers or who are already your customers. Start thinking in terms of precise targeting. Ask yourself who your prime prospects are. If your money is limited, whom will you approach first? This philosophy is one of the main differences between direct marketing and general advertising.

What Is Your Business?

One useful planning exercise is to ask yourself, "What business am I in?" If you publish an investment newsletter, are you in the publishing business or are you in the business of providing customers with financial advice? The classic example of failure to ask this question involves the railroads. Years ago, some railroad people decided they were in the railroad business, rather than in the transportation business, and thus failed to compete effectively against airlines, trucking, and other forms of transportation.

Write in This Book

Although you'll find hundreds of ideas in this book, some will be more appropriate for you than others. To make the book as useful to you as possible, underline or highlight points that are most important to you. Put stars around sections that give you ideas for techniques you can implement in your business. Make notes inside the front cover and, in short, turn this into a workbook customized to your business.

2 CONSTRUCTING YOUR STRATEGY

It Starts with Your Offer

Whether you're planning direct marketing strategy, evaluating a campaign, or simply writing an ad, much of the work revolves around three basic elements: *the offer, the list,* and *the creative.* These elements work together and separately to make direct mail work. This book is organized with these three elements in mind.

In this chapter we'll review *the offer* in detail and give you an introduction to *lists* and *creative.* We'll also examine how the three elements affect direct mail response rates and shape the primary direct marketing strategy.

THE OFFER

Direct response offers include the following elements:

1. The product or service being sold.
2. Any warranties, guarantees, service contracts, or other features that go with it.
3. The price including credit terms and finance charges.
4. The action someone needs to take to place an order or respond in some other way.

This sounds similar to the classic definition of marketing—product, price, promotion and place—and it is. After all, direct marketing is what its name implies, a straightforward form of marketing, not an *in*direct form of image-building advertising. The offer is the center of direct marketing. Without it, phrased to include the price and response method, you would not have direct marketing.

Offers separate general advertising from direct response. General advertising may tell you about the quality of a product, and may even mention a price, but other critical information is often missing. Direct response puts *all* the necessary information together in an offer and tells the reader or listener exactly how to respond. It is *the* focal point.

People expect offers, especially in direct mail, and they're quickly bored if they don't see one. People know you don't send out direct mail just to entertain. They look for offers. Without an offer, readers have no incentive, no sense of urgency to take action. They don't even know what action, if any, the advertiser is hoping to elicit.

Small business people, consultants, and professionals annually mail thousands of brochures about their services but fail to make an offer. They don't give prospective customers a reason to respond.

Failure to have a clear offer, or any offer at all, is a common mistake among direct marketing beginners. As we'll see many times, one of the purposes of direct mail is to overcome inertia. The way to do that is not with generalities about how important your services are or how modern your facilities. The way to get a response is to make people an offer they can't refuse. If you have samples of any unsuccessful direct mail you've used, read through them and see if the offers are clear and obvious. Adding a clear, attractive offer to a DM package is one way to multiply the response rate. Further, any sales you get unrelated to an offer cannot be attributed to your advertising; you won't know where they came from.

If you tell the public that you provide expert interior decorating services, you're advertising. If you tell promising potential customers that you'll give them a free color evaluation of their home if they return a postcard within two weeks, then you're *making an offer*. An offer does not necessarily require a customer to place an order. For instance, you may offer an information booklet to any prospective customer who calls your office.

Do you *have* to have an offer? Yes, if you want to practice direct marketing. Most general advertising, public relations, and marketing communications tell customers or the public about your firm and leave it to them to decide when they will contact you and which of your products or services they will inquire about. With a direct marketing offer, you decide which product or service you want to sell. (That gives you more control over your business.) You select your product, then create an attractive selling proposition.

Varieties of Offers

Offers come in different forms depending on a variety of factors, including whether you sell to individuals or companies. To paraphrase a book club's recent offer, "Six books, six bucks, no strings." There's no mistaking what they're offering you. Here are some other examples of offers taken out of my mailbox at home and at work.

Product: Four-in-one labor law posters for the workplace.
Price: $4.99 each or less with large quantity orders.
Ordering: By mail with delayed billing and credit options.
Details: A brochure shows other posters available on motivation and employee suggestion programs.

Product: Consumer magazine subscription.
Price: $49 per year
Ordering: Enclose no money now; billing to follow.
Details: Two-issue trial subscription with no obligation. If orders are received by a deadline, customers also get a book on conservation.

Product: Membership in the American Institute of Professional Book-keepers.

Price: One year at $37 (normally $56) or two years at $66 (normally $112).

Ordering: By mail with check or credit card card number.

Details: Includes membership diploma, two free bookkeeping information reports, monthly newsletter, telephone hotline for questions, tax calendar. Two-year membership also includes dictionary of bookkeeping terms. Guarantee with right to cancel after two months.

Product: Selection of 14-karat gold jewelry.

Price: Sixty percent off regular prices.

Ordering: Visit one of several local retail locations by a specified deadline.

Details: Special private sale, by invitation only, during specified days. Gift check enclosed for an additional $20 discount on any purchase over $65. No down payment required and credit terms available.

Product: Information portfolio on purchase plans for office equipment including computers, copiers, fax machines.

Price: Free

Ordering: Postcard

Details: Recipient also receives a chrome, 3-pound executive dumbbell exerciser/paper weight. Two ordering options: one requests the materials and a call from a salesperson; the other asks for the materials only.

Product: In-home carpet cleaning service.

Price: $53.50 for any two rooms and a hall; $95.95 for four rooms and a hall.

Ordering: Call. Local and 800 numbers provided.

Details: Prices good for three weeks, discount coupon required. Credit cards accepted. Residential customers only.

In direct marketing, offers are sometimes categorized by the method of payment. Offers with delayed billing, installment payments, and trial periods are called *soft offers*, probably because there's no immediate requirement of hard cash. Subscription offers, book clubs, and other "bill me later" propositions are examples of soft offers. The magazine subscription and labor poster offers above are soft offers. When up-front payment is required for a product or service, it's called a *hard offer*. Hard offers may include sale pricing, free gifts called *premiums*, and other incentives, but they require payment in advance by cash, credit card, or check. Many mail-order catalogs contain nothing but hard offers. You order merchandise and include a check or credit card number or you call an 800 number and give them your card number for quicker delivery. The American Institute of Professional Bookkeepers membership offer is an example of a hard offer.

Your steps in formulating an offer include:

1. *Narrow your focus if necessary.* If you offer a variety of products and services, you'll need to select *one* to feature in your offer.

2. *Specify the details.* Decide what specific action you want your customers/clients/prospects to take. Determine if you can provide delayed billing, an 800 number for calls, use of credit card payments (see Chapter 17 for more detail). Will this be a hard or soft offer, or a hybrid? Are you looking for a direct sale, a lead, trial acceptance or some other response?

3. *Make the offer better.* This is a key step. How can you make this as attractive as you can afford? Typical techniques for improving offers include premiums, discounts, trial orders, free samples, and money-back guarantees. An opportunity for no-obligation information only, makes an offer more attractive because there's little commitment required. These devices and others have proved to increase responses on various direct mail and mail-order offers.

4. *Determine costs and establish a budget.* This is the stage where you actually put a price to your offer. Depending on what you decide you can afford to offer, you may need to alter steps two and three. For example, if you decide you need to increase your prices, see if you can modify some other aspect of the offer to make it as valuable and attractive as you can.

Here's one example of how to formulate an offer for a small business. One of my clients, a financial counselor, wanted to attract new business. Rather than just advertise that he was available to give advice, he developed an offer that included a portfolio review and analysis of an individual's financial condition. The offer was made for a limited time and was made available to a select list of doctors and other professionals with sizable investment portfolios. This limited free offer gave people a reason to contact him and gave him the chance to convert interested people into clients.

So many pricing options and other techniques are available for improving offers that hundreds of offer variations are possible. To help you formulate and improve your offers, you can create your own offer matrix listing many of the variations and options.

To build your offer matrix, write your products and services across the top of a page, then list your offer and pricing options down the side of the page. Figure 2.1 shows an example of a simple offer matrix with just two products and five variables.

With just the five variations down the side of the matrix you could still create many different offers for each of the two products. A combination of some or all of the offer enhancements could be applied to either product. Following are more suggestions for offer enhancements for the products or services on your matrix. You'll want to tailor your matrix depending on

	Roofing Products	
	Fiberglass Shingles	*Ceramic Tile*
Free roof safety inspection Free estimates Special-purchase sale on materials 90 days delayed billing Off-season special		

FIGURE 2.1   An offer matrix.

whether you're looking for direct sales or for leads and whether you're selling to consumers or to business people. Consider these options:

Pricing Options

Seasonal pricing

Everyday low prices

Factory-direct sales

Limited-time sales

Specific sales, for example:

- Inventory reduction
- Passing on manufacturers' discounts
- End of model year
- Damaged, incomplete, flawed merchandise

Discount prices available to members of a special group, such as:

- Credit union members
- Membership in discount store or program
- Previous customers
- Volume buyers

Introductory/charter member offers

Price-increase-coming offers

Two-for-one sale

Buy one, get one free

One-penny sale ·

Membership fees or free membership

Payment Options

COD

30-90 days net

Pay as you go

Installment terms

Major bank or entertainment credit cards

Free trial
Delayed billing up to 30 days
Payment with order
Payment per unit delivered or job completed

Premium Offers

Free gift for responses such as the following:

- Single order
- Inquiry
- Referral
- Specified size of order
- Early order date (early bird reward)
- Trial order
- Membership fee

Choose your own free gift

Variations:

- Free accessories/supplies
- Free installation
- Free alterations
- Free upgrades, updates (software, for example)

More-Information Offers

Information fact kit

Free for initial orders
Free for the asking, no strings
Free, to be delivered by salesperson
Nominal charge
Free in exchange for a referral

Variations

- Free consultation
- Free inspection
- Free estimate
- Free evaluation
- Free exam or screening
- First hour free

Not all of the pricing and premium offers will be appropriate for all of your products, but developing a large matrix lets you examine the possibilities. As you fill in boxes on your matrix to represent the possible offers you could use, you'll have columns and rows full of new ideas. (*Note:* see Chapter 10 on pertinent regulations concerning advertising language.)

Even this list is just a portion of the many offers and variations you can use by themselves or in combination. With the variety of services and products in your business, what unique offers can you create? Let your imagination flow.

In a sense, the offer is a statement of your short-term marketing strategy. Say you have a travel agency and you want to build your customer base. You formulate an offer to appeal to consumers in your area. To develop your offer, identify some of the services you provide, such as airline ticketing, ocean cruise planning, and others. Then insert them across the top of your matrix to create a variety of possible offers. Let's say you decide to offer a percentage discount on a package trip to Mexico. Your short-term strategy then is to break even or make a profit on a discounted package in order to add customers. Depending on what you know about the loyalty of your existing customers and how often they use your services, you may be able to determine how much you can afford to spend to obtain a new customer.

Improve Your Offer

Once you have established your general strategy, try to improve your offer. Tests have shown that a consumer offer of "buy one, get one free" is often more attractive than a 50 percent discount offer. If you can afford it, change your Mexico trip pricing to reflect this approach, if not this percentage. Perhaps a premium would be a better, low-cost way to improve the offer. Try adding a free travel bag, shopping guide, or complimentary brunch. Once you start to formulate an offer, it almost forces you to think in an organized way, examining your costs and options as your strategy progresses. In this example the short-term strategy, and thus the offer, might have centered on obtaining company travel accounts or perhaps on selling high-profit package trips to repeat customers. Each short-term approach should be drawn from or developed to support your longer-term business plan.

Offers can help promote just about any business from mortuaries to nurseries to management consultants. Depending on your product or service, you may have to make operational or structural changes in your business to help you create offers. For example, a retail store might want to start offering some products by mail. Another company might need to create introductory services which can be used to create offers. Even a business with but a few products can devise a variety of different offers using variables on a matrix. If you are slightly diversified, however, you'll find it easier to create different offers that can boost your total business.

To summarize, offers should be as attractive as possible to get the most responses. They should appeal to the psychological needs of the readers, and they should be geared to generate a specific action. Further, they should be worded so that the reader clearly knows how to respond. Chapters 7 and 8 provide help in using the psychology of selling to create and write effective offers. To find a stack of offer examples, look through a co-op card deck mailing. This medium is explained in Chapter 5.

THE LIST

Even an unquestionably genuine and ludicrously inexpensive offer will be useless if it is presented to the wrong people. If you received a mailing at home offering you a 95% discount on oil drilling equipment, vintage fire engine parts, or a teak violin bow, chances are you still wouldn't be interested unless you were in the oil business, restored old fire fighting vehicles, or played the violin. On the other hand, an offer of only 5 percent off the above-mentioned merchandise could generate a big response if it were mailed to nothing but wildcatters, owners of antique fire engines, or violinists. An even better selection would be a list of oil drillers, fire engine collectors, or violinists who have responded to direct mail before.

Most lists available for rent fall into one of two categories: compiled lists and direct response lists. Compiled lists contain categories of people and are created from telephone books, business and industrial directories, and other sources. That is, the lists are *compiled* from outside sources. Compiled lists also include residential lists organized by ZIP codes and business lists organized by standard industrial code (SIC). If you were looking for people in the oil business, you might consult a compiled list.

Direct response lists are just what their name implies. They're lists of people who already have responded to a direct marketing offer. In general they are more likely to respond to another offer, especially if it is related to the one they already responded to. In many cases people get their names on direct response lists by subscribing to magazines. Not only does subscribing to a magazine show that you do respond to mail, but also it says something about your interests, depending on the subject of the magazine you read. If there were an *Antique Fire Truck Magazine,* you would probably find buyers for parts among its subscribers, or from a list of people who already had bought fire engine parts through the mail.

Working with lists gives you flexibility you can't find with any other medium. You can test portions of a list, you can rent only segments of a list, such as identifying drivers by age, and you can find out how recently a list has been updated.

In other forms of direct response advertising, the medium forms the "list." You select different periodicals, for example, because of the characteristics of their readers. You select radio stations on the basis of their listeners.

THE CREATIVE

Once you have your offer and your target list, or the publications you're going to use, you need to create the advertising. All the work that's left is generally lumped under the term *creative,* advertising agency jargon that refers to writing and designing ads. Some of the creative work includes the following activities:

Copywriting.   Penning the magic words that grab the reader's attention and lead him from the offer to the action required is the most important of the creative skills. Direct response advertising is a combination of words and pictures or graphics and, unlike some other forms of advertising, the words almost always carry the burden of persuasion.

Designing.   Direct mail ranges from thick catalogs generously illustrated with color photos to simple letters and even postcards. Elaborate and expensive designs are not a requirement. Most copywriters think the purpose of the design is to make the words easy to read. And they're partially correct. Lavish or unusual artistic techniques, which may work well in image advertising in magazines and other media, may distract from or inhibit readership of direct response sales messages. Even a simple layout, however, requires planning and a good eye for detail. Selecting the paper stock and the number and size of inserts is a part of the creative design work.

Printing and Personalizing. Ads in periodicals don't require preprinting unless they are inserted or bound into a publication. With direct mail, however, printing is, in essence, the medium. As the size and complexity of the mailing pieces increase, so do the skill and sophistication required of the printer.

A variety of services from printing and mailing to data processing and personalizing letters with high-speed laser printers are available from *letter shops,* production facilities that serve direct mail marketers. Production of direct mail packages may be a multistep process including printing, die cutting, embossing, stitching, gumming, labeling, personalizing, folding, inserting, sealing, stamping, and mailing. You can choose a full-service letter shop (also called a mailing house) to handle the majority of your work, or you can do some of the work yourself with help from smaller vendors.

Don't let the term *creative* make you think that the first two elements of direct mail do not require creativity. Although developing profit-making offers and selecting precise lists seem more a function of money, merchandising, and mathematics, creativity and ingenuity are also important. Often just a good idea for making an offer more attractive or valuable will make a big difference in the response.

Each of the three elements of direct marketing is required for success, and each is dependent on the effectiveness of the other two. Adjustments in one area will easily affect the others. The more attractive the offer, the greater the persuasive ammunition for copywriting. The more accurate and specific your lists, the more personalized your copywriting can be. Furthermore, offers are frequently tailored to specific lists. When I was a credit union marketing director, in addition to being responsible for the creative, I also helped develop offers that could be successfully marketed. Developing the offers was frequently more important to success than producing the advertising. With a little help, you and your staff should be able to plan, create, and implement all three elements of an effective direct mail program. How much you do yourself and how much outside help you get is up to you. Appendix A explains your options for getting specific tasks completed when you work with outside consultants, creative freelancers, and others.

RESPONSE RATES

Estimating direct mail response rates is one of the trickiest aspects of direct marketing, especially for beginners. Although it's difficult or impossible to predict a precise response rate without previous testing, responses must be considered in your initial direct marketing strategy.

You actually control the response rate the way you use the three main elements of direct marketing we've just discussed. For example, I've mentioned that it's easier to sell to existing customers than it is to market to a list of strangers; therefore you can set higher expectations for a *house list* mailing than you would when mailing to a list of outsiders.

But since there is no industry average, where do you start? If you haven't shaken the 1-percent-average-response myth, there's more to learn, but at least you're at the correct end of the spectrum. Your responses are going to be closer to 1 percent than to 90 percent, or 50 percent, or perhaps even 5 percent. Some direct marketers can make money day in and day out with *less* than a 1 percent response, but depending on your initial costs you may need much more than 1 percent just to break even.

A *successful* response rate should be more important to you than an average one. Take two examples: First, when you determine your costs for an initial mailing, you could discover that you need more than a 3 percent response just to cover expenses. Second, consider that you're doing a lead generation program and you know from experience that you will convert 20 percent of your leads into sales. If that's the case, then you have to divide *any* response percentage you'll get by five (20 percent is one-fifth) in order to determine the percentage or number of *sales* your campaign will generate. The lesson from these examples is that response rates are only relevant in terms of costs. Since advertising and production costs vary among businesses, so does the significance of a response rate.

One way to identify a successful response rate is to work backwards by determining your advertising costs, then estimating the number of responses/sales you need just to break even. You might decide, like many direct marketers do, that you're willing to conduct a campaign even if you expect it will not show a profit from the initial responses. In this case you do it to build a customer base you can sell to again and again, or to generate leads to be cultivated later.

If response rates of 1, 3, or even 5 percent still seem low to you, compare direct mail response rates to general advertising. Say you're placing an ad in a metropolitan newspaper. Your newspaper ad generates 58 leads. Sounds like a good response. But then consider that the newspaper has a circulation of 650,000. Your 58 leads represent a response rate of .009 percent. Compare that to a direct mail response rate of even a conservative .25 percent and you can see a substantial difference. To get 58 leads at the .25 percent response rate you'd have to mail to only 20,000 people. If we put your response rate at a respectable 1.5 percent, you'd have to mail to less than 4,000 people to get the same number of leads. Keep in mind, however, that while direct mail responses are high, so are the relative costs. It costs more to reach a potential customer through direct mail than through print advertising media.

To refine your response estimates you need to track and, if possible, test your mailings. Chapter 6 reviews the procedures.

STRATEGIES

The basic direct marketing strategy is simple: First, get an initial response and second, resell those same customers. Most direct marketing revolves around this concept. For most direct marketing professionals, the initial or *front-end* marketing of a product or service is just the beginning. The front end leads naturally to *back-end* marketing and the significant portion of the profits. The term *back end* refers to selling to identified customers or sometimes qualified prospects who have already responded in some way. The back end is the ultimate goal for most direct marketing programs. Successful front-end strategies, however, are important in the short term, since costs and risks are usually higher for front-end advertising. To compare direct marketing to sales again, the front end could be considered the prospecting stage where rejections are higher and planning and professional execution especially necessary.

You can use the three elements of direct marketing as an outline for developing your front-end strategies. You first select a target market, sometimes identified by a list you are able to obtain, other times by analyzing your existing customers. Then you formulate an offer that will appeal to your market segment. (In mail order the offer often comes first, then you find the most likely prospects.) Finally, you create the advertising (having already selected the media, i.e. DM, print ads, etc.) that presents your offer in language your prospects will understand.

In consumer mail-order marketing, front-end strategies are designed to establish a back end quickly. Attractive, low-cost offers are used by mail-order sellers to build a data base for back-end marketing. Sweepstakes, inexpensive memberships, and low-price offers are examples of short-term, front-end marketing designed to move quickly to the back end.

Many consumer direct marketers set their front-end offer prices high enough to cover their costs, yet low enough to generate a maximum number of responses. Free offers will produce even more responses, but they have two drawbacks. First, they don't give you income to offset your front-end costs. Second, when people respond to a free offer, they're not truly customers yet because they haven't bought anything. Conversion of someone who responded to a free offer may be more difficult than selling to someone who has already purchased from you. Low-priced or free front-end offers in consumer and business-to-business marketing are referred to as *lead generation* programs.

Back-end marketing is more efficient than prospecting. Response rates are usually much higher. You will obtain more orders at a lower cost than just about any front-end idea you may come up with. Back-end selling (to house lists) costs less than using outside lists or buying print ad space in publications to sell to first-time buyers.

Front-end strategies for small business people vary depending on the field of business. Among some common free lead generation offers are the seminars conducted by stockbrokers and real estate investment counselors and free gifts from builders to homeowners who order cost estimates for additions or improvements. People who respond are reached later via mail or phone or in person. Real estate agents offer free market evaluations of homes to find people who are thinking about selling. (Real estate agents have a further back-end market among people who have bought or sold homes through them before.) Offers of free information brochures or booklets on everything from nutrition to car care are perhaps the most common lead generation offers. Examples of low-cost front-end offers are also plentiful, especially in mail order. Cosmetic jewelry, inexpensive clothing and accessory items, and low-cost trial subscriptions are common in front-end offers.

Mail-order marketers often do front-end and back-end marketing at the same time via different media. While a catalog firm is serving existing customers through direct mail, for example, it might be using direct response magazine ads or direct response radio to expand its house list of customers. When people respond to the magazine or radio ads, they start receiving direct mail.

The front-end/back-end (and lead generation) strategy is appropriate for most direct marketing, regardless of your product or service. How you develop your front end will depend on many factors. In retailing, for example, your front end could develop in the normal course of business. Collect names, addresses, and other information on customers, then focus on the back end to increase your responses above what they are when you use conventional advertising to appeal to the general public.

Some retailers practice a form of direct marketing strategy through inexpensive traffic-building offers. There is usually no true back end to these offers, however. The only advantages come from further sales made at the time when people show up to buy the traffic builder product. Without a data base or tracking device, there is no effective way to capitalize further on front-end retail successes.

Building a business, whether it's mail order, retail, service, or a combination of types, requires not only developing a customer data base but also doing the repeat selling and servicing necessary to *keep* the customer base. Bankers know, for example, that the more services a customer uses, the more likely he is to remain a customer. Someone who has a checking account, savings account, home loan, and safety deposit box all through the same financial institution can almost be considered a lifetime customer because that person is linked to the bank in many ways. Similarly you can link your customers to yourself as you develop your back-end marketing.

The basic direct marketing strategy is effective, yet depending on your type of business you may not think it's for you. You might decide that a lead generation or two-step approach is too expensive, in spite of the increased response rates for back-end marketing. If you're only interested in making one sale to as many new customers as possible, you're making the marketing job more difficult. Such a strategy means you have to concentrate on using direct response techniques to advertise for one-time direct sales. Perhaps another form of advertising may be more effective or cost-efficient. It's difficult to imagine, however, any organization that cannot benefit from building a data base of customers, then using it to generate repeat sales, or at least referrals, in the future. In succeeding chapters we'll review a variety of strategy examples and demonstrate other ways you can categorize and market to your best customers or best potential customers. Concepts such as recency and frequency of purchasing will help.

One novel extension or application of the basic direct marketing strategy lies in the importance of the offer. To create the strongest direct response advertising, you sell the offer, whether or not it contains your product. If your offer is a free trial, low-cost sample, or similar front-end proposition, your advertising must focus on the benefits of the *offer,* not the product. The whole purpose of an introductory offer is to increase responses by providing a way people can reply without making a final commitment. If you focus on your product instead of the offer, you remind people that you're ultimately going to try to sell them your main product.

For Professionals and Business Marketers

Back-end strategy is equally important for self-employed business and professional people who serve consumers. In some cases, direct marketing may be more appropriate for the front-end portion, with the back end, that is the repeat selling, being done through personal contact with a customer/client/patient. Direct marketing may be used, however, for inactive customers or to sell an additional service to existing customers. For example, an accountant who has a large list of tax preparation customers could use direct mail to sell tax planning, trusts, financial planning, and general accounting services to them.

Direct mail shouldn't be a substitute for personal selling to existing customers, but it can supplement *cross-selling* efforts. Cross selling is a form of personal selling in which you cross over from the sale of one product to another. When clerks at McDonald's ask you if you want fries with your Big Mac™, they're using cross selling.

As you begin to develop a sense of direct marketing, look for additional services or products you can offer to your existing customers. If you are so specialized that you only offer one service, your back-end possibilities are limited unless customers require your services many times. Successful direct marketing/mail-order companies with large data bases actually develop or buy new products specifically for sale to their existing customers. In this case, the product is matched to the market, not vice versa. Obviously, the better you know your customers, the better you will be able to match a new product or service to them.

In the business-to-business field there are three fundamental strategies. First, business marketers who sell consumables such as office supplies, medical supplies, or some business services through mail order need to rely on building a data base and on back-end marketing to maintain profits, similar to consumer marketing. For many business marketers a second strategy is necessary. Many business and industrial products are so expensive or complex that they cannot be sold by mail order and require demonstrations or in-person sales calls. In this instance, direct marketing is used for lead generation, to identify and qualify prospects who can be contacted on the phone or in person later. The third basic business-to-business strategy involves sales support communications aimed at existing customers or prospects who are visited by salespeople. Direct mail to these people may support a salesperson's efforts and possibly obtain additional orders. Measuring the success of this third category may be difficult.

Regardless of the strategies that are appropriate for your business-to-business selling, a data base will be an important element in your success. If you're just starting a business or are a business consultant seeking to add customers, or if you're planning to enter a new market with an industrial product, you'll want to focus on adding leads or prospects to your data base first, rather than seeking one-time-only sales. In business marketing the average amount of a sale is often substantially greater than in consumer marketing, so you can afford to spend more money to generate leads.

Another key ingredient, of course, is finding the right list; the closer the prospects on a list are to your ideal company/customer profile, the better. Like consumer marketers, you need to control costs carefully by targeting mailings precisely. Some lead generation advertising in publications and DM can help you pre-qualify the leads you receive. You can sort leads according to the relative likelihood of their being converted to customers, among other factors. In Chapter 14 we'll review ways you can identify the right business lists and compile your own list of hot prospects.

POSTSCRIPTS....

Putting Three Factors Together

How do the three direct marketing factors work to increase (or decrease) responses? Here's an example of having all the factors in your favor: You mail to your house list of satisfied customers; you have a clear, valuable offer designed with your specific customers in mind; and you use compelling copy in your mailer that tells readers specifically what you want them to do.

To see all the factors working *against* you, imagine mailing to a list of residents you know nothing about, with a generic offer unrelated to the characteristics of the people on the list (such as sleet scrapers for residents of Phoenix, Arizona), using a message that doesn't do everything it can to overcome inertia and get action.

Peace of Mind Offers

In mail-order selling, the final part of your offer should be a money-back guarantee. Customers buying from the Land's End or Spiegel catalogs know they can return a product if they don't like it or find it is not what they expected. A guarantee is essential for items such as clothing, which people are used to trying on in a store. More than matching retail convenience, however, a prominent guarantee tells your customers something about the quality of your products and reputation of your company.

The Quill Corporation goes one step further: Included with every shipment of office supplies they send is a preapproved return slip. This helps to alleviate fear of hassles and red tape. In fact, with speedy, unquestioned return policies, some mail-order merchants have a better reputation regarding returns than do some department stores. See Chapter 10 for details of "full" warranties.

Familiar Offers, Unfamiliar Jargon

Continuity, load-ups, and negative options are three offers used primarily by book and record clubs and similar organizations. You may find a way to use them in your business, but they're presented here mainly because so many people associate direct mail with book and record clubs. Consumers find these offers in their mailboxes, so you should be aware of them. A *continuity series* offer covers the sale of a string of related products, such as one music CD or tape or volume in a book series per month. A version of the continuity series is used in fund raising. Contributors are asked to donate a certain amount periodically. A *load-up* offer gives the customer the opportunity to buy all the remaining units of a continuity series at one time. Load-ups usually result in a greater number of people buying an entire set. A *negative option* offer means that the publisher will continue to ship products unless the customer responds with a stop order.

Step-Up Offers

Another familiar direct mail offer is called a *step-up*. It simply asks customers to increase, or "step up," their orders. Magazines tell you to save money by increasing your subscription from one year to two years. Membership offers may have a "prestige member" level at a higher cost. You can increase your profits by adding one or two step-up levels to your basic offers. Discounts for extending the length of a contract or subscription or for substantially increasing an order are usually a sound proposition for marketers.

Keep Good Records

One of the secrets to direct mail success is to keep good records. If you do a mailing, don't just record the number of responses you get, but keep track of the number and percentage of sales you convert from leads. Keep careful track of costs. To build a successful strategy you need to learn from everything you do. Make sure you separate and identify all costs for *each* mailing you do. For example, don't pay for your postage from a general office account without itemizing the amounts spent on individual mailings.

An Overall Strategy

Never pass up an opportunity to promote. Every contact you have with a customer or potential customer—in the mail, on the phone, or in person—is an opportunity to sell. Make the most of every dollar you spend on your business. When you talk to a customer about one product or service, use cross-selling techniques to mention another product.

In the mail, you have many opportunities to promote. One example: When you ship merchandise, include a *bounce-back* offer, that is, an advertisement containing an offer for another of your products. When customers receive an order shipment from you, they may be in just the right frame of mind to order something else. Give them the opportunity.

3 FINDING YOUR MARKET, SELECTING THE MEDIA

Building a Customer Profile

Of 900 employees at BBD&O [an ad agency], there are 200 vice presidents.

—Judith Katz

One of the secrets of direct marketing is to identify your present customers, then reach more people just like them in the least expensive way possible.

Whether you use direct marketing for retail support, mail order, or business-to-business marketing, you need to define your market clearly, then select the appropriate media to carry your message to that market. The media may include magazine and newspaper ads, mailing lists, radio commercials, telemarketing, and other forms of communication. Although it may be less costly, and somewhat less time-consuming than creating the advertising, selecting the media is probably the most important of the three elements of direct marketing. All the creative and production work you put into your advertising will be based on the media decisions you make.

RESEARCH

In conventional advertising, research comes first, then the focus shifts to creating the commercials and ads. With direct marketing, particularly for small business, the research should be ongoing. The types of research you may associate with advertising, such as attitude and product surveys, are not used extensively in direct marketing. Research efforts are concentrated first on locating the best media and mailing lists to use, then on detailed analysis of complex test mailings and print advertising tests.

Using layers of tests to determine the effectiveness of different lists, different offers, different media, and other factors, large, established direct marketers search for the right combination for success. They test lists by mailing to tens or hundreds of thousands of people and they test print media and print advertising offers through direct response ads in many publications.

As a small business person you are limited by your budget in the number of tests you can conduct. Limited availability of testing is in fact one of the biggest differences between large and small direct marketers. Therefore, you should use a combination of conventional and direct response–style research.

Surveys, interviews, and other field/customer research will help you define your market and develop advertising keyed to your customers' needs.

To compensate for limited testing, two other steps are essential: researching your available media and lists to target your advertising as precisely as possible, and carefully tracking your results. Inaccurately targeted advertising and lack of methodical tracking are two of the most common pitfalls for small business marketers. Master these two techniques, combine them with testing and other research when possible, and you'll be miles ahead of the majority of small businesses—and many of the larger ones as well.

Customer Profile

No matter how you intend to use direct marketing, your first research step should be to draw a customer profile. The more information you can collect on your customers, the better you will be able to find new ones. In a sense, your entire media strategy will be based on your profile because you'll be looking for new customers among people who match the profile of your existing customers.

Your profile needs to be more than a guess as to who buys from you; it should be as exact and detailed as you can make it. The information you should gather about your customers is the same information you will examine when you're considering outside mailing lists or print media advertising. Here are some of the categories of information that will help you form a useful customer profile.

Demographics. The term *demographics* refers to various socioeconomic characteristics used to identify people. Information on age, gender, occupation, marital status, children, and income range are all important to predicting buying habits.

Geography. Where customers live is of prime importance for a variety of reasons. Retailers might consider it their *most* important factor. Where people live also tells a variety of other things about them, because people who are alike tend to live in the same neighborhoods. Census tract data and some sophisticated (neighborhood) cluster analysis programs let you make assumptions about individual customers' average annual incomes, home values, and a variety of other demographic factors. The term *geo-demographics* is used to combine the first two related categories.

Psychographics. People with similar demographic characteristics may have different lifestyles which lead them to be different types of consumers. *Psychographics* describe a person's habits, activities, interests, attitudes, and behavior patterns. People who live in the same type of neighborhoods may share some psychographic characteristics.

Naturally you don't have all this information about your customers at your fingertips, but it's not that difficult to collect, as we'll see. Until now you may not have cared whether the people who buy your products are married or single, so long as they buy. But what if you found out that 75 percent of your customers are single? Wouldn't that change your marketing plans and tell you something about where you should be advertising? That's just one example of how your customer profile will influence your decisions.

Fill in the details about your customers with hard facts. For example, you might assume that only people in a relatively high income bracket buy your product. Research may tell you, however, that many middle-income people buy your product too, as a status symbol, so they will be perceived as being a part of the upper-income group.

Try not to limit your market by distance. If you can find potential customers who fit your profile in every way except in proximity to your office or store, you can use mail order to reach them. The purpose of accurate targeting is to find people who are likely to buy. When you find them, distance may not be as important as you think. The way you will locate potential customers is through the media available to you, including mailing lists.

The exception to the profile plan comes when you want to develop a new market for a new product or service, or expand the market for an existing product. In this case you will want to build a prospect profile, comparing it to your original to find differences and similarities you can use. For example, if you sell PC software for business and home use and you decide to market educational software, your prospect profile will have to expand to include students, educators, and other new potential customers. You will probably also discover that your previous customers are also good prospects for the new products.

If you're just starting out in business, you'll have to draw a prospect profile, which describes the kind of person you *think* will buy your product or service. In that instance, competing companies would be one of the first places to start your research. Ideally, a copy of a competitor's mailing list would be a great source of information. You could analyze the list geo-demographically to find out how to reach these customers. Getting a copy of a competitor's list, however, is difficult at best. List owners ask to see your sample mailing pieces before they complete a list agreement with you.

As your start-up business grows, you should gather information on your customers and compare it to the prospect profile you began with. If your actual customers differ from your profile, change your profile. Keeping an updated profile is essential, no matter how long you have been in business; it's a useful by-product of maintaining an accurate data base on your customers.

If you sell to business, a profile is still helpful. Write up a list of characteristics of the companies that buy your products.

Marketing research is helpful in a variety of ways, including creating a customer profile, but research is not magic, nor is it mandatory for success. Some business people seem to conduct research because it's the astute thing to do, not necessarily because they need information. Unguided research simply consumes time. Before you begin a research project, ask yourself what it is you need to find out and what effect the results will have on your business and marketing plans.

• •

Why Research?

Here are some specific reasons why you may need research:

Select products. Conventional research may help you decide which new products to offer.

Identify new markets. For example, if you sell equipment for heavy duty printing presses and you only market to print shops and newspapers, research might tell you that some corporations have in-house printing facilities large enough to need your product.

Determine attitudes. How your customers feel about issues such as price increases and changes in service can be identified.

Discover buying patterns. Your customers order refills or replacement parts every four months and you want to know the national average frequency for reorders.

Evaluate ads. Certain types of research techniques can help you determine how people respond to different creative approaches.

Find media. Surveys among your customers can tell you quickly which publications they read.

Watch the competition. Keeping an eye on what your competitors are doing is a frequent research subject too.

• •

Ways to Gather Information

Marketing research is divided into two categories, primary and secondary. *Primary research* includes original surveys, questionnaires, and other methods you use to gather new information. These techniques can be costly. Many sources of secondary research, on the other hand, are free or cost very little. *Secondary research* is the analysis of data that has already been collected, organized, and printed. Reading news articles from back issues of trade journals is one example of secondary research.

Secondary Research. The U.S. Government is one of the largest sources of secondary data useful for marketing. Reams of studies and reports from U.S. agencies, including the departments of Labor, Commerce, Agriculture, and Education; the Federal Reserve Board; and many others, are available at local libraries or through the U.S. Government Printing Office. Information taken from the U.S. Census is minutely detailed. Specific geo-demographic information is available for any area of the country. An important portion of your customer profile information could come from comparing where your customers live with census information available at your library or from the U.S. Census Bureau. Census reports, for example, divide the country into small areas or geographic *tracts*. For each tract, averages are available for monthly housing costs, income, marital status, family size, and other demographics.

Marketing and geo-demographic information is available from a variety of other sources such as chambers of commerce, newspapers, and local governments. Private companies such as Dun & Bradstreet, which publishes many authoritative business directories, and Rand McNally, which publishes directories such as the annual *Commercial Atlas and Marketing Guide,* are also valuable research sources. Libraries at colleges with schools of business or marketing are especially good resources and have the additional advantage of providing access to current marketing research theses. Getting help from a research librarian at a college or public library could be as valuable to you as the full-time director of market research whom you probably can't afford yet. A friend of mine got so much marketing help from a librarian, he brought her a bouquet of flowers to say thanks. She told him it was a first, and now he gets special help.

Trade associations and trade journals often conduct research and publish the results. One recent publication produced by *American Banker,* a trade newspaper, contained enough marketing survey information to keep a financial institution marketing director busy for a week. It discussed consumers' attitudes toward various new services, satisfaction with different types of institutions, and consumers' opinions on a variety of other topics. Other industries have similar research publications.

Research-oriented computer data bases expand your possibilities further. Libraries are phasing out their old card catalogs in favor of computerized systems, which cut research down to a fraction of the time it used to take and thus give you more time to expand your searches. One periodical-based source, InfoTrac, from Information Access Co., is available at many libraries. In seconds you can search hundreds of thousands of articles from recent magazines for information on your particular topic. When you find the business or consumer publication with an article you want, copies are often available on convenient microfilm or microfiche. If you have a modem on your computer you can do some research from your office. Private on-line information services, which charge membership and access fees, such as those through Dow Jones & Co. Inc., provide business data that is updated daily. The vast computer catalog of the entire University of California library system is accessible free by modem from anyplace in the world.

Secondary research is cheaper and takes less time than primary research, but sometimes you need to ask all the questions and control the research process yourself. Here's a review of common primary research techniques.

Surveys.   For either phone or mail surveys, clear, unambiguous questions will encourage people to answer and will help you obtain unbiased results you can use to make marketing decisions. Focus on the purposes of your research and keep your questions short. Multiple-choice questions with several brief, possible answers are easy to respond to and easy to tabulate. For initial research, however, you may want to use some open-ended questions, which call for the respondent to provide his or her own answer. This lets people mention things you may not have thought of. For example, if you think that people make buying decisions about a particular product based on either price, convenience, or brand recognition, you would provide those possible answers on a survey. If in fact, product safety was the primary buying influence, your survey question would miss the majority of answers and would give you misleading information. Open-ended questions can give you ideas on which to base further research.

If you ask for a combination of customer opinions and preferences along with demographic information, it's a good idea to ask the demographic questions last. This gives the respondent time to become accustomed to answering questions, before more personal questions are posed. To find out income level, let customers pick ranges. This can give you enough information without requiring people to tell you their exact salaries.

The length of your survey will influence your costs, percentage of responses, and the time necessary to tabulate results. A shorter survey will encourage people to respond and make it easier for you to acquire the results.

Make sure your customers or survey subjects know the purpose of your research. You don't need to explain your marketing strategies, but you should clearly identify your company, tell them the survey is important to your firm, and assure customers that their responses will remain confidential. People are more likely to respond if they know the name of the company and the purpose of the research.

Mail Questionnaires.   One of the easiest ways to collect information and opinions from your customers is to mail them questionnaires. You don't even need to do a separate mailing; some companies include short questionnaires on product registration cards or insert them with statements and other routine customer mailings.

The more information you wish to find out, the more necessary a separate questionnaire becomes. With a mail survey, one of your biggest goals is to obtain a high return rate. To do this, be sure the questionnaire is clear and clean. It should appear easy to answer and the questions should require a minimum of instructions. Broad white margins at the top, bottom, and sides of the questionnaire will make it more appealing, and the questions themselves should not be jammed together on the page.

Include a cover letter that identifies your survey as a legitimate marketing research project. Encourage the readers to fill out the questionnaire as soon as they get it. If you plan to make changes in products or customer service based on the survey results, say so. If you include a postage-paid return envelope, you'll boost responses.

For most mail surveys, you will need to do a second mailing to people who don't respond. To get your responses as high as possible, you may even need to do a third mailing. The follow-ups should be received by your audience at two-week intervals.

One big advantage of mail surveys is their relatively low cost compared to telephone and in-person interviews. The major disadvantage is a low response rate. Your ability to attribute the opinions of the survey respondents to the group as a whole increases with your reply rate, but authorities differ widely on the level of responses necessary. Here's a suggested range:

- 60 percent and above—very good
- 35 to 60 percent—good
- 25 to 34 percent—questionable
- 24 percent and below—don't rely on this data

These figures assume you are mailing to your entire list of customers. Remember that people reply to surveys for different reasons. A small response rate may introduce a bias by having an unrepresentatively high percentage of people who turned in the questionnaire because they wanted to complain about a service.

Telephone Research. Although more expensive, telephone research yields higher reponse rates, and its results therefore have a greater validity than those of mail surveys. If you think it will be difficult to get people to answer your questions when you conduct a telephone survey, you may be pleasantly surprised. Whereas some people may respond to telemarketing calls by hanging up, most people are interested in being asked for their opinions. Phone surveys account for a majority of primary market research. People do take the time to answer surveys, if the person conducting the survey (1) clearly identifies the purpose of the call as a marketing survey and not sales, (2) treats the respondents in a courteous, businesslike way, and (3) allows time for answers to the questions, but keeps the respondent on track and the interview flowing forward.

It's important to work from a specific script and not to deviate from the script with different people. Everyone must be asked the same questions in the same way. A mixture of closed- and open-ended questions may be asked, but each question must not be so long, or have so many options, that the listener becomes confused.

Your response rate for a telephone survey should be substantially higher than for a mail questionnaire. You should receive a response from the vast majority of your survey subjects, excluding wrong numbers, answering machines, busy signals, disconnected numbers, and any circumstance that prevents you from reaching the person you wish to speak with. If you don't complete your survey with more than 80 percent of the target respondents you reach, then you may need to adjust your technique or script. Phone surveys of business people are often more time- consuming, depending on the occupation of the respondents. Business surveys often require callers to transfer through an organization to find the right person, only to discover that person is already on another call.

Another advantage of telephone surveys is time. Mail surveys take time for printing, addressing, mailing. They typically sit at the respondent's home or office before they're returned. The process can take weeks or months depending on the scope of the survey. Phone surveys can be done in a week or two, depending on the number of people in your audience and the number of people doing the calling. Also, when you do a phone survey, you can ask follow-up questions such as "Why?" to find out customer motivation.

An occasional side benefit from a phone survey is sales leads. When you contact an existing customer or a potential one, the respondents may ask you questions about products and may even ask to place an order. I recently conducted a brief telephone survey of personnel executives at large and medium-sized companies for a health industry client. Although I clearly identified the purpose of the call as just research, 20 percent of the company representatives I spoke with asked for more information on the service, and some asked to be contacted by a sales representative.

Don't expect this kind of response with every survey you do, but surveys have a way of getting through to potential customers. For this reason some telemarketing people pretend to be conducting a survey when they're actually selling. This, of course, makes it more difficult to conduct bona fide research on the phone.

Other Techniques. A variety of other primary research methods are available, including field observations, where you simply watch and record behavior, and field experiments, in which you control certain variables and record behavior. Testing techniques and focus groups are discussed in Chapter 6.

EVALUATING PUBLICATIONS

When your research helps you identify the people you want to reach, use that information to start narrowing down your possible media. Selecting media is not an either/or proposition. The best campaigns use a combination of advertising media. You can focus your search for publications two ways: geographically, primarily through newspapers; and demographically or psychographically, primarily through magazines.

Start at the library. Look at the publications that you think are read by your target customers. Read through a few issues of each publication, looking for ads for competing or similar products or services. Notice the editorial content of the publications as well and see if it gives you an idea of what the demographics of the readership might be. If you have a mail-order product, notice if the publications have special buy-by-mail advertising sections. Look for *reader service cards,* which allow people to request information from any advertiser simply by checking off a number on a postcard and returning it to the periodical. Bingo cards, as these postcards are known in the industry, give your potential buyers a simple response device.

When you have a partial list of advertising sources, it's time to gather more data. Three publications, available at most libraries, provide detailed information on periodicals.

1. *The Gale Directory of Publications and Broadcast Media,* organized geographically by state and city, provides the circulation, basic ad rates, and other information on most newspapers and magazines. It is especially useful in locating all publications in one community.

2. *Writer's Market,* arranged by magazine subject, doesn't contain any advertising information, but it provides detailed descriptions of editorial content and some demographics of readers for hundreds of business and consumer magazines.

3. The bibles of professional media buyers, however, are the directories published by Standard Rate and Data Service, Inc., abbreviated SRDS. Separate volumes are devoted to consumer magazines, business magazines, newspapers, mailing lists, and broadcast media. While the two other books mentioned are published annually, SRDS directories come out monthly, except for the mailing list book, which is issued bimonthly. Figure 3.1 shows a sample magazine listing in SRDS.

To do a thorough job of your periodical search, read through the directory listings for the publications you've selected. Search for additional newspapers in the same area as your targeted publications, and use indexes and tables of contents in the directories to help you find other magazines in the same or related fields as the ones you have selected. Look at the demographics of the readers and see if you can find the ones closest to your customer profile. Compare circulations and ad rates; the two are usually, but not always, closely related. You can also use local Yellow Pages to identify new publications or ones that are not listed in the national directories.

Magazines

To identify all possible magazines, you need to be specific and creative. For example, let's say you're selling a device that cleans guns. Obviously, you could advertise in mass circulation magazines such as *Time* or *Reader's Digest* to reach millions of people. But considering that a full-page, black-and-white ad in *Reader's Digest* costs more than $100,000, there must be a better way to reach gun owners without paying for the *Reader's Digest* readers who are not prospects. Next, you might think of firearms magazines such as *Guns and Ammo* or *American Hunter,* a publication of the National Rifle Association. Since your cleaning device is only good for pistols, however, you look further in the pages of SRDS and find *American Handgunner,* which sounds even more promising. In the latter publication, the price listed for a $\frac{1}{6}$-page ad, which would be appropriate for a mail-order device, is less than $500. Read the Publisher's Editorial Profile in SRDS for the gun magazines to see who their readers are.

Don't stop there. Who uses pistols regularly, in addition to hunters and hobbyists? What about military personnel and police officers? In a different classification of SRDS are the listings for a variety of law enforcement and active duty military magazines, such as *Leatherneck,* a Marine magazine. In skimming through the *Writer's Market* to research the readers of these magazines, you find a reference to magazines for soldiers of fortune—more likely prospects. (If there were a trade journal for gangsters and hit-men, that might be a good buy too!)

GUN DOG

THE MAGAZINE OF UPLAND BIRD AND WATERFOWL DOGS
A Stover Publishing Co., Inc. Publication

The Audit Bureau

Media Code 8 325 6975 6.00   **Ifd 006281-000**
Published bimonthly by The Stover Publishing Company, Inc., 1901 Bell Ave., Suite 4, Des Moines, IA 50315. Phone 515-243-2472. FAX: 515-243-0233, .
PUBLISHER'S EDITORIAL PROFILE
GUN DOG is edited for outdoorsmen who own upland bird and waterfowl dogs. Each issue contains stories and advice on dog food, health care, training techniques and devices, shotgunning, ammunition, travel and new products. Rec'd 10/6/89.

1. PERSONNEL
Chairman & C.E.O.—Roger D. Stover.
President and Publisher—Carrell E. Bunn.
Advertising—Rick Koskovick.
Production—Rollie Lee.

3. COMMISSION AND CASH DISCOUNT
15% to recognized agencies. 2% 10 days. Net 30.
ADVERTISING RATES
Effective January 01, 1989.
Rates received October 14, 1988.

5. BLACK/WHITE RATES

	1 ti	3 ti	6 ti
1 page	2100.	1880.	1690.
2/3 page	1435.	1290.	1150.
1/2 page	1090.	985.	885.
1/3 page	750.	695.	595.
1/4 page	590.	540.	475.
1/6 page	415.	365.	335.

5a. COMBINATION RATES
Gun Dog may be purchased in combination with Wing & Shot and Wildfowl. Receive a 10% discount for advertising in two of Stover Publishing Company magazines or for bigger discounts see The Big Three listing for advertising in Stover's big three hunting magazines. (To receive frequency discounts and combo discounts ads must be same unit size and color).

6. COLOR RATES
Black and 1 color, extra .... 375.

	1 ti	3 ti	6 ti
4 color:			
1 page	2835.	2620.	2420.
2/3 page	2175.	2030.	1880.
1/2 page	1825.	1720.	1620.
1/3 page	1485.	1425.	1330.

	1 ti	3 ti	6 ti
1/4 page	1320.	1270.	1205.
1/6 page	1145.	1095.	1065.

7. COVERS

	1 ti	3 ti	6 ti
4 color:			
2nd cover	3405.	3185.	3080.
3rd cover	3170.	3015.	2850.
4th cover	3640.	3470.	3255.

8. INSERTS
Available.

9. BLEED
No charge.

11. CLASSIFIED/MAIL ORDER/SPECIALTY RATES
CLASSIFIED:
1.75 per word. 20 word minimum. Cash with order.
DISPLAY CLASSIFICATIONS:
7-1/4 col. inches ... 340.00   2 col. inches 130.00
4 col. inches .... 220.00   1 col. inch 75.00
3 col. inches 180.00

15. MECH. REQUIREMENTS
Also see SRDS Print Media Production Data.
Printing Process: Web Offset.
Trim size: 8-1/4 x 10-7/8; No./Cols. 2&3.
Binding method: Saddle-Stitched.
Colors available: Publisher's standard, 4-Color Process (AAAA/MPA); 5-Color Process.
DIMENSIONS-AD PAGE

1	7-1/4	x 9-1/2	1/3	4-11/16	x 4-11/16
2/3	4-3/4	x 9-1/2	1/4	3-1/2	x 4-11/16
1/2	3-1/2	x 9-1/2	1/4	7-1/4	x 2-1/4
1/2	7-1/4	x 4-11/16	1/6	2-1/4	x 4-11/16
1/3	2-1/4	x 9-1/2	1/6	4-3/4	x 2-1/4

16. ISSUE AND CLOSING DATES
Published bimonthly.

Issue:	– Closing – (*) (+)	Issue:	– Closing – (*) (+)
Feb-Mar	12/14 12/1	Aug-Sep	6/14 6/1
Apr-May	2/8 2/1	Oct-Nov	8/16 8/1
Jun-Jul	4/12 4/1	Dec-Jan	10/11 10/1

(*) Material.
(+) Space.
No changes or cancellations accepted after closing date.

18. CIRCULATION
Established 1981. Single copy 3.50; per year 20.97.
A.B.C. 6-30-89 (6 mos. aver.—Magazine Form)

Tot.Pd.	(Subs.)	(Single)	[Assoc.]
55,524	55,240	284	...

Average Total Non-Paid Distribution (not incl. above):
Total 1,546
TERRITORIAL DISTRIBUTION 3/89—55,140

N.Eng.	Mid.Atl.	E.N.Cen.	W.N.Cen.	S.Atl.	E.S.Cen.
2,524	5,320	10,362	8,921	7,742	2,838
W.S.Cen.	Mtn.St.	Pac.St.	Canada	Foreign	Other
5,996	3,665	6,010	1,552	96	114

FIGURE 3.1 Sample magazine listing from SRDS. (*From Standard Rate and Data Service, Mar. 27, 1990 edition of Consumer Magazine and Agri-media Rates and Data. Reprinted with permission.*)

As you study magazines, you can learn several things from back issues. Look at the sizes and types of ads the magazines run. Pay special attention to mail-order and direct response ads, especially for products and services similar to yours. What size ads do your competitors use? Look for those small-space ads which are repeated month after month. Many of them are successful or the advertisers would not keep repeating them. Notice the types of articles. Would they appeal to people in your customer profile? Does the publication have special pages or sections devoted to mail-order shopping? Even if you're just looking for leads, not direct sales, presence of these sections tells you that people who read the publication are accustomed to seeing and using response-oriented advertising.

The next step is to call the publications and request rate cards and *media kits*. Most magazines will send you their advertising rates and a kit containing a sample issue, geo-demographic information on readers, circulation/readership figures, lists of advertisers, and other information. A recent media kit for *US Air Magazine* contained a 32-page supplement, comparing its readership and market share with other airline magazines in the major U.S. markets, and an equally long market research report. The report compared demographics and purchasing histories of *US Air Magazine* readers with those of other major airline and news magazines.

Family Circle's media kit includes a map showing its 26 regions and 56 subregions. It also includes a special insert for response media, listing the number of direct response ad pages they have run (a measure of magazine readers' responsiveness), circulation statistics, and testimonials from mail-order advertisers. Obviously smaller and regional publications will not have as elaborate materials available, but these are some things to look for.

Remember, a media kit is sales information and not a third-party analysis, but it does help you evaluate a publication. The kits also will contain deadlines (called closing dates) and mechanical requirements. The latter term refers to the form in which the magazine wants you to send the ad, usually camera-ready artwork or a negative.

Before you make any decision about a publication, ask to see its *audited* circulation figures. This *is* third-party information. Circulation for most publications is audited and certified by outside firms. The Audit Bureau of Circulations (ABC) audits consumer magazines and newspapers, and the Business Publications Audit of Circulation, Inc. (BPA) covers business and some consumer publications. Both organizations provide *publisher's statements* for each magazine or newspaper they audit. The statement describes the size and sources of the publication's circulation. A consumer publication that boasts of a 150,000 circulation, for example, may be giving away a substantial number of subscriptions in an effort to justify its ad rates. A magazine's BPA- or ABC-audited statement will give you the facts.

Many magazines allow you to buy advertising regionally. For example, on *Family Circle*'s rate card, a $\frac{1}{6}$-page, black-and-white direct response ad in the full magazine lists for about $11,500. If you want the same ad to run in just the Western United States, the price is about $2,500. *Family Circle* traditionally has been a good medium for direct response and usually carries many pages of it.

Some other publications which have been effective for direct mail advertisers include *TV Guide, Parade, Cosmopolitan, Money,* and *Prevention.* This is only a sample of many magazines that can be successful for you. As you examine rates, compare the costs of different-sized ads in the same publication.

The cost should be only one consideration in your decision on the size of your advertising. Here are some other factors:

- Balance size and frequency. For the same price as a large ad, you may be able to run smaller ads in several publications or run ads in consecutive issues of the same magazine.
- If you're just looking for leads, if you're selling a relatively simple product by mail order, or if you're offering a catalog, a small-space ad such as $\frac{1}{3}$- or $\frac{1}{6}$-page is probably all you need. If it's well designed and written, your small ad will probably attract as many readers as a larger one, at a substantial savings to you.

- Mail-order ads for complex products such as insurance or high-tech electronics, or new services or products that require explanations, call for large ads, such as a full page. See Chapters 8, 9, and 12 for samples and examples of large and small ads.

- In direct response you're looking for bottom-line results, so the income from most ads will be evaluated individually. Your ads also build on each other to add to your awareness. (You get awareness and orders.)

- If you have a complex offer and you're thinking about large ads, consider the law of diminishing returns. A full-page ad often costs twice as much as a half-page ad, but often doesn't give you twice the return. Some publications offer nearly-full-page ads, which leave a little room on the top and one side for editorial matter. These junior pages, as they're sometimes called, can have all the impact of a full page without the full cost. In addition, the editorial matter may draw more readers.

- If you want to add a reply card to your message, you can have a postcard bound into the magazine next to your ad. You usually have to buy a full-page ad to qualify for a card, and in larger-circulation magazines cards can be prohibitively expensive.

Media selection should be tied to your business plan and ultimate objectives. For example, if you need to generate many responses or make a big impression in a short time, you will probably advertise in the publications that have yielded the best response for you in the past. Without a track record to guide you, and under pressure for quick sales, you might buy the largest-circulation publication in your industry or spend where you will get the maximum circulation for your money. If business objectives allow you more time, test one medium or one publication against another before you commit to spending the bulk of your ad budget.

Newspapers

Local newspapers provide you with some of the fastest results of any print medium. If you get good results you can immediately repeat a winner; if you don't you'll know soon, and you can try something else.

Large newspapers have their own market research departments and can often provide detailed demographics for all the neighborhoods they serve. Depending on size, papers may offer customized research or special reports on various segments of the retail market such as apparel or automotive. In addition, a newspaper's media kit material can be as detailed as its magazine counterparts.

Rates and circulation vary dramatically depending on the size of the paper and the market. Your budget may allow you to consider weekly quarter-page (or larger) ads in smaller papers or a few infrequent ads in metro dailies. Some large metropolitan papers divide their circulation areas into zones and permit you to run an ad in one or more geographical areas.

With a newspaper, you pay for a mass circulation. You're not buying a narrow audience, as you are when you select special interest magazines. Being local publications, newspapers cater to local advertisers, charge national advertisers a higher rate, and are often willing to give you special services.

Free-standing inserts (FSIs) are another way to advertise in a paper. You pay a fee as if you were buying an ad, but instead you have a brochure, booklet, or other printed piece inserted into each newspaper. The *Orange County Register*, a large suburban Southern California daily, will find advertisers to share the cost of an $8\frac{1}{2}'' \times 11''$ FSI with you: you buy one side and the other advertiser buys the other. Sunday is by far the most popular day for FSIs, and many of the inserts feature coupons. On Sundays people tend to spend more time with the paper, so your insert has a better chance of being read—if it's not lost among a sea of other FSIs.

Newspapers will even do the typesetting and layout of ads for you at an additional cost. This is a great way to start if you have an ultra-skimpy budget and want to test an idea; however, it's usually more effective if you do your own production or hire a graphic artist to do it for you, because you have more control over the final product. Reproduction in newspapers is not as good as in magazines, so don't use minutely detailed artwork. Review papers for examples of ads similar to ones you might use.

RADIO AND TELEVISION

Radio advertising is increasing, the number of stations is growing, and broadcast formats are subdividing into increasingly specialized groups. All of these factors are in your favor. The increased competition tends to fragment listeners and reduce the audience of any one station, but it also helps keep commercial time reasonably priced.

While you can't buy as specialized an audience as you can with magazines, radio gives you a few distinct groups of listeners, based on stations' formats. All-news, rock, classical, country, easy listening, oldies, contemporary, and all-talk are some of the most common station formats today, but more are emerging. For example, some serve ethnic communities.

As with print, you need to become familiar with the medium. Listen to the music and types of commercials a station carries. If you hear nothing but commercials for blemish cream and slasher movies mixed with rap music, you have not found the right medium to advertise real estate investment trusts. Try a classical station or an all-news format.

You can identify radio stations and formats through SRDS and request rate cards and other information. Most radio advertising is bought on a spot basis locally, but you can make national and regional buys. Sales firms that represent groups of stations offer package deals.

You never buy just one commercial, but a series of spots spread out over several days. The advantage of radio is that it can deliver your message to people several times. This is called the medium's *frequency*. Since there are dozens of stations in large metropolitan areas, a station's *reach* or total audience is limited. Up to a point, the more spots you buy, the more listeners you reach. If your ads on one station in a market generate leads or sales for you, you should stick with that station. If you want to expand and you can find another station with similar demographics, then you will increase your reach by buying the second station.

Costs of radio commercials vary depending on the size of the audience. Spots on a small-town station in a rural area may be $20 or less. Commercials on a top-rated station in New York or Los Angeles can cost $500 or more.

The hours from 6 to 10 A.M. and from 3 to 7 P.M., known as drive time, are the most expensive because radio audiences tend to be highest at these times. The majority of listeners tune in while in their cars on the way to work. In the past, drive time has not been the best for direct response ads. However, with the popularity of cellular telephones, more people now have a means to respond, and in metropolitan areas they're not doing anything else at the time anyway, except inching along the highway. Products or services pegged at people who have phones in their cars might be good for drive-time radio; so might a product aimed at commuters, such as books recorded on cassettes, or anything else to make commutes easier.

A radio station will often produce commercials for you that are to be aired on that station. Some stations will do it for free depending on the number of spots you buy. Even if you have to pay an additional fee, you'll get professional commercials at a lower cost than if you did it yourself.

Television is far more expensive than radio and is usually outside the budget of small business, although it would be worthwhile for you to check the costs of local station spots if you live in a relatively small metropolitan area. Late night and other non–prime time hours might be affordable while delivering the responsive audiences you're looking for. In addition, no matter what size city you live in, cable stations, sometimes the video equivalent of a weekly home-town paper, can be an inexpensive buy.

COMPARING AND BUYING

Trying to compare the costs and values of different media is difficult. One common comparison figure is the cost per thousand impressions (CP/M), or the cost of getting your message to one thousand people. You can use CP/M to compare similar-sized ads in different publications. You can also use CP/M to compare two different direct mail packages.

No single comparison factor exists, however, to compare one medium with another. There is not enough common ground. For example, the size of an ad or the length of a commercial would change your cost without changing the number of impressions. With direct mail your CP/M is many times higher than for print advertising, but your results are much higher too. A better way of comparing different media is your cost per order or cost per lead. Unfortunately, a station or publication can't give you those figures. You have to find out for yourself by carefully tracking your results.

You have a choice of ways to buy media. If you use an advertising agency to do it for you, the publication or station will pay the agency a standard 15 percent commission. In other words, if an ad costs $100, the agency will pay $85 to the publication and pocket the commission. If you do the buying yourself as an advertiser, there's no commission involved. Depending on how much print or broadcast media you intend to buy, it might be beneficial to form your own in-house advertising agency, simply as a way of retaining the 15 percent agency commission for yourself.

Many large and small advertisers have their own in-house agencies, which are effectively advertising departments, agencies only in name. Most media outlets will recognize in-house agencies and give you the commission, provided you keep the transactions of your agency essentially separate from your company. To do that, have separate letterhead printed with the name of your in-house agency and use it for correspondence and insertion orders (orders for ad space). Keep a separate checking account to pay for your advertising space and commercials. Some in-house agencies at larger companies have actually accepted work from outside clients so that they have become profit centers for the parent companies.

When you're ready to negotiate the best prices, prepare to wheel and deal with radio station sales reps. More than with print media, the cost of radio station time is usually subject to negotiation. The rate card may be just a starting point. Open negotiating is so common that the 15 percent agency discount becomes a moot point. You simply negotiate for the lowest base price, period. Even though negotiation is common in radio, that doesn't mean it's easy.

A further option is the use of a media buying service. Even some advertising agencies that do not specialize in radio or TV buying use outside buying services. The services buy in such large quantities that they can often give you your commission, take their percentage, and still sell you a spot for the price you'd pay for it after you negotiated. The size of your radio buy will determine whether it's feasible to work with a buying service.

With print media, you should be able to negotiate some discounts, depending on the amount of space a publication has available and on your powers of persuasion. At a minimum, however, you can usually expect an automatic discount for direct response ads.

One thing to ask your media representatives about is per-inquiry (PI) ads or spots. To fill unsold air time, some stations sell spots for a price based solely on the number of inquiries received. Newspaper space may be available through similar arrangements.

PI agreements let you advertise without up-front media costs and they let the station or paper share in your success. The more you are willing to pay for each inquiry, the more likely your media representative may be to go along with a PI agreement. Many papers and stations will refuse under any circumstances, but it will pay you to ask. Incidentally, stations or papers that do PI advertising usually have an arrangement so they can monitor the responses.

When contracting for print media space, the location of your ad is important. If you have a small-space ad with a coupon, point that out to your sales representative. You don't want your coupon buried on the gutter (the inside fold of a newspaper) because it will be difficult for customers to cut it out. If you have other than a small-space, mail-order ad, the generally accepted philosophy is that right-hand pages, as close to the front of a magazine as possible are the best. "Far forward, right-hand page requested" is stock wording on some agency insertion orders.

Publications differ, however, and a prime location in one might not be as good in another. A left-hand page opposite a popular columnist or regular puzzle feature in a magazine might be better than a page toward the front of the magazine that was sandwiched between many pages of ads, remote from articles or other editorial matter. You can save money on a newspaper ad if you do not specify the location, but permit it to be printed anywhere in the paper.

POSTSCRIPTS ....

Research Help

If you're looking for research help, private market research firms abound. They come in all sizes and price ranges. To get help for a research project on a budget, contact the marketing, business, or communications department at a local college. Marketing professors often moonlight as consultants, and some marketing classes look for business research they can tackle as a class project.

Prices Change

As economic and market conditions change, so do advertising rates. Magazines and radio stations sometimes change formats or cease operations. What was a gospel station one day might start the next morning with an all-talk or heavy metal format. You can be sure that within a short time, the station's demographics will be transformed.

The prices and availability of media listed in this chapter are subject to change. Effectiveness of an individual magazine as a mail-order medium can change as well. Before developing a tentative ad budget, check the prices and availability of the media you're interested in by reviewing the current issue of SRDS, or better, by obtaining rate cards from the various media outlets. Also consider testing one publication against another.

4 BUYING, CREATING, AND USING LISTS FOR FUN AND PROFIT

Data Base Marketing

When Suzuki Motor Corporation debuted its new model motorcycles, direct mail was selected as a way to increase awareness and generate sales leads. The obvious target audience for the mailing was motorcycle owners; the list included 1.2 million people.

Rather than mail to that many people and hope for an acceptable 1 percent response, says Tim Maroney, president of HDM Worldwide Direct, Suzuki's direct marketing agency, they decided to get more specific.

To narrow their focus, they used what's called a *geographic overlay* to sort out all potential customers who did not live within a certain radius of a Suzuki dealer. That narrowed the list to 800,000. Then they eliminated people who did not match their customer profile, which had been established the previous year. That left them with 600,000 prospects.

They then decided that a prime candidate, based on their research, would be someone who had bought a bike two to five years ago and had not yet traded it in. That reduced the list to 400,000 names.

Next came brand loyalty. They agreed that owners of some brands of motorcycles, notably Harley-Davidson, would not be good candidates to buy a new Suzuki. The people who remained on the list were finally screened for creditworthiness, and those who qualified were sent a mail package offering them preapproved credit on the purchase of a new motorcycle.

The final list, says Maroney, was pared to 256,000 recipients, about one-fifth of the original. Their response rate? Six percent of the recipients took the offer to a dealer for a test ride, and another 1.5 percent called the 800 number.

While your mailing lists are probably not nearly the size of Suzuki's, you can apply the same principles to your list planning. By using careful list selection and segmentation you can aim right at your principal prospects or customers. Like Suzuki, you can be selective to increase your response rates while reducing your mailing costs.

Precise selection of potential customers is the key advantage of direct mail, yet surprisingly few small businesses do any list sorting or segmenting at all. According to list compilers, average small businesses don't even buy lists that can be corrected and enhanced by various, sometimes simple, computer techniques. Small business people usually just buy address labels for residents in defined neighborhoods or businesses in certain classifications.

With your customer profile you can identify print and broadcast media that have the best chance of reaching the prospects you want. Mailing lists let you be even more selective. You have thousands of lists from which to choose, and many lists are sliced into smaller sections based on various criteria from demographics to buying histories. Some lists are just that, lists. Others are vast data bases containing a variety of information on thousands or millions of potential customers.

Your house list of existing customers and prospects remains your best resource, but to learn more about using your house list you should learn how to use rental lists, which in many cases are other people's house lists. You can use other lists to add to your house list. As mentioned in Chapter 2, there are two types of outside lists you can rent: direct response lists and compiled lists.

Begin your exploration of lists with a directory. The SRDS direct mail list directory is the industry standard and is available in many public and college libraries. It's divided into business and consumer lists, and both direct response and compiled lists are represented. To find a list, look up your category in the index at the front.

Lists come in all types and sizes. For the inveterate entrepreneur, a stroll through a direct mail list directory will yield a variety of appealing potential markets. Some mail-order people base their marketing plans on finding a market (a large list) first, then figuring out a product to sell to that list. Here's a sample of some interesting direct response lists of consumers. The dollar amount following some lists is the average amount of sale, in other words, the average amount customers spent on mail-order purchases:

- People who bought or inquired about cast iron stoves, $1,250
- Vinyl upholstery repair kit buyers, $15
- Investors in horse-breeding business opportunities
- Business seminar attendees
- Buyers of arthritis pain relievers, $32
- Buyers of exercise apparel, $75
- Members of the National Association of the Self-Employed, $42 dues
- Spanish-speaking buyers of kitchen accessories and gift items
- Buyers of books about gay lifestyles, $20

As you look through the directory, you'll see hundreds of potential markets. Does the narrow focus of some available lists give you ideas for products? One compiling firm can give you a list of people sorted by birth dates. You could sell T-shirts and coffee mugs with deprecating slogans about turning 30, 40, 50, and so on. Does a look at *your* customers' characteristics give you ideas for additional products or services you could develop for them?

Although much of the data base marketing business is handled via computers, and the SRDS directory is now available on-line, the two main ways people gather information about compiled or direct response lists are on paper. Companies that compile lists publish their own catalogs of lists, which you can usually obtain for free with a phone call. Direct response lists are rented by list managers who issue separate *data cards* explaining each list.

THE CAREERTRACK MASTERFILE

CareerTrack

Location ID: 13 ICLS 45   **Mkd 031082-000**
CareerTrack Managed Lists.
3085 Center Green Dr., Boulder, CO 80301. Phone 303-447-2323, FAX, 303-939-8176.

1. PERSONNEL
President—James Calano.
List Manager—Connie Howard.
List Specialists—Michelle Silvers, Kinloch Dunlap.

2. DESCRIPTION
Managers, supervisors and administrative personnel who have attended or approved attendance at CareerTrack's professional-development training seminars.
ZIP Coded in numerical sequence 100%; Canadian postal coded.
List is computerized and maintained at CCX (U.S.); U.K. managed by Mardev I, Asia managed by mailing list Asia, Australia managed by logos.

3. LIST SOURCE
Direct mail sold through catalog and brochure mailings.

4. QUANTITY AND RENTAL RATES
Rec'd Aug. 3, 1990.

	Total Number	Price per/M
Total list	1,565,027	85.00
Product buyers	299,677	"
Consumers	234,299	"
Executive class	183,399	"
Business buyers	1,188,367	"
Professional women	1,022,417	"
Approving managers	359,434	"
Multi-buyers	377,499	"
Healthwatchers		
Mid-Management	350,230	"
Frontliners	151,230	"
Sales & Marketing	59,774	"

Technical	51,161	"
Financial	75,882	"
International		
Canadian	149,693	90.00
United Kingdom	77,704	185.00
Australia	50,808	"
New Zealand	1,921	"
Continental Europe	15,144	"
Asia	6,351	"

U.S. and Canada, net name arrangement upon approval (minimum 50,000), 85% plus 5.00/M running charge.
Selections (U.S. and Canada): job title, SIC code, state, SCF, seminar topic, title slugging, sex, year, maximum names per company, 5.00/M extra; bus/home, keying, 2.50/M extra; carrier route presort, 90 day hotlines, 10.00/M extra; splits, 25.00.
International: country, sex, 7.00/M extra; keying, 5.00/M extra. 15% value added tax (VAT) applicable on all U.K., Australian and European orders. All prices in U.S. dollars only.
Minimum order 5,000.

5. COMMISSION, CREDIT POLICY
20% commission to all recognized and reciprocal brokers. Net 30 days. Prepayment or broker letter of guarantee required with new mailers.

6. METHOD OF ADDRESSING
U.S. and Canada: 4-up Cheshire labels, no charge. Pressure sensitive labels, 10.00/M extra. Nonreturnable magnetic tape, 25.00/reel.
International: 4-up Cheshire labels, 5.00/M; pressures sensitive labels, 10.00/M; nonreturnable mag tape 40.00/reel.

7. DELIVERY SCHEDULE
Two weeks.

8. RESTRICTIONS
Sample mailing piece required for approval. Nonreciprocal and competitor mailers will not participate in CareerTrack's private database will be charged an additional 80.00/M (noncommissionable) on any requested segment.

11. MAINTENANCE
Updated quarterly.

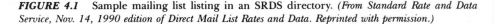

FIGURE 4.1   Sample mailing list listing in an SRDS directory. *(From Standard Rate and Data Service, Nov. 14, 1990 edition of Direct Mail List Rates and Data. Reprinted with permission.)*

DIRECT RESPONSE LISTS

If your business is strictly mail-order, direct response lists are your most important source of potential customers. Direct response lists are populated with people who have responded favorably to offers. Your job is to find people who have responded to offers similar to yours. Beyond that, you should narrow your search even further by using geo-demographics and other information often provided with rental lists; this allows you to try to match your customer profile.

Figure 4.1 shows a typical data base listing in SRDS. A variety of information is provided for each list. After you've studied the directory and selected some promising lists, you can call the firms that manage the lists and ask for data cards. When you review a list directory and data cards, you need to consider a variety of factors about each list.

If you sell crystal chandelier polish to an upscale market, and you find a list of people who have bought chandelier polish or even crystal polish before, that doesn't necessarily mean it's a good list. It could be out of date, too expensive, or flawed in other ways. When you identify a list that seems promising on the surface, you must scrutinize it. Here are the 12 elements a list broker uses to identify good and bad lists.

Professional List Broker's Criteria

Affinity.   This heading identifies the classification of merchandise a list represents. If you are selling business software, your ideal list would be buyers of business software. If you could not obtain such a list, perhaps a list of buyers of books about business software or business computer applications would be appropriate. If you have software that aids in inventory control and warehouse management, subscribers to magazines in the material-handling business or people who have bought books on the subject would be good prospects. You could expand your affinity market to include people who have attended seminars on business computing or on the specific topics, such as inventory control, that your software covers.

Some catalog and mass merchandise marketers who offer a variety of products can segment their lists by the type of merchandise purchased. You might, therefore, be able to rent just a list of people who bought a specific item from a general merchandise catalog.

Geo-demographics.   Owners/managers of large lists can sometimes provide segments of lists broken down by age, sex, income, and other factors. This allows you to pinpoint your potential prospects further through geo-demographic characteristics.

Owners can use census tract information to provide a variety of demographics on the people who populate their lists.

Psychographics.   Habits, attitudes, and behavior patterns can be helpful, if you have some of that information in your profile and if it's available to segment or define an outside list. Not all lists and data bases have psychographic information. Some basic psychographic information may be inferred from the other list criteria, such as the type of merchandise purchased.

Source.   People get their names on lists in different ways, and it's important to know how a list was created. Not all direct response lists are made up of direct mail, mail-order buyers. Many mail-order companies also rent lists of people who have inquired about their product (*inquires*), but who have not necessarily purchased it. Lists may also be made up of people who have subscribed to publications, attended seminars, responded to direct response print or broadcast advertising, or responded to telemarketing. Some lists also include retail customers. If you are doing a mail-order mailing, your best list would be made up primarily of people who have purchased as a result of direct mail offers.

Selections.   In some cases you may want to rent an entire list, but most of the time you want to be more selective and rent only a portion of the list that meets your requirements. Nearly all list managers offer *selects*, which are different ways of segmenting their lists, such as by merchandise purchased, or where customers live. Each of the other list criteria can be used as a select to segment a rental list, though rarely are all selection criteria available. The more ways you can sort a list, however, the more valuable it will be to you.

Recency. This list criterion, and the two that follow, make up what list professionals call the *RFM selection,* which stands for recency, frequency, and monetary. These criteria are based on the idea that people tend to repeat themselves. The recency factor is one of the most crucial in mail order. People who have ordered something through the mail recently are more likely to do it again than people who ordered a year ago.

Most rental lists have a *hot-line* selection that includes only those people who have ordered recently. "Recently" is usually defined as anywhere from one to six months, depending on the list. The hot-line time period will be spelled out.

Frequency. Naturally, people who order frequently are desirable customers. These *multi-buyers* are available on lists, but you need to know how recent the purchases were and the amount spent for the frequency criteria to have meaning. A recent multi-buyer who spends an above-average amount on each order would be a prime mail-order customer.

Monetary (Average Amount of Sale). This measurement tells you the average amount customers spend on individual orders or the amount of contributions in the case of fund raising. Some list selections are broken down by different average amounts spent. For example, you might rent a list of people who spend an average of $75 per order, or a list of people who spend only $20 per order.

Universe. How big is the total list? Knowing how big an entire list *universe* is will give you an idea of the depth of some selects. For example, suppose you want to select people whose average amount of sale is relatively high and to segment further by a limited number of ZIP codes. If the list you want to draw from has only 10,000 names from across the United States, chances are you'll find few names to match your criteria.

Size of the list universe is an important factor in testing. If you had to choose to test one of two similar lists, the larger list would provide greater possibilities for further sales.

Method of Payment. Not every list owner has information on how customers pay for merchandise, but when available it can be helpful to you in matching your customer profile. In addition, bank credit card purchasers are usually considered better prospects than people who pay cash or use a private retailer's credit card.

Mail Sorts. All lists are available in ZIP-code order, and many offer sorting according to carrier routes and regional postal centers, called Sectional Center Facility (SCF). Other possible geographic sortings include states and regions of the United States.

Continuations. When a major mailer runs a successful test of a small portion of a list, he will return to the list owner and ask for a *continuation.* The continuation is simply another batch of names from the same universe. If several mailers ask for continuations from the same list, that's a good indication that the list has responsive people in it.

```
EMPLOYEE BENEFIT NEWS                                      EB
```

```
DESCRIPTION:                                        FALL 1990
TARGET THE GROWING EMPLOYER MARKET.  EMPLOYEE
BENEFIT NEWS IS A NEWS MAGAZINE WHICH COVERS THE    UNIVERSE:  51,346
TOTAL EMPLOYEE BENEFITS FIELD WITH A FOCUS ON THE
LATEST TRENDS, PRODUCTS AND SERVICES.  EBN REACHES  PRICE:  $95/M
OVER 51,000 FINANCIAL OFFICERS, BENEFITS ADMINI-     AS OF 10-15-90
STRATORS, HUMAN RESOURCES DIRECTORS, PERSONNEL
EXECUTIVES AND OTHER KEY POSITIONS--MOSTLY IN       MINIMUM:  5,000
COMPANIES WITH MORE THAN 100 EMPLOYEES.
THESE ACTIVE EXECUTIVES ARE LOOKING FOR THE MOST    ADDRESSING:
CURRENT NEWS AND TRENDS WITHIN THE SPECTRUM OF      4-UP CHESHIRE
EMPLOYEE BENEFITS; INCLUDING---NEW PRODUCTS AND     MAG TAPE
SERVICES FOR BENEFIT PLANS; HOW TO OPERATE BENEFIT  P/S LABELS
PROGRAMS; ALL ASPECTS OF INSURANCE INCLUDING HMO/
PPOs, SUBSTANCE ABUSE, AIDS, STRESS, CORPORATE      SOURCE:
WELLNESS, CHILDCARES; MOTIVATIONAL MATERIALS;       100% DIRECT MAIL
RELATED SOFTWARE PACKAGES AND BUSINESS FORMS; PLUS
EDUC, SEMINARS, CONFERENCES, BOOKS, TAPES & VIDEOS

                                                    COMMISSION:
SELECTS AVAILABLE (PARTIAL LISTING)                 20% TO RECOGNIZED
1.  EMPLOYEE TITLE             QUANTITY             BROKERS
    HUMAN RESOURCE VP              9,373
    PERSONNEL, VP, MANAGER        7,465             SELECTIONS:
    EMPLOYEE BENEFIT MANAGERS    13,530             SPLITS     $3.50/M
    AND 7 OTHER TITLES                              STATE      $3.00/M
                                                    SCF/ZIP    $5.00/M
2.  TYPE OF COMPANY                                 P/S        $8.00/M
    MANUFACTURING               13,591             KEYING     $2.50/M
    FIN/INS./R.E.                9,713             TITLE     $10.00/M
    AND 10 OTHER COMPANY TYPES                      TYPE/CO   $10.00/M
                                                    SIZE/CO   $10.00/M
3.  SIZE BY NUMBER OF EMPLOYEES                     FREE OFFER$10.00/M
    SEE ATTACHED FOR COMPLETE LISTING OF SELECTS

LAST UPDATE 10/90. QUARTERLY UPDATES.               NON-REFUNDABLE MAG
                                                    TAPE SURCHARGE $25
RESTRICTIONS:  2 SAMPLE MAIL PIECES AND CLEAR MAIL
DATE IN ADVANCE.  A WRITTEN 30-DAY PAYMENT GUARAN-
TEE FROM MAIL DATE MUST ACCOMPANY ORDER.  ORDER
WILL NOT BE PROCESSED W/O RECEIPT OF GUARANTEE.
                                                    INFORMATION ON
USER HISTORY (CONTINUATIONS 1989-90):               THIS CARD IS
REMARKABLE PRODUCTS      SOCIETY FOR HUMAN RESOURCE  BELIEVED ACCURATE
S. NEIL CATALOGE         BENEFITS TODAY              BUT NOT GUARANTEED
COUNCIL ON EDUCATION     DUN & BRADSTREET            MAILING RESULTS
 IN MGMT                 CORP. COMPENSATION PLAN     ARE NOT GUARANTEED
CAREERTRACK SEMINARS     AT&T                        LIST RENTAL IS FOR
MORNINGSTAR              AMER. MANAGEMENT ASSOC.     ONE-TIME USE ONLY
BEHAVIORAL HEALTHCARE TOMORROW
```

Information on this card is believed accurate but not guaranteed. Mailing results are not guaranteed. List rental is for one-time use only unless otherwise indicated.

CMA CARNEGIE MARKETING ASSOCIATES

20695 So. Western Ave., Suite 200
Torrance, CA 90501
(213) 212-0771
* List Management   * List Brokering   * Consulting

FIGURE 4.2 Sample mailing list data card. (*Reprinted with permission from Carnegie Marketing Associates.*)

When you find a list that satisfies your requirements in other ways, if it has a substantial list of companies that have bought continuations, then the list is probably a good choice for you.

Most lists have a base price between $45 and $125 per thousand. Selects add an additional per-thousand charge of $5 and up, though some list prices include basic selects. The higher end of the price scale is reserved for lists the managers feel are particularly responsive, but cost is not always an indication of a list's value to you. You can best decide that by using the 12 list criteria. Some managers charge more for offers that compete with their own products or services. When you obtain a list, you don't buy it, you rent it, for one-time mail use only.

Figure 4.2 shows a typical list data card. Notice the description of the list, the selections available, the price, and the list universe.

COMPILED LISTS

Compiled lists are usually your second choice after direct response lists. If you can't find the people you're looking for through a direct response list, you're sure to find them on a compiled list. The difficulty is that you may not be able to identify them clearly. Compiled lists cover nearly every household and business in the United States, so although nearly everyone's address is available, you don't want to mail to 80 or 100 million addresses to reach a few hundred or a few thousand prime prospects.

Compiled lists drawn from city directories, public records (from government agencies such as state motor vehicle departments), phone books, and other sources are often used by retailers, service firms, and self-employed professionals such as accountants or dentists to reach a certain geographic area, without regard to other characteristics of the residents. Some compiled lists give you additional information about the people, such as demographics, automobile ownership, and other factors, but the lists do not tell you if the people have responded to a specific type of direct response offer. (Suzuki's direct marketing agency used motor vehicle lists to identify owners of different brands of motorcycles.)

Compilers also offer business lists, organized by standard industrial code (SIC). Again the emphasis is on large quantities, but depending on the list, various background information is usually available on each company. Lists of just about any business imaginable are available, from Thai restaurants to used brick dealers to industrial hygiene consultants. Paging through catalogs from large compiling firms can give you market ideas as well. Some compiler catalogs are 75 to 100 pages long.

Figure 4.3 shows one page from the catalog of R.L. Polk & Co., one of the largest compiling firms in the United States. This is an example of an enhanced compiled list. In an effort to create more precisely targeted lists, compilers are using questionnaires or other techniques to provide lists that have more information and therefore more available selections. The Polk list lets you choose from among 15 million households headed by women and

Polk's Female Head of Household List

An ever increasing number of women are working. Changing lifestyles also means that these women are now buying the products you may have only been selling to the man in the past. Don't miss this key market segment on your next mailing.

Coverage: Approximately 15 million households available in the United States.

Currency: Polk's Household List is updated, in its entirety, six times per year.

Selection Factors:

Geographical

State	Nth Selection
County	Postal Carrier Route
Town/City	Census Tract
Sectional Center Facility (SCF)	Metropolitan Marketing Area
Zip Code	

Household

Age of Household Head	*Motorcycle Ownership
Estimated Household Income	*Recreational Vehicle Ownership
Dwelling Type	*New Car Owner
Owner or Renter	*New Truck Owner
Occupations	Mail Order Buyers
Telephone Number	Mail Order Responders
Length of Residence	Mail Order Contributors
Families with Children	Credit Card Users/Bank
*Car Ownership	Credit Card Users/Retail
*Truck Ownership	Smokers

Consumer list pricing is as follows:

...Under 15,000 names $40.00/M base price.

...For geographical or individual household selection surcharges, please contact your Polk Representative.

...Minimum order is 5,000 names per state.

NOTE: For prices on larger quantites and/or multiple state selects please contact your Polk Representative.

...*For **Vehicle Registration Pricing** - Please contact your Polk Representative.

See opposite page for estimated metropolitan marketing area counts for the top 150 markets in the country.

24

FIGURE 4.3 Here's a sample page from the mailing list catalog of R.L. Polk and Co., one of the largest compilers in the United States. The list of women who are the heads of households has been enhanced to provide a variety of selections based on demographics and other factors. *(Reprinted with permission of R.L. Polk & Co. Marketing Services Division, Taylor Michigan.)*

provides a variety of selections based on demographics and other factors. On the opposite page of the catalog, not shown here, is a breakdown of the list showing the number of households headed by women in 150 different U.S. cities.

Some of the other large list-compiling firms are American Business Information, Metromail Corporation, R.R. Donnelley & Co., Dun & Bradstreet Corporation, and TRW, Inc. Dozens of smaller firms also rent compiled lists. Some small firms actually obtain their lists from one of the big firms and resell them to you.

COMPILING YOUR OWN LISTS

One further option for developing lists is to compile your own. If you're looking for a specific group of people and you can find a business directory, membership list, or other source that contains the names you need, you can create your own list. This should not be treated as your house list, because these people have not bought from you yet, but you won't have any limitations on use of the list as you would if you rented it.

Many business organizations, chambers of commerce, and community and civic clubs have membership lists available. Some organizations go a step further and sell address labels of members. Most government records are public information and, given the time, you could compile your own local lists based on business licenses, homes purchased, business consolidations, liquor licenses, and many other categories. (Many professional compilers use these same sources.) You can even use news publications to collect the names of people who are mentioned, then use phone books, city directories, or other sources to obtain addresses.

The advantages of compiling your own list include the list's uniqueness. No one will have a list identical to yours. You can also include only those people to whom you wish to mail. A considerable amount of labor is involved in researching and entering your list on a computer. If you don't count your own time, it's inexpensive, but most small business people would be better off to have someone else do the typing for them. While membership lists and similar sources probably aren't updated as often as even some of the more neglected compiled lists, you can update your own list using the telephone— providing the list you have has phone numbers. To promote the business writing training programs I conduct, I once created my own list of meeting planners from associations that had scheduled their annual conventions near where I live. I obtained the information from a local chamber of commerce, a directory of association executives, and from two association trade journals.

With the thousands of compiled and direct response lists, plus the possibilities for compiling your own, list decisions can be puzzling. If you make a living conducting seminars on business skills, the CareerTrack list (Figure 4.1) from SRDS might look promising. Notice the many interesting categories, especially the multi-buyers. Before you bought, however, you would need to find out about recency, monetary, and some of the other professional list criteria.

Let's take another example. You sell accessories for four-wheel-drive vehicles. To start, you might run ads in off-road magazines, make some sales, and develop a customer profile to give you clues about where to find other prospects. You might think that someone who has just bought a new Jeep or similar vehicle would be a good candidate for direct mail, and they might. From R.L. Polk you could buy a list of people who own four-wheel-drive vehicles. But owning a vehicle capable of being driven off-road is no indication the people would be willing to buy accessories. What are some other options? Direct response lists are available from the subscription files of off-road magazines. Lists of buyers from automotive accessory catalogs are also available. How about a list of people who have bought camping supplies? You would probably want to test some of these lists.

As a final example, consider the sale of pet supplies through a local store. Your list options include local resident lists; pet owners, compiled from registration files; readers of pet magazines; or buyers of pet supplies through mail-order catalogs.

WORKING WITH BROKERS

All these list decisions are good examples of situations in which you could benefit from the help of a qualified *list broker*. List brokerage firms are in business to rent, and often manage, lists. Sometimes a list manager will be an employee of a firm, such as a magazine, that owns a list. In many other cases, however, list owners hire private list brokers to manage their lists for them. When you want to rent lists, you could contact the manager of each list separately, or you could contact one broker to do the job for you. The relationship of brokers and clients is, in one respect, not unlike that of real estate agents and their customers. Agents can sell you a house they have listed, but can also arrange for you to buy any other house you're interested in.

Since you're probably going to be dealing with a broker one way or another, you should seek a broker's advice. Experienced brokers have detailed knowledge, not only of lists but of direct mail in general. Their advice can be invaluable. The cost to you? Essentially nothing. Brokers get a 20 percent commission from the list managers when they rent a list. Your list costs are the same whether or not you ask your broker for advice.

Since brokers handle many lists every day, they see how well various lists perform for different clients and different offers. A list that matches your demographics may look perfect when you see it in SRDS, but a broker may be able to tell you that the list is not pulling a strong response to offers such as yours, or that the list is not updated or cleaned as frequently as it should be.

While many compilers are large firms with extensive in-house computer capabilities and sales offices around the country, brokers are usually small, specialized firms. The brokers/managers with the widest list experience tend to be located in a few of the largest cities in the Unites States. Brokers in smaller cities often specialize in local or regional lists and may not have experience in evaluating national direct response lists in specialized fields. To find names of brokers, look in the brokers/compilers section of SRDS, the Direct Marketing

Marketplace (listed in Appendix B), and your local phone book under mailing lists.

Working Relationships

One way to evaluate brokers is to ask several for their list recommendations for your product or service, then compare the advice and service you receive. If you have experienced brokers nearby, talk with them, then if necessary, call brokers in other cities. Here are some of the things you might expect from a broker:

- He may ask to see a sample of your product and, if he is genuinely interested in working with you over a long period of time, he will ask you about your business plan and objectives. If he knows where you want to go, he can help you develop the strategies to get there.
- He may want to see samples of any direct mail advertising you have already created, and he may offer to help you prepare your materials. Some brokers provide creative services or can recommend copywriters and designers to work with you.
- The broker will want to review short-term testing tactics with you and may advise you to conduct as much testing as your budget will allow. A good broker will also be available to help you analyze the results of mailings.
- The broker might even offer some advice on other marketing possibilities such as package inserts, or telemarketing.

Not all brokers are going to be this thorough, but this gives you an idea of the type of help a broker can provide. Some of a broker's initial questions are designed to help you, and some are also designed to assure the broker that you have a reasonably substantial business that will be financially worthy of his time. Brokers are naturally more interested in working with a large client that might ultimately rent hundreds of thousands or perhaps millions of names, rather than a smaller business that can afford to rent only in much smaller quantities. You don't need to volunteer to a broker that you intend to rent no more than X number of names, but don't try to deceive him into thinking you're going to launch a gigantic campaign just to get his expert advice.

Not everyone recommends relying on a list broker. Although brokers are knowledgeable, they usually don't know as much about any given list as the list's manager does. To get the most accurate information about lists, Tim Maroney from HDM Worldwide Direct recommends working directly with managers, rather than a single list broker. In addition, some mailers think that brokers who are also managers might tend to favor their own lists over others.

Although most brokers will advise against Maroney's suggestion and recommend that you pick one broker and tell him everything about your business so he can help you, not all brokers are eager to devote hours and hours advising small business people. Furthermore, you may not be able to find a qualified broker in your area and may have to deal with someone on the phone. Regardless, considering all the options, if you can find an experienced broker who is interested in working with you, it is in your best interest to listen to his or her advice. A wise, experienced broker's list savvy may be the best advice you can get in direct marketing. Some brokers can look at your product or service and tell you exactly which lists to use, and when and how to conduct your initial mailings. This is not to say you should not learn as much as you can about using lists on your own. You should still do your own independent research first, then ask for recommendations from professionals.

When you contact a compiler for lists, don't expect the same service you get from a broker. When you work with a local office of a large, national list compiling firm, the sales representative you talk to may just take your order, period. Some sales reps, however, may answer your questions and give you limited advice. If the national compiling firm you want to work with does not have a local representative, you can place your order directly with the main office.

Smaller, local or regional list firms are located in most cities. These companies are often considered compilers because they usually offer lists of local residents and businesses compiled from public records. If you need a list of residents who have recently moved to your community, for example, or a list of all local real estate agents, contact a local compiler. A local, service-oriented compiler may provide you with more assistance and advice than a sales rep from a national compiling firm and if your mailing is going to be confined to several local ZIP codes, a local firm may be your best source of lists and list advice. While list brokers tend to be biased against compiled lists, they can still help you select compiled lists along with direct response lists.

List Rental Details

Here's how a list transaction takes place:

- You and your broker/compiler select lists and place an order. If you're doing it yourself or are a new customer of the list owner, you will have to pay in advance. Once you become an established list renter, fees can be paid after your mailing has been made, a cash-flow advantage for you.

- List managers usually require you to send them one or more copies of your mailer before they agree to rent a list to you. They want to see if your offer competes with their own. Some list owners will not rent to competitors, others charge more. List owners/managers also want to know when you're planning to mail so that they can coordinate any mailings they may be planning.

- Your rental agreement permits you to mail just once to everyone on the list. To be sure you don't abuse the agreement, list managers salt their lists with names and addresses so that they will receive your mailings. These *decoys* or *seeds* allow brokers to keep track of list activity and maintain files of all mailings sent out to their lists.

- You can specify the form in which you want your lists to be delivered. Magnetic computer tape is the preferred way. This allows you to use a data processing service bureau or letter shop to perform various operations on the list and to output the information to personalized letters and envelopes or to labels. You can also have your list provided on floppy disks for your microcomputer or on labels, paper lists, or telemarketing cards.

- All the people who respond to your mailing become your customers, and you can mail to them as many times as you like after that. You add them to your house list or data base.

If You Do It Yourself

If you decide to do your own list shopping, here are some questions you should ask list managers:

- Ask for details of any list criterion which is not clear in a directory or on a data card. For example, find out about continuations. Which mailers have rented continuation lists? You could take a further step and call some companies which have rented lists to find out their experiences. Remember what a broker once told me about information on data cards, "Sometimes there's promotional writing on data cards which has nothing to do with the list."
- Find out how hot the hotline is. Ask precise questions about the order dates that are reflected in the hotline. Are they really within the time period stated? A six-month hotline is not too hot.
- Be sure hotline names on magazine subscriptions represent paid subscribers, not just people who have responded to free trials or who have not made their payments yet.
- Ask specific questions about lists to be sure you get exactly what you want. This applies whether you're ordering from managers or compilers. For example, if you're mailing to banks, make sure you don't get addresses for 147 branches of the same bank if all you need to do is reach data processing managers at headquarters.
- Ask for the specific percentage of direct mail–generated names in a direct response list. You should also find out the sources of other names, such as direct response television or 900 telephone numbers.
- Ask for a net name arrangement. When you mail to segments of more than one list, you will want to cross-reference or compare each list to eliminate duplicates. This is done by a computer merge/purge operation. Since people who respond to direct mail often order from more than one company, duplications are common, sometimes amounting to 15 percent or more. When a merge/purge process reduces a given list, you should not have to pay for those names you will not use because they already appear on another list, possibly your house list.

List managers often will agree ahead of time to cut costs by 15 percent off the top to compensate for duplicates identified in a merge/purge, but they are often reluctant to grant further reductions, regardless of how many names are actually used. Unfortunately, if you are renting a small quantity of names you don't have a strong bargaining position.

What you can do as an alternative is tell the manager you want to mail twice to all the duplicates. Since multi-buyers are prime prospects, you can benefit by mailing a second time to this group anywhere from several days to a couple of weeks after the first mailing. List managers are generally more inclined to agree to this arrangement. Also subject to negotiation is whether you mail the multi-buyers the same offer twice or a different one the second time. Mailing a different offer to the same list of multi-buyers would make an interesting, inexpensive test. If you do mail the same offer twice, wait a week between mailings.

DOING IT YOURSELF ON A MAC OR PC

Computers are giving direct marketers more and more options every day, and the methods of selecting, renting, and using lists are changing. Depending on your list needs, microcomputers may some day replace your broker or your compiler's representative. You can actually become your own broker/compiler today if you use lists or data bases available on media accessible with a microcomputer.

Many companies offer lists on computer diskettes, but your main advantage comes from products that allow you unlimited use of names and addresses. One such product, from American Business Information, Inc., is called Business Lists-on-Disc™. This product gives you access to data on 9.2 million U.S. businesses via compact disc.

The compact discs are similar to the ones that play music, except these CD-ROM (read-only memory) disks contain millions of bytes of information and have storage capacities many times larger than floppy disks or traditional PC-size hard disks. For this reason firms are adopting CD-ROM for data base storage.

With the Lists-on-Disc product, the CD-ROM storage lets you view names of companies before you buy them. Listings by company name and the names of individual contact people at those companies are available. You can sort the lists by geography, type of company, and other factors. The prices, at approximately $160/M, are more expensive than for simple compiled business lists on labels, but substantially cheaper than some similar services. One company that offers business names through your PC charges nearly $1 per name.

Other companies offering information on CDs include TRW, Inc., which collects credit information on millions of companies. NYNEX Information Resources offers a CD-ROM product containing all the information in white pages telephone listings for New York and the New England states. This NYNEX Fast Track™ also contains ZIP codes so that you can create mailing lists from the information. U.S. Census information from the 1990 census is available on CD-ROM disks. Other data, including address correction software with a U.S. ZIP + 4 directory, is also available in this computer medium. Prices on CD-ROM list products are subject to change. When you're developing a marketing budget, contact suppliers for up-to-date quotes.

If your computer doesn't have a CD-ROM disk reader, you can buy one for less than $1000, and, like most microcomputer hardware, prices are coming down. This new technology can give small businesses in-house capabilities that only major data processing companies or large corporation management information systems (MIS) departments have had in the past. Potentially PCs and CDs can drastically reduce your data base acquisition costs, but one issue stands in the way: privacy.

In early 1991 the Lotus Development Corp., famous for its Lotus 1-2-3™ software program, scrapped two CD-ROM products that would have made extraordinary data base resources available at a price within the budget of millions of small businesses. One of the products gave a small business person the ability to access inexpensively a data base of literally tens of millions of American households. It was this ease of access, however, that contributed to the demise of the product.

When Lotus announced it was halting its Lotus Marketplace products, it cited consumer privacy complaints as a major factor in the decision. Lotus received more than 30,000 letters from consumers complaining that the new product constituted a violation of privacy.

In spite of these concerns, CDs and similar technology will someday provide an inexpensive alternative to the way lists are rented today, and new products are already in the planning stages. Low-cost business data bases will come first because they are less affected by the privacy issues. For household data bases, privacy safeguards will need to be combined with publicity campaigns that position inexpensive CD-ROM data bases as strictly monitored business tools.

In addition to giving you access to lists, advanced personal computers give your small business enough computing power to manage nearly all functions of your direct marketing program. Among the uses of a PC in small business direct marketing are:

- Creating and managing lists
- Tracking sales and leads and analyzing test results
- Designing, setting type, and creating finished layouts for ads and direct mail
- Formatting and producing labels and personalized letters
- Conducting *list hygiene* operations such as correcting addresses and eliminating duplicates
- Keeping track of orders and shipments and performing other customer service functions

You can choose from a variety of prepackaged software to handle these jobs, with some programs performing more than one of the above-listed tasks. I'll mention specialized software elsewhere in the book. Appendix B contains a list of suppliers.

Read industry trade journals, also listed in Appendix B, to keep on top of the latest technological advancements and new products available. Although many of the precepts of direct marketing are seemingly inflexible, the way you obtain, analyze, and use lists and data bases is constantly changing and improving.

PROFESSIONAL DATA BASE TECHNIQUES

Several of the list and data processing tasks are best left to professionals. A variety of operations can be performed on your list and rented lists to eliminate duplicates, correct data, and to sort, enhance, and expand the information. **Service bureau** is the generic name for the data processing companies that do these tasks for you. A list broker with whom you have established a relationship can refer you to a service bureau he or she has worked with.

Before you do a mailing, the first step is usually a merge/purge. To have a merge/purge conducted, all the lists must be transferred to compatible formats. Most commercial lists are available on computer tape, which is the medium that service bureaus use. You'll have to talk to the service bureau before you order your lists to find out which format they prefer. SRDS and data cards usually specify available data formats.

To eliminate certain names from the final list, your data processing service will perform a *suppression*. You could suppress bad credit risks stored in your house files. In addition, outside services provide suppression files of people with bad credit. To narrow your mailing area, you might also want to suppress a particular geographic area such as a state or a ZIP code.

Further, you can have the list run through various programs to standardize or modify the addresses, add ZIP + 4 codes, and otherwise clean up the files.

To improve the list even more you can process it with the National Change of Address (NCOA) file and Delivery Sequence File (DSF), which represent nationwide data bases maintained by the U.S. Postal Service. NCOA contains millions of address changes; DSF contains a list of about 120 million actual, deliverable addresses. Your list can be compared to both files to correct outdated, inaccurate addresses. When your list is compared ZIP + 4 is also added.

Before the process is complete, all your names from all your lists are sorted into ZIP code order for mailing. Your list may be further sorted to receive the discounts from the U.S. Postal Service. When finished, the tape will be in the proper format to print labels, personalize letters, or imprint whatever advertising format you're using. Some service bureaus will be able to do the addressing/imprinting for you, or you may have it done by a letter shop.

The above processing is not extremely expensive, and it saves you money on postage by allowing you to qualify for the postal discounts. Merge/purge processing costs vary from about $2 to $10 per thousand, depending on the quantity and complexity. ZIP sorts and some types of suppression are included in the cost. NCOA and DSF processing is offered by vendors throughout the United States. Service bureaus that do not offer the service directly can obtain it for you. Processing prices are based on your list size. The USPS has a low-cost option for small lists. See page 78.

In addition to these services, which are considered routine by major mailers in the industry, there are a number of enhancement techniques. Some of these may exceed the budgets of small businesses. Here's a summary of some techniques that may become financially feasible for you as costs come down and your business grows.

A few companies offer lifestyle overlays. Prizm™, from Claritas Corp., is a program that separates the United States into more than 500,000 neighborhoods and places each in one of 40 different categories. Each category, given a descriptive, albeit overly colorful name, is a lifestyle cluster based on demographic and behavior analysis. Within one ZIP code in Manhattan, for example, are eight separate neighborhood lifestyle clusters, such as Gray Power, New Melting Pot, and Downtown Dixie-Style.

One way to use Prizm, or similar geo-demographic clustering, is to analyze your house list, attaching Prizm codes to each customer. Then you identify the cluster types or lifestyle categories of your best customers. When you go shopping for lists, some compilers and list managers offer Prizm clusters as a select. You buy the addresses of people who have the same cluster codes as your prime customers.

For example, a western medical clinic wanted to establish a reputation and clientele beyond the region where it was known, so it analyzed its list of past patients to see what geo-demographic characteristics they had in common. They used the information to purchase national lists, buying names in neighborhoods that matched their enhanced customer profile.

Prizm codes can also be used to identify a variety of other information about consumers, based on the neighborhoods in which they live. By matching Prizm codes, based on addresses, with lists of motor vehicle owners, compiled by R.L. Polk and Co., you can predict the type of automobile a person is likely to buy, based simply on where he or she lives.

Costs for Prizm and similar analysis programs depend on how you use them. You can pay a per-item fee to have your house list encoded, or you can obtain a licensing agreement to use special software yourself. Expect to spend about $20,000 annually for licensing agreements alone.

Overlay and list-enhancement programs can be successful enough to cover their substantial costs provided you are mailing in large quantities. It's best to gather some experience in direct mail before tackling advanced data processing techniques.

While gathering a quantity of information about prospects and customers is important, some companies thrive just knowing a few key facts about their customers. Before you launch into an expensive data processing journey, be sure you will *use* the information you plan to gather or buy. Often the RFM trio is all you need to know. At the other extreme from the complex Prizm analyses, for example, is a method of data base marketing that targets people who eat pizza. See Chapter 13 for an example of data base marketing simplified.

BUILDING YOUR OWN DATA BASE

Data base marketing seems so logical, so rooted in common sense that an explanation of the purpose of maintaining an in-house data base seems unnecessary. Except for some veteran mail-order sellers, however, few people in business, large or small, maintain the information they should. If it hasn't been clear before now, the purpose of building and maintaining your data base is to (1) sell more to existing customers and (2) find more highly profitable customers. To do this you need to establish and regularly update your customer files. Here are some suggestions for building your own data base:

1. *Computerize it.* Unless you can count your customers/clients on your fingers and toes, you need to get rid of your paper system and get a computer. If you already have customer lists or files on paper, you may be able to transfer them to a computer medium without keyboarding. Scanners combined with optical character-reading software will do the job. This process can be used to transfer data that is routinely typed rather than entered into a computer.

   Your data base program should give you wide latitude for sorting and segmenting. Your software should allow you to do the following basic functions: entering, editing, updating, and deleting information, as well as coding various data to allow you to segment your files in many ways. For example, you might want to assign a special code to your customers who have children so you can send them information on family services or products for children. You also need to treat prospects separately from established customers, so you may want to establish several codes for potential customers.

   You should be able to expand your data base in two directions. For each customer file you should have sufficient storage spaces, called *fields,* to record a variety of data, beyond the usual name, address, phone, and credit information. When you set up a system, you should have empty fields available for future use. Should you decide later that you want to record something else about customers, you need room to record it. The second direction for growth is in the number of customers and prospects. Don't start off with a 20-megabyte hard disk and think that it will last you for the foreseeable future.

2. *Record information on your customers and their buying histories, then look for similarities.* Some things may be obvious. A large percentage of your customers may come from the same ZIP code, for example. Doing a geographical sort of your customers or prospects would be similar to the geographic screening that was done for the Suzuki motorcycle campaign mentioned at the beginning of this chapter.

3. *When setting up your data base, keep the 12 list criteria in mind.* Those criteria are more important when applied to your own customers than they are for people on a rented list. The RFM factors are especially important because they help you predict what your customers will do. Using these factors you can create a sublist of your most frequent and highest-spending customers, knowing that it will pull an even greater response than your house list in general. When you're able to identify your best customers, you have a better idea of the characteristics to look for when you rent outside lists.

4. *Sorting and segmenting your data base saves you money.* You can mail more frequently to your best customers, and you can avoid wasted mailings to particular segments, such as offering backyard play equipment to apartment dwellers or customers without children. It also lets you create special, high-percentage response promotions based on some of your customers' unique characteristics. In addition to obvious savings on printing and mailing, your data base becomes a source of continuing research as you analyze results, look for patterns, and constantly revise your customer profile.

Here's one example of how a company uses a customer data base to create unique, personalized offers. I recently bought an RCA television, and I filled out and returned the product registration card. Just before the labor portion of the TV's warranty expired, I received a mailing from RCA. I opened the envelope right away because it said "warranty notification" on the outside. The letter inside told me the warranty was about to end and offered me an extended service contact. An accurate data base permits RCA to expand its business by making back-end, mail-order offers to retail customers.

Your data base software should also allow you to import and export data to and from other programs. For instance, you should be able to access your address files with your word processing software so that you can create personalized letters.

To prosper in direct marketing you need to do two things to your data base constantly: update it and add to it. The Postal Service, your customers, the NCOA system, and your staff will provide you with a stream of corrections and additions to keep your files current. You need to set up office procedures that ensure that updates are made regularly. An outdated list will waste money every time you use it.

One of the modifications you invariably make on your list is deleting people who move, change interests, or for some reason cease to be customers or clients. In pure data base marketing, customers are continuously lost, so they also need to be regularly added. It's important to develop as many ways as you can to add to your data base. Ways to do this include ads and commercials, rented lists, retail sales, referrals from existing customers, telemarketing, unsolicited inquiries you received by phone or mail, and leads from trade show booths or other types of public exhibits.

You need to be constantly adding not only customers, but also prospects. The prospects you put on your list are more likely to become customers than the people on a rented list. Even if you're self-employed, think for a minute of the number of people you're in touch with every day or every week. If you kept track of your colleagues, people who have called you with a question, contacts you have made at meetings, and so on, you would find you'd soon have the beginnings of an attractive data base. You and your employees should get in the habit of asking for referrals and watching for data base sources such as guest lists from meetings.

By building, segmenting, and refining your own list, you reduce your dependence on outside lists and increase your mailing response.

POSTSCRIPTS....

Rent Your Own List

As we've seen, some of the best and most expensive rental lists are house lists of other firms. List rentals are a source of substantial income for some companies. When your house list reaches 5,000 or more, you should consider renting it out as a source of income with a high profit margin. If you take the precautions other list owners do, your list rental will not affect your doing business with your customers.

The size, segmentation, and specialized nature of your list may make it attractive to others. If you manage the list yourself, you'll have to (1) advertise it via direct mail and telemarketing to list brokers, (2) see that it's listed in SRDS and other directories, and (3) maintain the list in different DP formats. Alternatively, you can hire a list manager to do this for you in exchange for a 10 percent commission.

More List Sources

Local businesses may be a source of lists, outside the normal list channels. Talk to local firms to see if they would be willing to rent you their customer lists. Some may have never thought of it before, but someone in a related business to yours might be an ideal source of prospects. For instance, people who have just bought swimming pools or spas would be good prospects for pool supplies and services.

To keep your list rental costs down, you can also trade lists, either locally on your own or through a list broker. If your list is good enough to rent, you can also trade it with other list owners in exchange for a chance to test their lists.

Ask for Help

Always ask people who respond to your direct mail to correct their addresses to help you maintain a clean, less costly data base. Provide space on your order blanks and reply cards for customers to add new addresses.

A Reason to Use "Smith"

Data base marketing has its own built-in hazards, depending on the business you're in. The marketing manager of a Las Vegas hotel once received a negative response to one of the hotel's mailings to past customers. It seems a gentleman and his girlfriend stayed at the hotel, registering with his name and her address.

Later the hotel sent out a card thanking them for their stay and giving them an offer for their next visit. The complaint? The woman, who happened to be married to someone else, was alarmed that her husband might see the direct mail that the hotel sent to her address with her boyfriend's name on it. The boyfriend called the hotel asking that he *please* be deleted from the data base.

5 LIST-RELATED MEDIA

Try a Secret Weapon

> *Advertising is eighty-five percent confusion and fifteen percent commission.*
>
> —Fred Allen

Mailing a single offer in its own envelope is just one way to use lists. This chapter explains ways you can use well-known list-related direct marketing techniques, such as telemarketing and catalogs. It also explores opportunities available in marketing methods I like to call secret weapons, because they are simple, inexpensive, and not widely used by small business.

CO-OPS

A co-op mailing contains offers from a variety of companies, usually collected by one vendor and mailed to a specified list or lists. The advantages for a small business are that you can reach a large audience for a fraction of the cost you would pay to send out your own separate direct mail and that you can usually look as good as larger companies. Donnelley Marketing's Carol Wright co-op mailing is familiar to millions of Americans. Filled with money-saving coupons from a variety of advertisers, it's delivered to 30 million homes in the United States.

Similar co-ops are produced for regional and local markets all over North America. They're conducted by large national companies such as Harte-Hanks Corp. and by local direct mail entrepreneurs. Residential co-ops often contain inexpensive flyers printed on paper that is one-third or one-half of an $8\frac{1}{2}'' \times 11''$ sheet. You can ask a broker about the larger co-ops or simply look in your local phone directory under advertising, direct mail.

A word of caution about local mail co-ops: the small firms that offer these mailings sometimes have a limited life span. Don't spend money buying space in several future co-ops unless you are familiar with the company and comfortable that it will be around when all of your mailings are supposed to be posted.

Availability of local business co-ops varies. Formats are often similar to residential co-ops. The range of costs for co-ops is so broad that it's impossible to set an average price. It's best to compare costs of the local co-ops you're considering. Ask questions about circulation, demographics, and deliverability percentages. Ask to see samples of previous mailings so that you can identify the other companies that use the medium and the types of offers used. Call some of those companies and see whether they have obtained good results.

Following are some other, lesser known, co-op opportunities.

Package Inserts

This medium grew, perhaps, out of a need to save postage and find a new way to reach mail-order shoppers. You have seen this form of advertising if you've ever ordered something and found advertisements for other products in the package. Instead of buying a list, you simply send a certain number of brochures or other inserts to a mail-order merchandising company. The company inserts your brochures (or other advertising format) in packages it sends out to customers. You don't know exactly how long it will take for them to send out all of your inserts, but most companies can tell you the average number of packages they mail in a week.

Here are the positives: Remember the RFM list criteria? Obviously, a package insert is sent to as recent a customer as possible! While you can't select a monetary level, you can find out what the company's average amount of sale is. There are other positives as well. Your offer receives an implied endorsement simply because it's contained in the other company's shipment. Furthermore, you pay no postage, just a cost per thousand that's on a par with many list prices. You don't need an outside envelope, the services of a data processing bureau, or a letter shop to stuff your direct mail and take it to the post office. You don't have to worry about bad addresses on lists; you get an almost 100 percent delivery rate. Perhaps best of all, you know your piece will be delivered to people who buy through the mail.

Sound too good to be true? Now for the negatives. You may have competition in the box, because companies can include multiple inserts, including their own catalog, which will siphon attention from your information. Your inserts are mailed on an irregular schedule and you don't know where your insert will be in each box, Jiffy bag, or other outer wrap. Selects are usually not available. You study the company's customer profile and take it or leave it.

Inserts are also listed in Standard Rate and Data Service (SRDS) directories. Just as a sample, insert opportunities are available in packages containing carry-all bags for new mothers, fishing gear, backyard cooking equipment and gas grills, and gift assortments of fruit.

Figure 5.1 shows a data card for an insert program in packages containing bicycle parts and accessories.

While response rates for inserts are often well below those for separate direct mail, an implied endorsement from the right company could build your prestige and collect orders at the same time. Typical costs of package inserts are $45 to $60/M.

Card Decks

Here's a medium that virtually didn't exist before 1980, yet today approximately 750 different card decks are available. A card deck or pack is a collection of from 30 to 100, $3\frac{1}{2}'' \times 5\frac{1}{2}''$ business reply cards, all representing offers from different companies. They're bundled in polyethylene envelopes and mailed to a specified list. Many of these are listed in SRDS under co-ops, and new offerings are listed in direct mail trade journals.

LH INC

Performance Bicycle

PACKAGES

535M/Year $55/M

5329

MAX SIZE:
5-1/2 x 8-1/2"

MAX WT: 1/4 oz.
(Overweight - Inq.)

Reach the upscale active buyer purchasing from the
Performance Bicycle catalog. Inserts are collated in
a 6 x 9" envelope and shipped with the merchandise.

SEX: 85% men

UNIT OF SALE: $70/Avg.

This mostly male audience spends an average of $300-$400
a year on cycling equipment, has an average age of 35
years and an average household income of $40,000-$50,000.
75% are homeowners and 80% have college degrees. They are
outdoor sports enthusiasts with many related interests.

SOURCE: Direct
mail & space ads

SELECTIVITY: None

Max. # of inserts: 5

MINIMUM TEST: 10M

20% COMMISSION TO RECOGNIZED BROKERS
SAMPLE MAILING PIECE MUST BE SUBMITTED FOR APPROVAL

ent 12/87 tb
Upd 5/30/90 tb

We believe this information to be accurate as stated, but we cannot guarantee its accuracy or the outcome of the mailing.

LH MANAGEMENT DIVISION   455 Central Avenue, Scarsdale, New York 10583   914-723-3176   Fax#: 914-723-0205

FIGURE 5.1   This data card for a package insert program is similar to a mailing list data card.
Notice that there are no selections available, however, because package inserts are placed in every
package the firm sends out. *(Reprinted with permission from Leon Henry Inc.)*

Lists for decks are as varied and specialized as mailing lists themselves.
There are card decks for Pentecostal ministers, plastics engineers, and women
who have bought sportswear through the mail. Card packs for compiled and
direct response lists are available for both businesses and consumers.

You can't expect a card in a deck to pull a response similar to a solo mailing,
but the costs are substantially less. Card packs are a good medium for generating sales leads because they provide a simple response device and because
the limited copy space doesn't leave room for complicated descriptions.

Select a card pack with the same care you give to a mailing list. Packs are
a good medium for small business because you can look as professional and
appealing as any large or well-established company. No one knows that you
just started your firm. They can't tell by the look of your card that you're a
fraction the size of your competition. A deck can be an especially good buy
for you if you can find a pack that goes to just the specialized audience you're
looking for.

Deck circulation is usually between 50,000 and 100,000. You buy space in
the entire mailing for prices from about $1,000 to $2,000, although some cost
more. Prices vary according to the perceived value of the list, not just on the
amount of circulation. Printing and postage are included. Ask for samples
from the deck manager and find out how many cards will be competing with
yours. You want the deck large enough to look inviting and catch attention,
but not so large that your offer is lost. Pick one with about 50 or so cards.

Statement Stuffers

This medium is an institution for financial institutions. The marketing rationale is: When you're already sending a customer a bank statement, why not add some advertising too, at no increase in postage?

More and more firms are taking advantage of this practice by paying to have their advertising inserted in billings and routine mailings of other companies. For example, you could have your inserts placed in statements sent to holders of major credit cards. An advantage of course is that your message could go to someone who is prosperous enough to have a MasterCard, for example, and if you honor the card, your offer ties in nicely.

Prices are similar to those for package inserts, but instead of arriving with merchandise someone has been looking forward to receiving, your notice arrives with a bill.

CATALOGS

Large, national, full-color catalogs are complex, expensive, and highly competitive. Start-up costs can be staggering. Just the merchandising costs alone can be prohibitive for a fledgling company. In light of the competition, sophistication of the market, and rising postal and paper costs, starting a national clothing or general merchandise catalog operation is not in the realm of small business.

Don't ignore this popular format, though, because you can learn creative marketing and customer service techniques from the large catalogers and because small specialty catalogs might work for your business. Small-business catalog opportunities include the following:

- Branching out into mail order if you already have a successful retail business base.
- Starting a specialty catalog for a particular type of merchandise or a technical field with which you have detailed experience.
- Using a specialty catalog for double duty as a traffic builder for your retail product or service business and as a mail-order medium.

There are other areas of opportunity as well, including specialty business catalogs. While the majority of catalogs today seem to be in full color, there are notable, successful exceptions. Depending on your products, you could create a one- or two-color catalog and make substantial savings on production. Nor does a catalog have to be the size of a small phone book or even a magazine. A small booklet showing a collection of merchandise can be inexpensive and effective.

Some large national firms use mail order to enhance their substantial retail efforts. Catalogs for Eddie Bauer and The Sharper Image create direct sales and also act as store advertising. You can do the same, or use your catalog as many firms do simply to support store sales. With a knowledge of mailing lists, you can do more efficient mailings than the traditional department store strategy of blanketing a city or mailing only to charge customers.

OUTBOUND TELEMARKETING

Outbound telemarketing can be conducted with or without rental lists. Telephone numbers are available on many lists, so you can combine direct mail and telemarketing. Phone numbers are frequently available in business and organization directories as well. You can even pay to have phone numbers added to your house list if you don't normally obtain that information from customers. Telematch, a data processing company, uses its data base of 65 million residential phone numbers to match numbers to the names and addresses you provide on computer tape. A subsidiary of R.R. Donnelley & Sons Co. has a similar service.

As with most direct marketing techniques, telemarketing is flexible in scope, message, and the things it can accomplish. You can establish a telemarketing department to implement extensive campaigns. You can also use telemarketing techniques to fill in the spare time you or your employees may have. If you have a target list of prospects always handy, spend those spare minutes on the phone generating more business. Of course nearly every successful small business must be good at *inbound* telemarketing, that is, the technique you use when responding to customer and prospect calls. Details of this part of your business are covered in Chapter 17.

Telemarketing gives you immediate feedback from customers and prospects as no other medium does. You find out what prospective customers want, what they like, and what they don't like. While telephone research may sometimes yield sales, telemarketing almost always yields useful information as well as sales. The head of a medium-size company I know occasionally spends a few hours doing telemarketing to keep in touch with what potential customers think about the company.

Lists play an important part in telemarketing too. You can expect a more favorable reception and a much higher response rate when you phone your existing customers than when you make *cold calls* to strangers. Both types of calls are an integral part of telemarketing, but the better your list is targeted to your prime prospects, the more productive telemarketing will be.

Answering inquiries is another form of outbound telemarketing. A phone call is the quickest way to respond to a request for more information, and it's more personal than sending literature, which you can do anyway, after the call. The sooner you respond to an inquiry, the better your odds are of making a sale.

In addition to identifying prospects, telemarketing also helps you qualify them. You might discover they are top candidates and send a salesperson out to visit them. You might target them for further calls, or you might simply send literature and flag them for follow up. Telemarketing is often used in conjunction with other types of marketing. It works well with direct mail because you can identify prospects and reach them directly through two media.

Telemarketing is one of the most expensive forms of direct marketing. If you hire an outside firm to do your calling, or if you hire staff telemarketers, your costs per call will be higher than the cost per piece of direct mail you send out, but the results also should be higher—much higher. This surprises some people. One communications professional I know told me that when she began her career she was a telemarketing representative. When she started her job she had the usual negative image of telemarketing. But she said she was surprised at the large number of people who *did not* hang up on her and at the large number who actually placed orders.

The reason for the success of telemarketing is clear: It's a personal, interactive medium. As a caller you can answer questions, overcome objections, and tailor the sales message to the individual you're talking to. The essence of effective phone sales is promoting *customer benefits*—individual reasons why someone needs your product or service. The use of benefits is a key element of all direct marketing and is described in detail in Chapter 7. Using customer benefits, you should develop a script, which you and your employees will use for all outbound calls. Modify or update it as you use it, but the purpose of a fixed, written approach is to find the words that work best and use them again and again.

You can get started with outbound telemarketing in three ways. First, you can use it occasionally to supplement your other marketing with little additional expense. You take advantage of free time. Second, you can make a commitment to use telemarketing effectively as an in-house marketing function. To do this you can either hire one or more telemarketing professionals, or you can obtain training for yourself and other people you designate to spend time regularly calling.

Practice and training are necessary to become adept at telemarketing. You can't expect a secretary, a clerk, or even a marketing person simply to pick up the phone and become an instant hit as a telemarketer. Many local telephone companies offer free or low-cost telemarketing seminars. Call your phone company and ask. If they don't provide the training, they may be able to refer you to an outside firm which does. In addition, some community colleges and adult education centers offer telephone sales classes.

The third, and perhaps the most expensive, way to use telemarketing is to hire an outside telemarketing company. Hiring outside firms is discussed in detail in Appendix A.

900 PHONE NUMBERS

Ideally, 900 phone numbers are tailor-made for your direct marketing efforts: Customers call you to hear information on a recording or to place an order. Then the phone company bills them for the call, collects the money, and sends it to you.

Two techniques are used for 900-number programs; you earn income with both. In the passive programs, you provide information on a recording (called *audiotext* in the trade), and customers are billed automatically each time they call. Passive phone services include sports update programs, news and information lines, children's stories, and horoscopes. In interactive 900 programs, your customer service representatives talk to callers, taking orders, providing information, and making note of callers' names and addresses to send them merchandise or information about products or services. Again, callers are billed per call. This latter service is a new way in which marketers are adding names to their data bases, for which the callers subsidize the costs.

In theory this sounds like a marketer's delight. In practice, 900 numbers started out with less than a positive image and have slowly come back toward mainstream use. In many metropolitan areas, 900 numbers are used for "chat lines" advertised on cable TV. In the commercials, breathy-voiced women in negligées urge male callers to phone in and talk with them. Callers are connected to what amounts to a telephone open forum. Some 900 numbers have also been used for sexually explicit recordings. This "sleaze factor," as one trade journal writer called it, initially kept other companies from experimenting with the new medium.

As more well-known, reputable firms use 900-number programs for legitimate marketing, the tarnish should wear off this medium quickly. Using 900 numbers may be beneficial for you, but you'll have to evaluate the costs carefully. Here are some of the expenses you can expect in setting up a 900-number program:

- For passive services, you need automatic answering and recording equipment plus professionally recorded messages, which need to be changed regularly depending on the type of information you provide.

- If you set up an interactive system, you need to have operators available to handle all the incoming calls.

- MCI Communications Corp., Sprint Gateways, and AT&T are major suppliers of 900-number programs, and all have service charges and other requirements. AT&T, for example, has transport, billing, and collection fees, as well as minimum daily call requirements high enough to discourage many small businesses.

- Add to all this substantial costs for the advertising necessary to generate enough calls to make your program profitable. In addition, you will have some costs in collecting the information you provide or in purchasing the products you sell via the calls.

In spite of the drawbacks, the service still holds possibilities. Rather than charge customers directly for catalogs, direct merchants have offered catalogs to people who call a 900 number. Warner Bros. set up a unique birthday service which uses 900 numbers effectively: Customers call a 900 number and give the name and phone number of a friend who is having a birthday. The friend then receives a (recorded) call from Bugs Bunny wishing him or her a happy birthday.

Keep this medium in mind. Monitor the image of 900 numbers in your region. Check with your local representatives of the phone companies offering 900 services to see what their current minimums are. Compare the costs of replacing the ordering system you're using now with 900 service. For information on using toll-free 800 numbers, see Chapter 17.

FACSIMILE TRANSMISSIONS

Advertising by fax is limited to business applications because most consumers do not have the machines at home (yet). When ads by fax were first transmitted, they created a backlash and cries for prohibitive legislation. At the same time, some marketers who use "junk fax" were announcing response rates of 10 percent or more, especially for fax-related products such as rolls of paper.

Since some of the novelty of the medium has worn off and several state legislatures have passed laws banning unsolicited fax ads, use has dwindled. The machine still has some benefits for your marketing program even if you don't send off unsolicited messages.

Fax transmissions still carry immediacy that is hard to beat with a letter. You can, therefore, use fax messages for your existing clients when you really want to get their attention. Use a fax message to call attention to specials you may be having. Tell existing customers when you have remnant quantities of some items, which they can have at reduced prices if they act right away. If you clearly identify yourself and show that you're a supplier for the firm you're contacting, your fax will not be treated like an unsolicited message.

Fax transmissions are also a good way to respond to a customer's or prospect's request for product or service information. Use a fax message in conjunction with a phone call or mailer. This way you'll be using a big-budget advertiser's technique of reaching prospective buyers through more than one medium.

POSTSCRIPTS....

States Regulate Technology

More than a dozen states have laws regulating unsolicited fax advertising and the use of computerized, automatic dialers for telephone advertising. Unsolicited fax advertising is banned in Oregon, Connecticut, Florida, and Maryland. Since several more states are considering regulations on forms of electronic advertising, you need to consult local authorities before using auto-dialers or facsimile machines. At the federal level, restrictive legislation has been discussed, but not approved.

Start Your Own Deck

Here is another way to use card deck advertising: Mail your own deck to customers. Some card pack advertisers, notably John Wiley and Sons, Inc., publishers of this book, send out their own decks filled with their own offers, each on a separate business reply card. If you have a variety of products or services to offer, you could send your deck to promising rental lists or your house list. Decks generate interest because they're an uncommon format and if recipients order *anything* from your deck, you will be the winner. Another way to profit from decks is to sell space in a deck that you mail to your house list. When you think your list is big enough, talk with a list manager about what it takes to start a deck.

Do Your Own Co-op

Instead of starting your own card pack, try your own co-op. Share the cost of a mailing with one or more local merchants who offer related products. A pizza shop and video rental store would be a good paring. A nursery and a patio supply store could complement each other in a mailing.

Charge for Your Catalog

Some catalog companies find that they get better leads and more orders per catalog if they charge a nominal fee. If you refund the cost of the catalog with the first purchase, you provide an additional incentive for someone to place an order.

Not for Children

The Federal Trade Commission recently adopted tough rules regulating the advertising and use of 900 phone numbers. The new regulations prohibit pay-per-call services aimed at children under 12 and require specific cost disclosures in ads, commercials, and in the 900 messages themselves. If you are thinking about getting into this business, a call to your nearest FTC office for a copy of the new rules is advisable.

6 TRACKING AND TESTING

Learning from Your Past

Testing pays off. If all variables are carefully controlled and sample sizes large enough, testing can help you predict the results of direct marketing better than any form of conventional advertising research. In spite of high costs in time and money, methodical testing of lists, offers, and other major advertising elements is the closest way to ensure success.

When a jewelry import company started marketing through catalogs, it evaluated lists in a 300,000-piece test mailing. The company president said she was willing to lose $60,000 on the test.[1] Tests are not designed to lose money, but many of them may be structured to gather information first and add to the bottom line second. Testing can easily continue for a year or more.

Conducting extensive tests is sound advice, but it's just not practical for most small business marketers. If a 300,000-piece test sounds like your mailing schedule for the next few years—or perhaps the next few lifetimes—you need to adopt what I call the "second-best" approach to testing, a mixture of limited tests and careful tracking. By meticulously recording your results you can build a data base of valuable customers and learn which marketing techniques work best for you. This chapter presents a variety of ways to capture data and track your results, and it provides an introduction to different testing methods. The applicability of the testing methods will vary with the size of your lists, the number of your potential customers, and of course, your budget.

TRACKING RESULTS

As you know by now, a major benefit of direct marketing is its accountability. You can repeat advertising that brings in the most money and dump the flops immediately. To do this, however, you need a foolproof tracking system so you can clearly identify what works and what doesn't. It won't cost you a mountain of money to keep good records; it just takes planning and the discipline to follow through.

As I mentioned earlier, research in direct marketing is an ongoing task. You record results, make decisions, and maintain your files as a resource for when you do another mailing, place another ad, or build a campaign. Even though your advertising may be focused on accomplishing a specific short-term objective, you should track it carefully enough so you can learn from it. Try to learn as much as you can from every step you take.

To get started, make a new file folder for every mailing you do, ad you place, and commercial you create. The file should contain copies of your ad taken from the publication in which it appeared, plus an ad schedule if it ran in more than one issue. In the case of direct mail, include several copies of the mailing pieces, stuffed and addressed exactly as they were sent out.

Here are other things your file should include:

Cost, quantity, description, and source of each list used

Circulation and edition of the publication in which your ad appeared

Description and explanation of any coding used in tabulating the results

Names and addresses of vendors who supplied lists, data processing, graphics, printing, inserting, or other services

Other advertising or sales/promotional work, if any, which supported the campaign

Details of any difficulties in production or tabulation

Result totals: number of responses, percentages, costs, and other amounts

If your advertising is successful and you want to repeat the winner, you will have all the information on file to re-create the campaign the way it was or to modify it as circumstances dictate. Of course the key elements of this file will be the results—the figures generated by the mailing or ad.

Figure 6.1 shows you an example of a simplified form for recording totals from a campaign. Not all the categories in this form may be appropriate for your business but this gives you a good starting point. Be careful not to mix results from more than one ad or medium. Keep separate tracking sheets for each. When you test one ad against another or one list against another, you'll need to keep two sets of figures for responses, as we'll review later in this chapter.

What to Record

The totals are just one part of tracking. You need the details behind the percentage totals to tell you who bought your product or service, how they paid for it, and other information. Let's start with basics. One way to remember the essential information you should record is to remember seven questions: Who? Where? What? When? Why? How? and How much? The basics you need are:

Who:	Names of prospects or customers
Where:	Addresses (and phone numbers)
What:	Which merchandise or service they bought
When:	Date when the order or response was received
Why:	Positive incentives or premiums used
How:	Method of response (such as mail coupon, 800 telephone number, walk-in) and source of response (which ad or mailing generated the response)
How much:	Dollar amount of order

The president of a direct marketing service company told me he formed a partnership with a friend to sell a new product via mail order. They began by

DIRECT RESPONSE TRACKING/ANALYZING			
Job title:			
Date mailed:			
How mailed			
Class: _____			
Rate: _____			
List sources/media:			
Quantity:			
Circ./Impressions			

Cost	Quantity	CP/M

	Gross responses	Percent	Conversions (Sales)	Conversion Percentage
Mail				
Phone				
In-person				
Fax./etc.				
Totals				

Cost Per Response	Cost per sale	Average Order

	A.	B.

FIGURE 6.1   Direct marketing tracking/analysis form. Be sure to include all expenses, including outside expenditures, in the cost of a mailing or an ad.

advertising in several publications. When the first orders came in, his partner, also a veteran direct marketer, called excitedly to report results.

"We got several orders in today," he said.

"Which publications did they come from?" asked the president.

"Who cares?" he said. "We made ten sales!"

The same thing happened to me when I ventured into direct marketing as an entrepreneur rather than as a marketing director. When you're emotionally involved in the results of a campaign, it's easy to let the paperwork slide while you momentarily revel in the success. The lesson to learn is that even while you're celebrating, you can still record the details.

Those details often include information beyond the basic seven questions. How much more you need to record depends on your business. Remember the 12 list criteria? The information that makes a rental list valuable to you also makes your house list a storehouse of opportunity. Your data base should include information on the RFM trio of recency, frequency, and monetary (value of purchases). Some small businesses may not need to know much more; however, demographic information is often helpful.

In business marketing you'll need to record the name of the company, the name and title of the person who made the order, and any other details about the company that may be pertinent to your business. If you conduct lead generation programs, you'll need to expand the seven questions listed earlier to include when initial and follow-up contacts are made, by whom, and by which method, such as in-person sales, direct mail, or telemarketing. You should record all steps taken to convert someone from a prospect to customer.

When you track your results, keep running totals of sales, segmented by advertising medium, average size of orders, and other necessary factors such as geography.

All the data you record, which becomes a part of your data base, gives you the information you need to evaluate the success of current advertising and marketing and to develop your customer profile. It also gives you the resources you need to solve problems. For example, assume you're selling toner cartridges for laser printers. When you get ready to do a mailing to companies, to whom should it be addressed? By reviewing your files you might find out that, say, 68 percent of your buyers have had the title of office manager. If that's the case, you know the business title that should appear on your labels.

Remember, a goal of all this tracking is to turn customers into repeat customers.

Software Help

Keeping track of all this data is routine and time-consuming yet critically important to your success. Fortunately, computers make the process easier. At first you may be able to get by with a word processing add-on program such as WordStar's MailList™, which helps you maintain simple mailing lists and create personalized boilerplate letters. If you have more complex requirements, and you're adept at using a general data base program such as Ashton-Tate's dBASE IV, you may be able to create your own record-keeping data management system.

Instead of making do with something you already have, you can select from a variety of special data base marketing software, ranging from mailing list programs to sophisticated lead-tracking programs that truly simplify marketing and sales functions. Many programs in the new generation of specific direct marketing and direct mail software are easy to learn and easy to use.

Simplicity is a requirement for a tracking system. Many of your marketing decisions are only as good as the accuracy and timeliness of your data. To insure that the data you need gets entered rapidly and correctly, select an understandable computer program and use simple codes to track results of advertising.

Surprisingly, direct marketing software for a personal computer doesn't have to be expensive. You can buy an expandable, multifunction program for $300 to $1,000.

Here are some of the different categories of data base and tracking software available. Information on suppliers is in Appendix B.

Multifunction List Management. Programs such as Mail Order Manager (MOM) from Dydacomp Development Corp. will track sales and leads and perform a variety of other functions. MOM provides list management, inventory control, profit analysis, and other detailed operations, as shown in Figure 6.2. Some list management programs are so thorough that they prompt you to record information you might have missed. Then they provide up-to-date totals and analyses. The Mail Order Wizard from the Haven Corp. is a similar product.

Special Mailing Programs. Sorting your list in ZIP order and according to carrier routes will help you get substantial postal savings. Costs for address-sorting software range from a few hundred dollars to several thousand, depending on the sophistication and capabilities of the programs. The Mailer's Software catalog includes ZIP-code based software.

Standardizing or Cleaning Up Names. Ever wonder how lists from different sources are put in a standard mailing format? How do mailers decide to address someone "Dear Mr. Smith" or "Dear Ms. Smith?" A company called Peoplesmith Software has a variety of inexpensive programs that perform these tasks. DataLift, for example, cleans up addresses by converting information that is in the unprofessional-looking all caps format into proper upper and lower case letters suitable for personalized letters. Another program differentiates between addresses that begin with a company name and those that start with the name of a person. This helps you avoid personalized letters that begin, "Dear Mr. Allied Wrench Company." US Sprint could have used this program when they printed the letter in Figure 8.2.

Telemarketing and Other Categories. PC software that contains fields for customer records and that prompts telemarketers with scripts and questions to ask while they're on the phone can help you set up an outbound telemarketing program. Mapping software will help you conduct geo-demographic

```
    12/06/                       List Management System
                                CATALOG MUSIC SUPPLY, CO.

                               DEFINED LIST CONTROLS
    10 - Count Names on Defined List        11 - Print Labels for Defined List
    12 - Perform "n" th Name Sampling       13 - Reset List of Names
    14 - Export Defined List                15 - Increment Mailing Counter
    16 - Save Defined List                  17 - Load a Previously Saved List
    18 - Print Notices for Defined List
                               LIST DEFINITION CONTROLS
            INCLUDE IN LIST :                        EXCLUDE FROM LIST :
    30 - All Orders by Query...              50 - All Orders by Query...
    31 - All Orders of Products/Type...      51 - All Orders of Products/Type...
    32 - All Orders by Source Key...         52 - All Orders by Source Key...
    33 - All Prospects                       53 - All Prospects
    34 - All Prospects by Source Key...      54 - All Prospects by Source Key...
    35 - All Customers by Gross Amount       55 - All Customers by Gross Amount
    36 - All Customers by Order Freq.        56 - All Customers by Order Freq.
    37 - All Names by Customer Type...       57 - All Names by Customer Type...
    38 - All Names by State/Zip Range..      58 - All Names by State/Zip Range..
    39 - All Names on Saved List ...         59 - All Names on Saved List ...
                                             60 - Names by Date of Last Activity
    99 - Exit to DOS                              ENTER CHOICE ▮
```

FIGURE 6.2   Look at the variety of options you have to sort and segment customers in your house data base on this menu from the Mail Order Manager program by Dydacomp Development Corp. This is what one screen from the program looks like. Many of the list options refer to some of the 12 criteria for list selection explained in Chapter 4. List management is one of many operations of this multifunction program *(Copyright 1985 Dydacomp Development Corporation. Mail Order Manager is a Trademark of Dydacomp Development Corporation. Used with permission.)*

marketing research. Other available programs support and track field sales force efforts. Many software companies will send you demonstration diskettes which let you sample a program before you buy it.

National Change of Address (NCOA) Processing. If you maintain your lists or data base on diskettes you can still take advantage of valuable NCOA processing and get it at rock-bottom prices through the Postal Service. The processing is actually done by a contracting firm, FDC, Inc., but you send your diskettes to the U.S. Postal Service National Customer Support Center in Memphis, Tennessee. There's no minimum list size requirement; ZIP + 4 is included in the service; and it takes two to three weeks. For the address and phone number of this service please see Appendix B.

TESTING

Testing means different things to different people, depending on how they use direct marketing. You can test the three major elements of direct marketing: the offer, the list and media, and the creative work. You can also test a variety of other factors, from the time of year that you mail to the color of your envelopes. When you test, you compare one direct marketing option against another to see which is the more successful. You may judge success by the most responses, highest quality of leads, highest net income, or other factors.

Ideally, once a test is completed it should tell you which road to follow for the next step of your marketing. As a simple example, say you mail one offer to equal numbers of sample names from two different lists. If List A yields a much higher response than List B, you might reasonably assume that when you mail to more people you will get better results by selecting further names from List A. You should plan your tests so that you know ahead of time what the test is designed to measure.

That's the theory, but it takes care and large enough sample sizes to maintain the theory in the real world. Here are some common forms tests can take:

Lists: Mail the same offer to different lists. (Actually, you just mail to *samples* of names from large lists.)

Direct mail offers: Mail different offers to different sets of names taken from the same list.

Print ad offers: Create two ads with different offers. A magazine or newspaper will print one ad in half of their issues and the other in the other half of the issues. This is known as an A–B split test.

Creative mail test: Use the same offer, but use a different copy or graphics approach when you send it to different sets of names on the same list.

Creative print test: Use two different approaches to sell essentially the same offer in magazine or newspaper ads. A publication alternates the ads as mentioned above.

To make testing work for you,

1. Try to control all the variables.
2. Test only important marketing details.
3. Be skeptical of your tests.
4. Keep the tests and tracking methods as simple as possible.

The purpose of testing is to identify those factors or variables (such as one list over another) that make your responses and your profits go up. In practice, however, you always have many variables at work. The challenge of testing is to control all the variables except one, so that when you get your results back you can be reasonably sure that the one variable in question (for instance, the difference in lists) was the *only* difference between your two test mailings. In a simple two-list test, if List One is mailed one month and List Two is mailed a few months later, the difference in time could influence the test more than the difference in the lists.

To compare samples of two lists, every recipient on both sample lists should receive the same mailing, promoting the same offer, at the same time of the same month. The environment and conditions for each mailing should be as identical as possible. By doing this you try to control *intervening variables* which may influence a test without your knowledge.

Random selection of names on a list to be tested is also important to maintain your control of variables and give you valid test results. In testing one list against another, for example, you want to see how responsive an entire list is by sampling a portion of each list. You wouldn't want to select groups of people from the list according to the neighborhoods they live in, because the area of residence would be an additional variable. And, as we have seen, where someone lives reflects other differences in demographics and buying preferences. You *could* do a test mailing to determine which areas of the nation, state, or city are most responsive to your offer, but then the geography would be the variable, not the choice of one list over another.

The 5,000-Name Test

It's relatively easy to select random samples for tests, because list brokers, managers, and advertising managers of publications have systems already set up to assist you. To help you obtain a sample large enough to conduct a reliable test, list managers will rent you 5,000 randomly selected names to form a *test panel*. In practice, 5,000 names is a minimum order for many lists. The names are selected via a computer process which identifies every *Nth name*. The symbol *N* stands for a number. If the number selected was nine, then every ninth name on a list would be selected. In statistical terms, a *reliable* test is one that consistently gives the same answer each time it is conducted.

In the case of magazines and newspapers, testing is more simple. As mentioned above, an A–B split test means that you provide two different ads, each of which is printed in alternate copies of the publication as it comes off the press. The randomness here is that every other reader sees only version A or version B. In a publication test, the only variable should be the difference in your ad design and copy. You don't want a publisher to split up your ads by assigning one to one regional edition and the other ad to a different part of the country. It should also appear in the same place in each publication.

With as many of the variables as possible under control, you can proceed to test factors that normally affect your results. Some direct marketers and paper companies have conducted tests that show that changing the color of an outside envelope can increase responses. A test mailing by PaineWebber, the nationwide securities firm, showed that shading portions of a mailer with blue ink increased responses. These changes may make a slight difference, but when you're testing it's best to focus on elements that can make or break your advertising. Avoid testing minor issues. Even if you limit yourself to testing only offers and lists, you will have more than enough possibilities to keep you occupied.

After you've controlled the variables and focused on testing only major marketing factors, you should still be skeptical of your tests. Just because a test mailing of 5,000 names from a large list turned out to be successful is not a good enough reason to spend your life savings to mail to the 250,000 people left in the entire list. The test is a good indication that subsequent identical mailings will do well, but it's best to progress slowly. Increase your mailing in small increments. At this point a skilled, professional list broker can provide valuable direction. Many brokers would advise you increase your next mailing to 10,000 names. Some might say 20,000 or 25,000, depending on the type of list you're using and your offer.

One of the reasons for increasing your sample size on a follow-up test is that, statistically speaking, the larger the sample, the greater the confidence level of the results. Although few if any tests can be 100 percent certain, your 10,000-name test should be a better gauge of the responsiveness of a list than a 5,000-name sample. Often a cost-effective 5,000-name sample is sufficient to give you a 90 percent confidence level or above. It's a good starting point, but remember that this is a simplification of a complex operation. A handbook on statistical analysis will give you much more detail on the principles and operations involved.

There is an additional reason for skepticism. Since the 5,000-name test is so common, list managers routinely have their data processors keep tapes of 5,000 names ready for rental. Sometimes, either intentionally or unintentionally, these tapes contain names that are more recent than the list as a whole. Therefore, a 5,000-name test will frequently give a higher response than subsequent mailings.

For this reason, brokers sometimes recommend requesting more than 5,000 names so that list managers will have to do a new Nth-name computer run to create your test list. If you want to try to avoid artificially high responses on tests, request a test of 6,500 names, for example. Alternatively, if you sample from a number of lists, those 5,000-name test samples with high recency factors might provide you with enough responses to make your mailing not just a test, but a successful campaign.

One way of testing the uniformity or homogeneity of a list is to mail to two separate Nth-name samples of the same list. By coding your mailings, you should be able to tell whether the results are identical, which would indicate a homogenous list.

Keep It Simple

One last reason for skepticism is that you cannot truly control all variables in any test. Weather, variations in postal service, news events, changes in the economy, and numerous other variables may be at work on your test sample. Thus, you need to proceed cautiously.

Trying to make your marketing efforts as simple as possible, when in fact they are a mixture of an almost unlimited number of ingredients, is the last part of the testing formula. According to a Southern California list compiler, a client once tested 40 different offers by mailing each offer to separate 10,000-name list samples. Can you imagine trying to track responses to 40 separate offers in a 400,000-piece mailing? And what would be the next step if, say 23 of the offers drew substantially better than the rest? Would the next test have 23 separate segments?

If you're running two or more tests at once, it's easy to get sidetracked when you're supposed to be tracking. Add a few wrinkles, and keeping track of your results gets to be complex. If you have never used direct marketing testing methods, start small and work up.

One of the drawbacks to layers of direct mail testing is the expanded printing costs you incur when you print your materials in small quantities. One example: You're trying to test three offers, so you mail a different package to each of three different Nth-number samples of one or more rental lists. Depending on how different the packages are, you could nearly triple some of your design and printing costs. For large mailers who plan to mail ultimately to hundreds of thousands or millions of people, the unit costs are relatively small when spread over the entire mailing. But in quantities of 5,000, 10,000 or even 20,000, unit printing costs rise dramatically.

Here are a couple of ways to save: If you test different offers, see if you can put the variable details of the offer on only one or two printed pieces, such as the first page of a letter and the inside face of a brochure. That way you minimize costs for new typesetting, printing plates, and negatives. If you test offers with a self-mailer, you might only have to redesign and reprint one page or printed surface.

When you test lists only, you could print in advance all the mailing pieces you'd need for the test and the continuation (follow-up). That could be economical, providing that one of the lists you tested gave good enough results to warrant sending out the rest of the mailers to additional names. If your test showed poor results on all lists, you could be stuck with excess mailers.

Another way to save money testing is to test a cheaper version of a successful mailer. Take a mailer that has been successful for you and use a lower quality of paper and a cheaper envelope. Leave out one piece from the package, perhaps. Don't print everything in as many colors. If your cheaper package yields good results, you can save on subsequent mailings.

Publication testing is quite different, because there are no printing costs and the only additional cost of doing an A–B test in a magazine is to write and design the artwork, which chapters 7–12 will show you how to do for yourself. When you test in a print medium, it's a good idea to begin with several ads. Test different offers and different creative approaches until you find one combination that provides the highest responses. In direct marketing jargon, this ad becomes your *control*, which means your most successful creative effort.

In print or direct mail, once you establish a control—the very reason for testing—you should keep repeating it for as long as it's successful. You may get tired of the ad or mailer, but that is no reason to change. Neither is the fact that friends or colleagues may tell you that your ad isn't current. There's no need to update a winner. You can, however, challenge it periodically by conducting tests against the control. If the control wins, it remains. If a new offer or creative package wins, then you have a new control.

Testing Two Variables

While list and offer testing through the mail can be effective, it's not for everyone. For example, if you sell to business buyers in a unique field or limited geographical area and have a list of 7,000 total potential customers, it makes no sense to do a test mailing of 5,000, or even 3,000. Marketers who do mailings of this size or smaller, should simply mail to their entire list each time, but carefully track results.

If you do larger mailings, however, and your budget can justify some testing, it's possible to test more than one variable at a time. So, at the risk of introducing a more complex form of testing, here are some additional suggestions. You can conduct, for example, a test of lists simultaneously with a test of offers. The technique can be easily explained with a matrix. First, let's look at a single-variable test conducted by a small company that was introducing a new product to customers. To see if the addition of a free tape player would increase response, a test was conducted. One group of 3,000 customers received one offer and the other group received a different offer.

	House List Names	*Responses*	*Percentage*
New product offer	3,000	69	2.3
Offer with premium	3,000	129	4.3

The addition of the premium nearly doubled the response. On the surface, the test showed that the premium should be used for the remainder of the mailing, but even simple tests require careful cost analysis. One other factor that doesn't show up on the chart is the additional cost of the tape player, including shipping. Only if the increased cost of the premium was worth nearly doubling the response rate would the mailing proceed with the premium. Before the test was conducted, the marketers should have been able to determine how much an increase in response would be necessary to justify the premium costs.

Here's a more complex test, in which a newsletter publisher tested three different rental lists to expand his circulation. He selected three 6,000-name list samples, but at the same time he wanted to test two different subscription offers. Offer One included 14 months for the price of 12, whereas Offer Two included the same subscription deal but added a how-to booklet as a premium. To test the offers and the lists, each list sample of 6,000 names was divided in half.

	Offer One	*Offer Two*
List A	3,000	3,000
List B	3,000	3,000
List C	3,000	3,000

The results from the test were as follows:

	Offer 1		**Offer 2**	
	Responses	*Percentages*	*Responses*	*Percentages*
List A	36	1.2	39	1.3
List B	84	2.8	87	2.9
List C	18	.6	15	.5

A brief review of the results shows first that List C is not promising and that List B is substantially better than A. The differences between the offers are not as clear cut. In the test for Lists A and B, the second offer pulled only a slightly higher percentage than the first one; for List C the first offer actually pulled a higher percentage than the second offer.

If List B offers a large universe, it would be worth another, larger test. The results for the offers, however, don't give a clear signal. In this case, addition of the information booklet was not enough to boost response very much. If the marketer is satisfied with the responses without the premium, the booklet can be eliminated, although in this case the premium was retained for a following test since it was of minimal cost.

Using a similar simple matrix you could test more lists and more offers, depending on your budget and objectives. Remember to follow your tracking one step further when testing in a lead generation program. The meaningful numbers will be the percentage of sales (not leads), the lowest cost per lead, and the highest sales per lead.

Codes are necessary to track all results. You can use simple number or letter codes which are printed on mailing labels at the same time that the names and addresses are printed. Some PC software will code labels for you, and service bureaus are set up to do the same. If you are providing a telephone response option, you will need to ask callers for the code from their mailers. For publication ads, you can simply add a department code to your address. Dept. FH in the address, for example, would mean that the response came from *Family Handyman* magazine. If you're performing a simple A–B, or two-variable mail test, you could use differently colored reply cards. In magazine ads you can have your responses directed to different P.O. box numbers or simply pick two names of fictitious people to represent your two groups. You tell people to order by sending to Mr. Aames or Mr. Zorn.

FOCUS GROUPS

Bring a handful of people together to get their opinions of and reactions to advertising, and you have a focus group. This technique has recently gained new popularity. Whenever people discuss direct marketing testing techniques, the term *focus group* seems to pop up with increasing frequency among beginners and direct marketing veterans alike. The surprising, or perhaps alarming, aspect is that so many people misunderstand the limits and purposes of this research and testing method.

Focus groups are used to find out what consumers think. They're designed to answer the question of why consumers do what they do. The technique is helpful in providing spontaneous reactions to ads, direct mail packages, or even campaign themes. You can ask focus group members if they would pay more for your product or what benefits they think your competition provides which you do not. Compared to the other research techniques mentioned, focus groups provide far more details and more explanations of consumer behavior.

The results of focus groups, however, are qualitative, not quantitative. That means no matter how reasoned or logical-sounding the results from a focus group might be, there is no way to project the conclusions directly to the population of potential customers you're studying. Ideally, random-sample list tests will give you a reasonable idea of how the balance of a given list will perform. That's quantitative information. Focus group members are not usually randomly selected, nor are the groups large enough to provide any quantitative information that can be generalized to a larger group.

Focus groups and related techniques can be extremely valuable, however, so don't ignore the technique, just use it wisely. Don't expect to get any figures or percentages out of the discussions, but do expect to get detailed reactions, comments, opinions, and suggestions from the participants.

A focus group is a discussion group of 6 to 12 people who are generally representative of the same audience or population. For example, if you are marketing products to high school students, then you would want to recruit high school students for your group. You can use any geo-demographic factors you like in selecting your focus group members to match the profile of your customers or prospects.

Outside specialists often conduct focus groups, using meeting rooms equipped with two-way mirrors so that participants can be observed during the discussion. If you hire a research specialist to conduct a focus group, you can watch the meeting from behind the mirror. This observation is helpful to see how people react to your product, your advertising, or other subjects for discussion. Meetings are always recorded on audio tape and are frequently videotaped.

A skilled moderator is the most important element to the success of a focus group. While it is intended for open discussion, a focus group needs to be led. The moderator works from a list of questions and topics to be covered and keeps discussions from digressing too much or from being monopolized by one person. The moderator can ask follow-up questions, if answers are not self-explanatory, and can draw out participants who don't volunteer enough information.

Results from focus group meetings take many forms. Some of the information may help you develop ideas for campaigns. Comments and ideas from participants are sometimes used directly in print and broadcast advertising copy. Focus group results can also point out little details you may have missed. Krupp Taylor, USA, a direct marketing agency, uses focus groups. In one test, direct mail packages were reviewed by a group of people over 40, the target audience for the product to be sold. One benefit from the group, says Craig Walker, executive creative director for the agency, is that they discovered that some of the printing in the package was too small to be read comfortably by the recipients. The package had been written and designed by people in their 20s and 30s who had no trouble reading fine print.

A major software firm used focus groups in another way. Group participants were asked to identify what they saw as the most appealing benefits of a software program. Those benefits were given to the direct mail copywriters to incorporate in the advertising.

Focus groups usually last about two hours, and participants are paid from $25 to $100 each. To hire an outside research firm to conduct the program costs from $1,000 to $2,000 and sometimes more, depending on the experience of the company and the services requested, such as videotaping, recruiting participants, and providing the meeting facilities.

It's important not to use friends or relatives in a focus group, or anyone who is involved in any way professionally with your company or your product or service. Viewing a focus group session and analyzing tapes or transcripts can tell you what customers might find objectionable about your product or advertising, why they buy your product, and a variety of detailed information that other types of testing or research will not reveal.

WAYS TO SAVE MONEY ON TESTING

The best way to save money on testing is to incorporate a testing mindset in everything you do. When you can, vary some normal direct marketing function, then carefully monitor it to see if the results are different from those you've experienced in the past. Better yet, perform mini-tests when it's economically feasible.

A small, community-based credit union did a mailing to people who lived within a certain radius of the office. The purpose was to generate new members. Since the staff didn't want to generate more business than they could handle, they mailed the advertising in segments. The segments were not sorted in any particular way, except by quantity. What was there to be learned?

Because the credit union recorded the addresses of new members, and of people who just inquired but did not join, they got an idea of which local neighborhoods yielded the most new members, and the largest volume of loans and savings. A retail business that did not routinely record customer addresses, however, would not have known which residential areas yielded the most customers. Segmenting the list by neighborhood would have been necessary to turn a standard mailing into a low-cost test.

Since the credit union already segmented the mailing, it could have made a split test of different offers. It might have learned, for example, whether a no-fee checking account or a low-rate open-end loan was more effective in attracting new members. If the credit union used stock (existing) service brochures, the only additional cost for the test might have been to print a second letter.

Each time you do a mailing, develop print advertising, on use some other medium, look for ways you can test inexpensively to find out just a little more information about your business and your customers. To help you keep from straining your budget, here are some additional, inexpensive testing suggestions:

- Test a new product by mailing to samples of rental lists that have traditionally been good for your other products, and to a sample of your house list. If those tests are successful, you might try a continuation, with testing of new outside lists to follow.

- Telemarketing is a swift and inexpensive way to test offers. You can test the same offer variables you would via the mail, but with telemarketing you get instantaneous answers. To keep costs down, you need to use a tiny sample of names, much smaller than you would use with a mail test. With a small sample you cannot be confident of the reliability of the test, but a limited telephone test can give you preliminary data you can use to decide if a mail test is warranted.

- If focus groups sound too expensive, try similar testing methods, some using the telephone. To test copy, offers, or other aspects of your advertising informally, select individuals who are members of your target market and ask them questions. Have them give you their opinions of your offer over the phone. If you have a direct mail package that didn't get the kind of results you expected, ask people in person to look through the mailer. Have them read your response coupon and tell you whether they know what they are supposed to do. You could even conduct your own discussion group to get reactions from people in your target audience. As with focus groups, don't ask friends or relatives for their opinions. People who know nothing about your company or offer make the best test subjects.

- To find out how much appeal your product or offer has before you commit money to a mailing or mail test, use a small-space ad in a publication with demographics similar to the lists you would be using.

- To make your testing generate as much income as possible, stick to your best prospect lists, so that you will likely get a respectable number of sales even if one list doesn't pull dramatically more than another. In this case you're "testing" lists you might otherwise mail to without testing. In other words, if you need to get maximum profits, avoid risky tests.

- Here are some inexpensive media for price testing: self-mailers, small-space print ads, card decks, co-op coupons.

- For that matter, a card deck is a way to test various elements (not all at once, of course). For less than $2,000 you can do an A–B test in a large-circulation deck to test offers, prices, even a list.

- To make maximum use of the strong recency factor, you might only test hotline lists. Test one list's hotline against another's. Some rental lists have monthly hotlines large enough to be the only source of potential customers you need.

POSTSCRIPTS....

Why Sort House Names?

A further reason for sorting and segmenting your own list is so that you can appeal to different people differently. Chapters 7 and 8 tell you how to use the information you know about your customers to create advertising that will appeal especially to them. For example, you may want to talk to a new customer differently than to one who has bought from you for years.

Keep Track of the Monetary Factor

Be sure to keep close tabs on the third part of the RFM list criteria related to your customer activity. Keep track of how much your customers spend. The ones who spend the most are your prime customers. Your data base software should allow you to sort them separately because they need to receive special treatment. Compare your average sale per customer and your number of customers to see whether you are governed by the 80/20 rule. Many firms find that 80 percent of their business comes from 20 percent of their customers. Direct marketers know exactly *who* those 20 percent are.

7 CREATIVE PERSUASION
Explain What's in It for Them

That's the trouble with advertising, it makes you want to buy *stuff.*

—One teenager to another, overheard in a store

Advertising may possess what some consider mystical powers, but unfortunately you can't mesmerize your potential customers into ordering your product or flocking into your store or office. What you can do is understand basic human motivation and focus your advertising messages on concepts that most influence people's attitudes and buying decisions. Good direct marketing should overcome inertia, appeal to the emotions, and tell potential customers how they will benefit from buying.

After developing your offer and selecting the specific media or carefully targeted list, creating a persuasive message is the third major element of successful direct mail. To create effective direct response messages, you need to understand a little of the psychology of advertising. This and the following five chapters are closely linked to what has come before. In developing your creative advertising ideas, and in writing the copy, you need to concentrate on the offer and write directly to the people on your target list or data bases, using everything you know about them.

Motivational appeals and the other basic elements of direct mail persuasion are reviewed in this chapter. Chapter 8 shows how to apply the persuasive appeals when you write your advertising. Chapter 9 reviews the different formats you have to choose from. Chapter 10 combines information on direct mail's urgency devices and legal requirements. Chapter 11 focuses on writing direct mail letters, perhaps the most persuasive direct response medium of all. Chapter 12 shows you the essentials of layout and design, ways to get people to read your persuasive words.

The sales techniques and psychology covered in this and the next few chapters are applicable to most direct marketing situations. Most effective direct marketing creative methods have universal appeal because they're all designed for *people*. Whether your target market is made up of tool and die buyers, homemakers, or corporate presidents, they're all human and they're all motivated by basic human wants and needs.

Several years ago I heard Richard Thalheimer, president of The Sharper Image, Inc., speak at a direct marketing conference. He said that one of the reasons he was successful in marketing to an upscale audience is the knowledge that even affluent buyers love a bargain. No matter what their demographic status, people have many things in common, including an interest in saving money.

ARE YOU READY TO SELL?

You may be the most qualified person to write your direct response messages. As the owner or senior officer of a small business, you may already possess some or all of the information you need. You must know your *customers* and your *product*. That knowledge is essential, because it helps you identify the persuasive appeals and product benefits that go into successful direct response advertising. Creating effective advertising is another reason for your customer profile.

When direct mail copywriters tackle work for a new client, they often do their own research to find out as much about the new product or service as possible. They want to know how people use it and why. They want to know what the competition is like, what the sales history has been, and how similar products are priced. As a small business person you probably have all that information already.

A good copywriter needs to know not only the product, but also how to sell. Writing direct response copy is akin to putting personal selling on paper. General advertising aims at making an impression or positioning a product. Direct mail must *sell* it. You'll find no greater training ground for direct response advertising than behind the counter in a store or on the pavement of a field sales territory. Person-to-person selling gives you experience in overcoming customer objections, discovering the persuasive arguments that work best on different prospects, and closing sales. All these techniques are necessary in direct response advertising.

If you have sales experience, you probably already have a good idea of what makes people buy. If you don't have the experience, consider spending some time selling your product or service person-to-person. As a credit union marketing director, I initially had little personal contact with members (customers). It was not until I got involved in promotional campaigns that brought me into regular day-to-day contact with members that I developed an understanding of just how people feel about financial services and what benefits they look for from their financial institution. Savers at a credit union really are members because when they open an account, they become a part-owner of the credit union. The more I met with members, the more I became sensitive to the fact that it was the *members'* money that ran the credit union, not the credit union's money. In other words, the members were the first and only reason the institution existed.

To sum it up, your data base and customer profile are important, but to create effective advertising you need to learn about your customers on a one-on-one, gut level. If you sell to companies rather than consumers, get out and call on the people who authorize the purchase of your product and find out what they think. When I started my own business, I was my own sales manager. I learned, among other things, that the people at the companies I called on were looking for ways to solve their problems and not interested in my reasons for calling on them.

When you develop a direct marketing campaign, focus on your customers and not on yourself. People are interested first in what is important to *themselves*. This isn't selfishness; it's just human nature. When you write advertising in terms of what your customers or clients are interested in, you'll attract your reader's attention.

Some of the lessons you learn from personal selling are hard to explain with theory alone. Practical, hands-on experience is valuable. Rejection can be a powerful teacher. Consider getting out in the field or on the sales floor as soon as you can. Although it's not a substitute for real-life experience, reading a good book on personal sales can also help your advertising. *How to Master the Art of Selling* by Tom Hopkins (1982, Warner Books) is a good choice. Hopkins continually stresses the need to appeal to emotions, even in business selling. "Don't sell logic, sell emotions," he says.

As an example, here are two of many sales techniques which work well in direct marketing:

- The first technique is to get your prospects to start visualizing or even fantasizing about your product. Through conversation or through written marketing materials, you build an emotional bridge from the prospect to your product. Your prospects actually start selling to themselves when they make an emotional attachment.

- The other technique is simple and can be used to start that fantasizing. Simply ask your prospects which color (model, size, style) they would like. In direct response advertising, when you ask your reader to pick a color you're asking him to become involved with the product. In sales jargon this is called *assumptive selling*.

MOTIVATION

Everyone has basic needs such as those for food, clothing, shelter, and companionship. The inner drive we all have to obtain these things is a potent force. In a sense, our lives are controlled or motivated by our quest to satisfy these basic needs. You must appeal to a strong human drive in order to sell your products and services. The traditional way of putting psychological drives to commercial use is to show how someone can satisfy a basic human need by using your product or service.

On a simple level, if you're selling food, you want to make it as appetizing as possible so that people will connect it with the need to satisfy their hunger. Maintaining health is another basic need and is often linked directly and indirectly to a multitude of products today, from running shoes to gasolines that reduce smog.

Some psychological needs are stronger than others. One useful way of organizing the basic drives we all have is the *hierarchy of needs* described by psychologist and researcher Abraham Maslow. Dr. Maslow's theories of motivation have become standards in business and advertising psychology. He identified five levels of needs. Starting at the bottom, they are: (1) food and shelter, the physiological needs for sustaining life; (2) safety and security; (3) social acceptance, friendship, belonging to a group; (4) the ego needs, esteem and status; and (5) self-actualization or self-fulfillment, making a contribution to humanity.

According to Maslow, people try to satisfy lower-level human needs first before they move on to higher levels. When a person has satisfied one level of need, its power of motivation diminishes as the individual focuses on a higher level.

Not all motivational factors will be appropriate for your products or services, but many will. Sometimes you may need to point out potential customers' needs of which they may not be fully aware on a conscious level, then show how your product will satisfy that need. In other cases, research or your personal knowledge may tell you that your potential customers are especially vulnerable to a specific motivational hierarchy level. In that instance, zero in on that motivator and ignore the lower levels which are no longer strong influences. When you are unsure of the motivators necessary to push your prospects' "buy" buttons, stick to the basic mid-level motivators or use more than one in a specific ad or mailer. Ads that include more than one motivational factor are common.

Within each of Maslow's five levels are a variety of motivators you can use. Here are some of the motivators used in direct response advertising:

Exclusivity	Physical/Emotional Pleasure
Money (Greed)	Advancement
Pride of Ownership	Praise
Security	Accomplishment
Status	Recognition
Peer Pressure/Acceptance	Sympathy, Pity
Belonging	Guilt
Self-improvement	Fear of:
Beauty	Death
Sexual Attraction/Satisfaction	Poor Health
Family Love	Embarrassment, Criticism
Power	Losing Money
Prestige	Losing Attractiveness
Comfort (Status Quo)	Losing Friends (Lack of
Health	Belonging)
	Worry, Anxiety

Many motivational factors can be classified as either positive or negative, that is, factors which are either related to pleasure or associated with fear or pain. Nearly every one of the pleasure-based motivators has its opposite number in the possible loss of that source of pleasure. You can say your product promotes good health or that it helps users avoid the ravages of age and disease. Rather than tell you how much you can earn at a particular bank, some marketers will tell you how you will lose by banking somewhere else. Generally, fear and avoidance of pain are the strongest motivators. People are more interested in protecting what they have than in reaching out for something more. Describing what will happen if your potential customer does not respond may be stronger than explaining to him why he should, although a complete advertising message should tell both.

Whether you're writing about pleasure or avoidance of pain, remember Hopkins' advice. These motivators are primarily emotional factors, and emotions play a big part in daily decision making. Fear, and perhaps the strongest positive motivator, praise, are emotional concepts. The thought of love and affection could be the trigger to get someone to make a decision about your product. Buying is rarely based on cold hard facts alone, regardless what someone may say.

Here are some examples of how advertisers have used motivational factors in direct mail:

Money

The new tax acts...drastically changed the tax treatment of closely held companies and their owners!

These tax acts have brought new tax-saving opportunities for you and your closely held business!

Now you can cash in on these unprecedented opportunities with Panel's completely revised and continually updated guide....[1]

Saving money is one of the strongest and most universal motivators. It is the reason why stores and companies have special sales and why people postpone or make buying decisions. Providing ways to save your customers, clients, or prospects money should be a prime consideration when you formulate your offers. (This motivator, and most of the others, are also useful to consider in the offer-planning stage, *before* you formulate specific advertising.)

To some people, money is the only motivator in marketing. If you focus solely on price, however, you'll attract bargain hunters who will leave you quickly if they find something just a little lower-priced.

Exclusivity, Status

Every Monday morning, a rather unusual publication arrives at the desks of a select circle of individuals in positions of power and influence.

The readers of this...newsweekly include presidents (of countries, banks, universities and Fortune 500 companies), ranking executives (in business, government, and industry), and prominent thinkers (in law, science, economics, and military strategy).

...only a relative handful of Americans are aware of the existence of this exclusive publication, much less the intelligence it provides.

But now, with this letter, you are cordially invited to join the extremely select circle of men and women who wouldn't think of beginning each business week without the incomparable insight and reporting of ... *The Economist.*[2]

Of the many ways exclusivity is used as a motivator, few advertisers do it better than *The Economist*. The product, a British publication, *is* relatively unknown in the United States, so the exclusive appeal has the ring of truth. In addition, an underlying motivator here is the implication that if you don't subscribe you're not important or accepted.

One way you can offer exclusivity to your customers is by virtue of the fact that you don't serve everyone. Whoever is in your market can become part of a select, exclusive group. You could say your offer is only being made to college professors, executives, or residents of Baltimore, Maryland.

Fear

Every year, diseases of the heart and blood vessels lead to more deaths than all other causes combined, over 89,087 in California alone. Right now the chances are 50–50 that you, Mr. Jones, or someone you love will be a victim.[3]

Did you figure out that the advertiser here is the American Heart Association? It's easy to come up with dramatic, emotionally charged motivational copy for health and public service organizations, because life itself is the most basic of all human needs. But can you use a fear motivator to sell an everyday product or service? Advertisers do it all the time.

Here, fear is used to sell a newsletter:

Outstanding opportunities will open up for business and investors over the next few years in California. By taking advantage *now* of the continuing expansion in California, you can ride the crest of one of the biggest waves of growth in the nation.

But dangers lie ahead as well.[4]

Fear can be of the gut-wrenching variety, or simply fear of falling behind in business:

You can't take it any more.

Something is terribly wrong with your child and it's making your life a living hell.

While you hope and pray it's a typical case of teen-age rebellion, you fear it could be a serious drug, alcohol, or emotional problem.[5]

If you're only reading *O'Dwyer's*, you're missing the biggest PR opportunities in the United States.

You're missing dozens and dozens of editorial personnel changes at leading media—information you need to keep your Rolodex up to the minute.[6]

The first example, a front-end mailing, uses fear to promote a drug abuse awareness program for parents. The second tells readers they may miss important business tips if they don't read a public relations industry publication.

This next, rather outlandish example, demonstrates a necessary principle when using fear: Always provide a solution to the problem or situation which you present. The solution includes your product or service.

> . . . the financial markets are about to heat up like never before. The money-laundering gangsters have a time crunch—and record amounts of "dirty" money to clean up! The fires on Wall Street, Bonn, and Tokyo are going to burn bright and hot for a short time, and then the entire economy will collapse into something you won't easily recognize. Unless you know what to expect.
>
> . . . some investors are going to be ruined . . . while others (with inside info) stand to make the largest profits. . . . [7]

Guilt

When a child tries to influence (or manipulate) parents by laying a guilt trip on them, he or she has picked a powerful motivator. Guilt is often used in charity fund raising. Readers receive "free" Christmas cards, holiday stamps, or other items and are motivated by guilt to send some money. Appeals which remind readers how much they have and how little others have can be compelling.

Guilt seems to be overlooked in general direct marketing, especially by small business people. It can be used effectively for subscription renewals and in a variety of back-end strategies designed to activate dormant customers.

Praise

Negative, fear-based motivators are powerful. Positive factors, however, can be effective in some circumstances. With praise, you're restricted in some respects because you need to know something about your praisees (readers). Praise can be more effective with your house list, because the house list tells you more about your target audience than a rented list does. One of the most common uses of praise is in granting credit. "Dear Mr. Smith, because of your outstanding credit record we're pleased to offer you a preapproved MasterCard." Variations on those magic words of praise, linked to preapproval, have successfully sold hundreds of thousands of credit cards. One of many such letters I've written began this way:

> In recognition of your financial position, we are pleased to tell you that you have been preapproved to receive one of our first VISA Cards. It's special! There's no annual fee.
>
> This letter to you and a very small group of other members, is the first announcement of our new VISA Card program. To become a Charter Cardholder, please return the Reservation Form promptly.[8]

This letter combines praise with an appeal of exclusivity. Telling people they are part of a select group is effective.

While the major credit cards have substantially penetrated the market with their praise-filled letters, similar offers still yield results. You can use direct mail to tell customers or potential customers that they can buy from you using a preapproved line of credit. To put a preapproval plan into operation, you can establish your own credit criteria using your own files based on your customers' previous purchases. Alternatively, you can obtain assistance from a credit bureau such as TRW to evaluate the credit records of your existing customers. You can also develop a preapproved credit mailing to noncustomers using credit bureau lists.

Recently, special-interest groups have pressed Congress for laws banning prescreening and preapproved credit, but to date the practice is still accepted. See the end of this chapter for more information on advertising credit terms.

Indirect praise and praise unrelated to financial standing can be effective as well. *Sunset Magazine* used this lead paragraph (*lead* in writers' jargon) in a subscription offer:

> You're the kind of person SUNSET wants as a subscriber: a Westerner with a love of the Western Lifestyle. Someone looking for ideas that are practical, enjoyable and money-saving. Someone willing to try something new.[9]

BENEFITS

Reaching your prospective buyers on an emotional level is essential to your success. When you know how to do that, you're ready to provide substance to your advertising in the form of *benefits*. Benefits are the reason people buy products and services. A benefit is the personal advantage that your product or offer has for a customer. Benefits answer the customer's question, "What's in it for me?" They also tell him what he will miss if he doesn't buy.

Benefits of a product are often confused with *features*. The latter represents only the characteristics or specifications of a product, not the advantages it holds for buyers. When vinyl floors with permanent glossy surfaces were introduced, some bright marketing-minded person said the product had a No-wax surface, and thus the name told you the benefit. The fact that it had a permanent shine was attractive, but the *benefit,* the reason the product sold, was that it eliminated the work of regular waxing—it saved people time.

Benefits, not features, satisfy human needs and are related to motivators and emotions. Bare product specifications are dry and unconvincing; benefits are rich with personal satisfactions. Details of products should be delivered to readers in a way that will appeal to them as human beings. Benefits come in all varieties. A benefit might be the prestige the product gives the owner, or a specific amount of money that can be saved, or functional superiority over other brands.

For a simple example of the use of benefits, let's take a new bicycle and review some of its attributes:

Zoom XG-1000 Bicycle

Product Features	*Benefits*
Ergonomically designed, seat filled with gel material	Comfort. Lets you ride a long time without soreness.
Cantilever brakes.	Safety; brake design provides short stopping distance.
Folds in half.	Convenience for storage and travel.
Available colors include electric yellow and passion pink	Stylish; you're in fashion. (Social acceptance.)
27 gears for every terrain.	Ease of use, convenience; saves your energy so you can ride farther; possible safety benefits too.
Made in USA.	Built for quality and dependability in the United States.

You may be tempted, especially when writing about a commonly understood product such as a bicycle, to simply list features. You assume everyone knows the benefits. But even though the benefits seem obvious to you, explain them anyway. You can never err by describing your product or service in terms of benefits. Stating the benefit also makes the link from your product to basic human needs and wants. No one has a basic need for cantilever brakes, but everyone wants to be safe and secure.

Patriotism is another motivator used in advertising today. American-made products create local jobs and help the U.S. economy, thus more advertisers are emphasizing the home-grown nature of products. American-made products may have other benefits too, such as implied quality or availability of parts.

Even technical office products can (and should) be described with benefits. Here are some specifications for a facsimile machine:

Acme Facsimile Machine

Product Features	*Benefits*
10-page feeder.	Saves time, adds convenience. Operator doesn't have to wait while pages are transmitted.
Transmission delay sends documents at night unattended.	Saves money on long-distance charges, which are cheaper at night.
Activity journal.	Simplifies office record keeping, saves time for fax operator; avoids confusion and helps trace missing documents by automatically recording all incoming and outgoing transmissions.
One-button, memory operation.	Saves time and hassle for operator; transmits messages faster.

Each one of these features must be phrased in terms that show advantages for people. In your field or specialization there may be a place for listing specifications or other technical information. When you analyze the need to provide this data in an advertisement, however, you will probably find that the technical specifications or product attributes lead to satisfying a human need; therefore, you can also discuss specifications in terms of benefits.

Be careful to spell out the benefits in clear, direct language. Your technical language for a benefit may seem obvious to you, but still be a mystery to prospective buyers. You can't communicate benefits solely with jargon.

Here are a few examples of product benefits used in direct marketing.

DM advertising for *Communications Concepts,* a newsletter for people in the corporate communications business, lists ten benefits for customers, all linked to human needs. See if you can identify which motivator the writer is using in the following excerpts:

1. Improves your status as a communications expert in the eyes of management. You'll be more knowledgeable....
2. Improves your management skills ... often the hardest skills to master. They can open doors for you, help advance your career.
4. Saves your time. Quick-reading articles cut through an information flood to bring you only the best ideas and methods, without a lot of extra words....
7. Lets you in on hidden freebies and hard-to-find discounts.
9. Helps you build your personal VIP contacts file.[10]

A direct mail solicitation for membership in the Los Angeles County Museum of Art carries a variety of benefits, spelled out in direct language:

Let's take a closer look at the benefits you'll receive....

1. Private parties: The Board of Trustees invites you and your guest to an evening at the Museum we're planning *in your honor....*
2. Privileges: Your membership card will admit you and your guest to any exhibition in the museum—FREE....
3. Priorities: You'll receive advance ticket order forms and two free tickets to selected....

In direct mail to business people, AT&T sells the benefits of its cordless telephone by calling it a unique time-saver, something that lets you wander around the office and still use the phone. The copy says, "I'd like to introduce you to something that lets you be in two places at once.... It's the first and only cordless phone designed exclusively to be a business phone."[11]

If you're in a service business, you'll want to focus on benefits even more strongly, because without a tangible product, benefits are all you have to sell. Even though it's necessary to show that you have expertise and experience in your service field, you can do it in a way that emphasizes the benefits people will derive *from* your expertise. Here are some benefits to keep in mind when developing an advertising strategy for services:

Saving time: A business person or home owner doesn't have to perform a task herself; you do it for her.

Saving money: As an expert you can do it at a lower cost than your customer could do it for himself. With your experience you can find ways to save money the customer doesn't know about. Since you're a small business, with lower overhead, your service is more cost-effective than your larger competitors.

Enjoyment/pleasure: You'll do the job and your customer can avoid an unpleasant task.

Fear avoidance: When you provide your expert service it will protect your customer against breakdowns, delays, embarrassment, thefts, etc.

Knowledge, opportunities: Training, education and information services offer knowledge and a chance for personal advancement.

UNIQUE ADVANTAGES

Everyone would like to think his or her product or service is unique and different from the competition. If you have a distinct advantage over others, emphasize that in your advertising. Much conventional and direct response advertising focuses on product advantages. When the advantage arises from an exclusive aspect of a product, it's called a unique selling advantage or a *unique selling proposition* (USP).

One long-distance phone company tells you they're the only ones with the fiber optic network to make calls sound better. One airline says it has the best on-time record in the industry. One credit card is accepted at more places than any other. All of these are USPs and because they represent specific, unique benefits to consumers, advertising that uses them will have strong appeal.

Years ago, as a beginning copywriter, I learned how to identify and use unique selling propositions when I was writing ads for a company that made frozen onion rings. At the time, major food companies made onion rings out of chopped, processed onions. The small company I was writing for made onion rings the home-made way with actual sliced onions. Thus I came up with all sorts of advertising concepts that emphasized the USP, such as "The only onion rings made from onion rings," and "Are your onion rings made from onion rings?"

Notice that most USPs include the use of the word *only* or a superlative such as *biggest, fastest, most frequent.* If you can describe your product or service in those terms, chances are you have a USP you can use. It's not just large corporations that can preempt the market; you may have advantages your larger competitors don't have. For example, the *smallest* bank, consulting firm, or laboratory may have service advantages simply because they are smaller, more friendly, and more responsive.

Unique selling propositions will work equally well in mail order. Your distinctiveness may be in how your company works or in the uniqueness of your product. Many small mail-order firms get started by marketing one new, unique product, frequently one invented or developed by the company founder. It is the company's guiding unique advantage that brings it success.

Many USPs aren't discovered, they're synthesized by marketing executives. In other words, if a company doesn't have a dramatic advantage, marketers often invent them. One way they do it is simply to qualify their advertising statements. One airline may have the best on-time record *among the major air carriers* or the best record *to the Southwest*. One automobile may be advertised as the only sedan *made in America, selling for under $11,000* that has an air bag as standard equipment. These qualified USPs may be dubious distinctions, but with many similar products and services competing with each other today, advertisers are becoming more creative in trying to differentiate their offerings. This sameness of products, though, gives you an opportunity if you can discover or develop advantages that will benefit buyers.

Advertisers use other ways to develop unique advantages or give the impression of USPs. One way is through price: "The lowest priced home security you can buy," or "The only discount real estate broker in the three-county area." Also, you may no longer be unique, but you may have been the first, the pioneer in your field. Perhaps the strongest statements a small business can fashion are those that identify it as a specialty firm. Here's another way a limitation may be an advantage. If you're limited to one type of customer, if you sell a narrow product line, or if your business is limited by economic or geographic factors, identify yourself as a specialist. Examples are financial counselors who specialize in trusts, auto repair shops that fix only one or two types of cars, a training firm that offers only secretarial seminars, travel agents who book only cruises, catalogers who sell only pens, consultants who advise only on quality control techniques, and graphic designers who do only annual reports.

Unique selling propositions are strongest, and will show your superiority or advantages, if your USP does not need qualifying statements. Giant companies with multiple benefits and sizable resources can afford to grasp at weaker product statements occasionally. You should identify a solid USP before you base your advertising (and your financial success) on it. Don't stretch your credibility or advantage too far. If you're the only office supply store in East Winnebago that delivers, that's a good USP. But if you're the only office supply store in East Winnebago that features file folders in taupe and puce and delivers, then you'll have to look for another USP or just stick to benefits.

SUPPLYING THE PROOF

Is offering benefits and appealing to your potential customers' basic human needs all you need to do to close the sale? Sometimes, but not always. When you're asking for a direct response from prospects—especially when you're asking for an order—potential buyers want more. They want proof.

"Honesty works best, and when you learn to fake that you've got it made," said the late veteran copywriter Chris Stagg at a direct marketing conference years ago. He was being facetious, but being honest with yourself and your potential customers is the way to maintain credibility, particularly in a medium we've already said does not have the best reputation in the world. If one of your purposes in business is to provide quality and honest value to your customers, then that attitude will come through naturally in your direct response advertising. You won't have to fake it.

Having conducted direct marketing for nonprofit, member-owned credit unions for years, I have seen how organizations that advertise honest values and sincere service can prosper and grow tremendously. If you don't have to hedge your quality statements and if you back up your guarantees, it will make it all the easier to create effective direct response advertising. Remember, the most successful direct marketers are those who build a base of loyal customers and continue to sell to them month after month and year after year.

One way to deal with potential skepticism is to meet it head on. If your product or service sounds too good to be true, explain why you actually *can* provide the same service that your competitors do, but at a lower price. On one hand you want to build up a strong line of benefits to promote your product, but if your benefits appear too strong, your readers or prospects may become skeptical.

Does the warranty cover everything? Will they have the style I want in stock or will they try to move me up to a higher priced item? Do they have the expertise and experience necessary? These are some of the many questions that recipients of direct response advertising may ask. Anticipating questions is a good technique to help you write advertising that provides full details. In some cases, you may want to pose some obvious questions in your advertising, then provide the answer immediately.

Prices are often the focus point of skepticism. A low price is attractive, but if it's too low, buyers may wonder about your quality or honesty. One advertiser that always seems to provide logical reasons for low prices is Trader Joe's, a Pasadena, California specialty grocery chain. For instance, in its mail catalogs Trader Joe's frequently supports low-price offers by explaining special purchases from growers or packagers. Often the catalogs even list the number of cases the store buys. In one catalog, instead of just advertising a $3.45 regularly priced frozen dinner on sale for $2.19, the catalog carried a detailed explanation. The company that made the dinners packaged them for the professional diet food market, then withdrew from the business before selling out. The catalog copy said,

> They approached us with the offer to run fresh Healthy Choice dinners for us in the Professional Choice boxes and sell them to us at a substantial discount. We agreed, if we could be guaranteed that the dinners were identical, freshly run, first quality product. So now we have 80,000 cases. . . .

Good direct marketing tactics are usually based on common sense. If it sounds plausible, it's going to be more successful than outlandish, insupportable claims. Occasionally you may want to counter skepticism by telling the readers, not just what's in it for them, but what's in it for you. An ad agency I worked for created mail advertising for a company that leased out architectural antiques at what seemed to be surprisingly low prices. How could they do it? The copy explained that during the term of the lease the antiques would appreciate, and at the end of the lease the leasing company would still own them.

To back up your offers and promises you can choose from a variety of other techniques. Sometimes you need to use more than one:

Testimonials.   If you've ever looked at the back of a book jacket, read a flyer for a business training seminar, or seen ads for diet programs or health clubs, you know some of the uses of these third-party endorsements. Because the persons making recommendations or comments are customers, and not associated with the advertiser, their words seem to carry more strength. In many instances, if advertisers said the things satisfied customers say, the advertisers would not be believed. Testimonials are effective because they're a form of word-of-mouth advertising.

Endorsements can take many forms: the comments of homemakers who use your household services, or the words of company executives who endorse your mail-order computer accessories. The more original, spontaneous, and unsolicited a testimonial sounds, the greater its persuasive powers. Many products and services will benefit from testimonials. If they make sense for your industry, collect them. If you get thank-you letters, ask the writers to give you written permission to quote them in your advertising.

Thankful quotes from satisfied students seem to be the stock in trade of business seminar companies. They solicit comments on seminar critique forms and ask the participants to agree to let the company use the comments in ads. You can do the same thing by asking your customers for their written comments on your products or services.

If you use consumer endorsements, here are a few regulatory guidelines to keep in mind. Sect. 255.2 of the Federal Trade Commission's *Guides Concerning Use of Endorsements and Testimonials in Advertising* says that a consumer's endorsement generally means that the endorser's experience "is representative of what consumers generally achieve with the advertised product in actual, albeit variable, conditions of use." If you use a testimonial that is not necessarily representative of what most consumers will achieve with your product, or if you cannot clearly substantiate all claims made in endorsements, you should, according to the FTC guide, "conspicuously disclose what the generally expected performance would be in the depicted circumstances or clearly and conspicuously disclose the limited applicability of the endorser's experience to what consumers may generally expect to achieve."

Celebrity endorsements, of course, are also subject to government scrutiny. Although you see celebrities pitching everything from motor oil to facial cream, you should avoid the practice, not because it may create regulatory problems, which it might, but because it's not effective advertising.

Guarantees   Providing a warranty for your product is solid proof that (1) it will last, or, if it doesn't, that (2) you will replace it, repair it, or refund the customer's money. In mail order, guarantees with only a few qualifications have become the standard. Anything less than a full money-back guarantee will sound questionable. Here are typical guarantees from direct response magazine ads. The first, from an order form, is for a collector's model car, and the second is for flower bulbs.

> My satisfaction is guaranteed. If I am not satisfied with my replica, I may return it within 30 days of receipt for prompt replacement or refund, whichever I prefer.[12]

> If you are not satisfied with any product you buy from us, you may return it within 15 days with your shipping label for a full refund or replacement, whichever you prefer. Any plant not growing to your complete satisfaction will be replaced FREE! (3-year limit.)[13]

Legal considerations regarding warranties are discussed in Chapter 10.

Test results   Your product or service may be subject to government inspection or periodic testing; if so, use that in your advertising. If you have private test results that show your product's safety, superiority, or economy, use them. Testing by an outside authority carries more weight. The legal caution here is that you should have complete documented substantiation of your test claims *before* you advertise them. Don't write advertising based on reports and other documentation you know you could get, *if* you're questioned.

Client lists   Companies that sell to businesses often list the names of recognized clients. Client lists act as indirect endorsements.

Awards, professional designations   Any honors or awards your firm has won could be added to support your advertising material. The more well-known the awards and the more relevant they are to your particular product or service, the better. If you or any of your staff have earned licenses, certifications, or professional designations, that information also lends credence to your company's quality claims.

Associations   If you belong to a trade association, professional society, or even the Better Business Bureau, that indicates a commitment to your industry or profession. Some direct marketers identify themselves as members of the Direct Marketing Association, the national trade group. The DMA provides educational, legislative, and other services to members and publishes ethical standards for the industry. See Appendix B for information.

Regulation   Until the collapse of many savings and loan associations, simply saying that you were regulated by an agency of the federal government was an indication of safety in the financial industry. In other industries, regulation by a government agency can still add to your credentials.

POSTSCRIPTS....

How to Determine Best Motivators

To select the most effective motivational factors, consider *who* you're appealing to. Study your customer profile or the selects on the list you're renting. Yuppies, minority group members, senior citizens, business owners, salesmen, and renters will respond differently to different advertising appeals. Be sure to match your motivators to your audience. If you're mailing to lists of significantly different types of people, try either writing different versions of your material or sticking with more universal appeals.

FTC and Advertising Credit Terms

If you advertise credit or credit terms or terms of certain leases you must comply with the Federal Truth In Lending Act (Regulation Z). The law is administered by a variety of agencies for different industries, but most small businesses fall under the enforcement power of the Federal Trade Commission.

Under Regulation Z, if you advertise the amount of monthly payments, interest rates, or other "trigger" terms, you must comply with disclosure sections of the law which require you to provide an annual percentage rate (APR) and other information. Using general terms such as "budget payments" or "financing available" is not sufficient to require disclosures. If you plan to offer and advertise credit terms, obtain a copy of the FTC's booklet on how to comply with the law. See Appendix B.

Is It Credit?

Some mail-order sellers offer monthly payments for merchandise, but still are not considered credit grantors if the lump sum cash price and the extended payment price are the same. This is one way of giving customers a payment option without having to comply with Truth In Lending disclosures.

If you are going to offer credit and charge interest, however, and you have not done so before, you should know there are other federal regulatory requirements which await you, such as the Equal Credit Opportunity Act, Regulation B. Consulting, or perhaps hiring, an experienced credit manager with extensive regulatory knowledge may be advisable. You may also need to obtain advice from an attorney who specializes in advertising credit.

Negative Advertising

It's one thing to hit skepticism head on in a portion of an ad or mail package and quite another to base a campaign around a negative perception. In a backwards attempt to improve its image, an insurance company ran an ad featuring a large photo of a man's upper arm. On the underside of his forearm was a tattoo with a lightening bolt crossed with a dagger. In the center of the tattoo were the words, "Born to Raise Rates." The accompanying copy pointed out that some health insurers were raising rates but that the advertiser was "trying to get a grip" on controlling costs. The ad then asked you to write or call for a booklet on cost controls.

The ad focused so much on the negative impact, however, that "Born to Raise Rates" is all that stuck in the mind after reading the ad. With the limited budget of a small business, you don't want to take the risk that your company's image will be negative.

Challenge or Dare?

Sometimes a slight change in wording can make substantial differences in your results. Direct mail from small businesses sometimes uses the phrase "we dare you" as an attempt to inject fear. Daring someone to try your service is an indirect slam at your quality. Daring someone to not try your service is phony fear. A real-life explanation of what customers might expect if they *don't* use your product will be more effective. If what you really want to do is challenge your readers to test your products, do that. Then offer some incentive or reward exclusively for customers who try your service for the first time.

You Have to Ask

Ask for testimonials and referrals. Many small business people live off referrals. Savvy sales people ask for referrals regularly. Experienced direct marketers do it too, with forms in direct mail packages and inserts in fulfillment packages. Sometimes direct marketers even provide bonuses for customers who provide the names of potential customers. Some, such as Books on Tape, Inc., provide bonuses to customers *after* a referral customer has placed his first order.

When making an offer to encourage existing customers to provide referrals, be sure your terms explaining that the bonus is contingent on a referral sale are conspicuous and clear to the customers. Further, a referral bonus may be considered a free offer and thus it is covered by the FTC's "free" rules. See Chapter 10 and Appendix B.

8 CREATE YOUR HEADLINE AND START WRITING

Personal, Friendly, Yet Specific

When you get the mail at home, where do you open it? If you're like many people, you probably open it while standing in the kitchen. When you're *writing* consumer direct mail, imagine your prospects standing in their kitchens with your mailer in their hands. What are they going to do with it? How much time do you have to capture their interest before they toss your carefully written message in the trash?

Keeping a vision of a bored, uninterested reader in your mind when you compose your advertising is a good way to make you get to the point quickly and focus on benefits for the reader. When someone looks at your direct response message, they're looking for what's in it for them: What are the advantages? Why should I read further? Isn't that what goes through your mind too as you read direct response mail? You want to know why someone is writing; what's the offer?

STARTING THE CREATIVE PROCESS

Rather than starting out to write an ad or direct mail package from beginning to end, it's a good idea to write down or outline several important elements that will go into your copywriting strategy. Start with your readers. Whether you're writing an ad or direct mail, write down the characteristics of the most favorable prospects who will read your message. How old are they? Where do they live? What do they do for a living and how much do they earn? Depending on your product, you may want to include other demographic or psychographic information you know about your prospects. For example, if you're selling camping gear, presumably you should be writing to people who like the outdoors.

Focusing on the Buyer

Aim your thinking not at everyone on your target list, not at everyone who buys the publication in which your ad will appear, but only at your prime prospects. Unless you're selling a consumable that everyone uses, not every person on your list will be ready to buy no matter how attractive your offer. Therefore, by focusing on those people who are either about ready to buy, or at least likely candidates, you'll be writing directly to the people who are the most interested in and open to what you have to say.

In print advertising, the temptation is to make the ad as appealing as possible to a wide audience. When you do that, however, you often neglect the benefits or advantages that will appeal to your prime potential buyers. For example, say you have a small ranch resort that offers mainly strenuous outdoor activities. In your ad you could appeal to your primary customers by showing someone working up a sweat along with a headline that promises exercise. But if you worry that not enough people will read your ad, you might be tempted to write an attention-getting headline about a "romantic vacation" and couple it with a picture of someone relaxing with a drink. This might boost readership of the ad. Average vacationers might start reading, but ultimately they will not buy. Unfortunately the strategy intended to broaden the appeal will also lose the attention of many prime prospects who *want* exercise on vacation. By trying to sell the whole world, you dilute the appeal for your prime prospects.

Aiming directly at your prime prospects also makes it easier to write an ad or mailer. Rather than trying to dream up reasons and benefits for all, level your sights on those people you know are potential customers. For example, when I write direct mail packages for auto loans, I don't write to sell everyone. I know that no matter how attractive loans are, someone who doesn't need a new car will not borrow the money. Therefore, I aim at those people who are thinking about buying a car. I try to imagine their motivations. I remind them that they've probably been looking at the new models as they drive down the freeway. I ask them if they're wondering how difficult or expensive it will be to get a loan for a new car. The people who will get a car loan *somewhere* soon are the ones I want to reach.

Although this strategy may not sound universal, because people often try to sell everyone, it's difficult to find exceptions. Even retailers seeking traffic, or catalogers selling impulse items, are going to find some potential customers more susceptible to their persuasions than others. The closer you can focus your writing on probable, not just possible buyers, the stronger your persuasive prose will be. The better your list selection, of course, the higher the percentage of prime buyers you'll be writing to. The ideal list would be made up of nothing but these prime buyers.

Some professional copywriters go a step further than just writing down the characteristics of their prospects. They find a picture of them. One writer I know skims through magazines until he finds a picture of people who look like his ideal prospects. He puts the photo next to his word processor to give him a visual reminder of just *who* he's writing to.

After visualizing your prime prospects, write down your offer. Refer to the examples in Chapter 2 to help you identify *all* parts of your offer.

The next step is to write up a list of benefits and unique advantages. Start with a list of product or service features and draw one or more benefits from each. Write down as many benefits as you can think of, even ones that seem remote or far-fetched. You may not use them all in your direct response message, but you don't want to limit your thinking at this stage. Try to get as many ideas as you can.

When you jot down the benefits, write them as if you were writing a letter to explain them to a friend. Use personal language to show exactly how the reader will benefit. To determine your unique advantages, see if you can use the word "only" in a benefit statement.

Here's what you should have on paper so far:

1. Description of prime buyers
2. Outline of the offer, including pricing and ordering information
3. Long list of benefits
4. Any unique advantages
5. What you want the reader to do

Number 5 may seem obvious to you and it may already be included in your offer. I've listed it as a separate item so that you will not forget why you're writing the ad or mailer in the first place. What you want the reader to do should be crystal clear, not just to you, but to your prospects.

Brainstorming

After completing the five steps above, you may be ready to write your advertising. In fact, the process of putting all this information down on paper should have prompted you to start thinking of ways you can describe and expand on your product's benefits. If you still need a few good ideas to get started, do what professional copywriters do: Brainstorm.

The technique of brainstorming goes back decades and is simply a term to describe random association of facts and thoughts, much like word association games. The purpose of brainstorming is to dislodge the many good ideas you have stuck in in your head and slap them down on paper. Brainstorming rules are simple: There are no rules. Without rules, you're free to write down anything that comes into you head about your product or service—or anything else! Try not to be too conventional and don't try to think about a particular advertising format. The purpose is to create as many possibilities as you can.

To get started, take a few deep breaths and relax. Let your mind wander. Be as detached as you can from the normal ways you think about your business. Look at your products from a different perspective.

Don't judge any idea you come up with. Just note it and see what that idea leads you to. If you need a starting point, use one of your product benefits. Let's say your product is an inexpensive upper-arm exercise device that you're selling via mail order. One of the product benefits you wrote down is portability. Here's an example of some material that brainstorming might yield:

Maxi-Bod Exerciser: Portable

Fits in a suitcase . . . you can use it in the car (not while driving!), on trains, planes . . . would it be detected on X-rays at airport security? . . . Should/Do law enforcement people use it? Crooks? It would work in prison . . . in hotel rooms when salesmen are on the road...even in meeting rooms?!), Arnold Schwarzenegger exercising at a business meeting in a conference room...build your muscles on the road, take it from room to room at home, exercise while watching (diet programs on) TV....Where else can it go? Church?...beach...neighbor's barbecue...mini-suitcase—product package could be a mini-suitcase to show the go-anywhere advantages. ...The "Go Anywhere Exerciser"...More benefits: light, uncomplicated, folds in half to take up even less space....Would it fit in a purse, a big purse, briefcase, glove compartment, lunch box, Haystack Calhoun's lunch box...would wrestlers use it?...

Some of this is nonsense, but sprinkled here and there are ideas that might be developed into ways of showcasing the portability of the product. Keep in mind that at the brainstorming stage you don't evaluate any idea, just write it down. When you've got a list of ideas under one benefit heading, move on to another and see what that makes you think of.

Imagine all your product benefits as being important to the sale, even those far-fetched benefits that seemed impractical. When you have an extensive list, then you can start editing and deciding what will make good advertising copy and what will not. You don't make any of those judgments during brainstorming because that would inhibit the flow of ideas in your mind. You can become analytical again only when you're focusing on getting all the necessary information in your ad or mailer.

Usually brainstorming is best with two people, provided they both agree to leave inhibitions behind and simply recite anything that comes into their minds as they exchange product and advertising ideas. One unrelated, abstract comment one person makes may be just the spark you need to jot down an idea that may make an perfect headline. I've sometimes brainstormed for hours with graphic designers or other writers as we tried to come up with raw material or even to polish an ad that just needed a few more words. You can use brainstorming as an early step to prime your creative pump, or at any time while you're writing to find the exact words you need.

Words or Pictures

By this stage in the writing, you may have started to wonder about the design and layout of your ad or mailing package. How much space do you have for the copy? Welcome to one of the most common dilemmas in advertising. Which comes first, the copy or the design? The words or the pictures? In direct marketing the words usually come first. You may be able to *show* some of your product benefits, and thus some pictures, charts, graphs, or illustrations may occur to you when you're listing benefits or brainstorming. That's good. Keep track of all your visual ideas along with the ideas for copy.

There are many ways to bring the words and pictures together for direct response advertising. I suggest you concentrate on the words first and turn to visual ideas after you have a rough draft of your copy. Obviously, before you start writing you'll have to have an idea of the approximate size of your ad or the type of inserts you'll use in your mailing, but an approximation is close enough for now. Your goals are to (1) write a rough draft, (2) consider the artwork and layout, and (3) edit your copy carefully. Most copywriters think of ways to use visual elements as they're writing. They usually note them in a margin and later sketch out a rough idea of what their ad might look like.

Words, rather than photos and illustrations, have long been the prime ingredient of direct response advertising. DM letters and direct response print ads are often 85 to 100 percent copy. Thus words and the ideas they convey have been expected to do most of the selling. They still are in many cases, and it is a direct mail dictum that you should use artwork only in spaces left over after the copy is approved. Today, however, you should also consider your audience and not automatically discount the value of the artwork.

Until relatively recently, people grew up getting the majority of their news and information through the printed word. All people born after 1960, however, have lived their entire lives in a society dominated by television, and they tend to be more visually oriented. That doesn't mean they don't read. What it means is that you need to keep in mind that members of younger target markets are used to getting their information visually. There are other factors, such as education and economic level, which also indicate how likely your target market will be to respond to a written message with few visual highlights. This, of course, brings us back to the importance of considering your list or target audience as you create your advertising message.

With some experience you will be able to decide how large a role visuals should play in your advertising. Sometimes you will want to draw a rough layout of your materials as you're writing. Depending on how visually oriented *you* are, an idea of what your ad will look like may help you write the words.

HEADLINES

The headline is the most important part of your advertising and deserves careful attention. Professional copywriters probably use brainstorming more for headlines than for anything else. When I'm writing a direct response ad, I may spend nearly as much time on the headline as I do on the rest of the ad. If a headline doesn't succeed in getting the reader's interest, the rest of the ad is worthless. The headline is the one part of an ad that most people read. When you're reading through a magazine, you probably glance at most of the ad headlines, at least on the larger ads. Few, if any of the headlines, however, contain something to make you read further.

When you think of headlines (heads or headings) you may think primarily of print ads, although heads are just as important for letters, brochures, envelopes, and other formats. The purpose of a head, in any format, is to attract the reader's attention *and* lead him into the body copy, usually with an idea of what the product or service promises to do. What's the best way to do that? Looking at much of the advertising today, you might get the idea that using clever plays on words, slogans, or rhymes is the best way to write headlines.

Wrong.

Headlines should include the primary direct response persuaders: benefits, motivators, and unique selling propositions. You want to attract the reader's attention, but you need to do it in a way that is linked to your product or service. There are plenty of ways to attract attention, as you can see by looking through any magazine, but when the attention-getter in the head doesn't explain a benefit, the reader has little reason to read on—or buy the product.

Unfortunately, even people in the direct response business, who should know that benefits are the driving force, sometimes think that a clever ad is better than one that tells the reader why he or she should buy the product. For example, a direct mail list company ran a series of ads in a DM trade journal using just the names of famous composers for the main headlines. After the main heads were subheadings:

LISZT Marketing.
Passionate. Harmonious. Bravissimo!

HANDEL
your package inserts with a virtuoso cast. Hallelujah!

These ads featured a music staff across the bottom and the copy carried out the musical theme. The notion of Liszt marketing may have seemed hilarious to someone, but I doubt if the ads struck a responsive chord with many readers, because this allegedly clever approach has nothing to do with the service being offered. Slogans, catchy sayings, and jingles are a product of conventional advertising, which colors many persons' thinking when they create their own ads. Even though you see this technique over and over, avoid cleverness for the sake of cleverness. It will waste your advertising money. Rhymes, jokes, and cartoon banter have no place in direct response advertising, *unless* they're directly related to benefits or the offer.

To write effective headlines, concentrate on benefits and your advantages. Here are five techniques for writing profitable headlines. Each is fundamental, yet has room for creativity:

1. State your strongest benefit.

2. Make a promise that will benefit your reader.

3. Dramatically highlight a big advantage or USP.

4. Make an appeal to the emotions that leads directly to a benefit.

5. State your offer.

Using these techniques, it shouldn't be difficult to come up with effective direct response headlines. Perhaps the most effective (and uncomplicated) headline is one that communicates the biggest benefit, or the offer, in clear language. The headline for Soundview Executive Book Summaries (Fig. 8.1) clearly states the main benefit of the product, yet it doesn't tell the complete story. It makes you want to read the ad to find out how you *could* read a book in 15 minutes.

Now You Can Read the Best Business Books of 1990—in Just 15 Minutes Each

Too much to read! It's impossible to find time to read today's top business books—and thousands are published each year.

Yet not keeping up with those books could be a serious, and expensive mistake. Often the ideas and insights they contain are available nowhere else.

But how can you even know which titles are worthwhile—let alone find time to read them?

Fortunately, there's a solution . . . *Soundview Executive Book Summaries*. It really works. In fact, it's guaranteed to work.

Ingenious. Essential. Every month, you receive two or three quick-reading, time-saving summaries of the best new business books.

Each *Executive Book Summary* contains all the key points in the original book. The big difference: instead of 200 to 500 pages, the summary is only 8 pages. Instead of taking five, ten or more hours to read, it takes just 15 minutes!

Which Business Books Should You Read?

Of the thousands of business books published annually, only a handful are really worth reading.

To save your time, our Editorial Board plows through them all, eliminating 99%. Our standards are high, the criteria rigorous.

When a book meets all our tests, we prepare a *Summary*. Not a review (somebody's opinion). Not a digest (book excerpts strung together). You get a skillful distillation that preserves the content and spirit of the entire book.

How Many of These Outstanding Business Books Have You Read?

The titles you'll find summarized cover every subject of concern to business people today. Management techniques, advertising and marketing, productivity, leadership and motivation, career advice, effective communication, hiring and firing, tax reduction, health and fitness,

negotiation, time management, small business tactics, computers, strategic planning, personal finance, and much more.

Some of the many superb business titles summarized for subscribers include:

**In Search of Excellence
At America's Service
Cracking the Global Market
Thriving on Chaos
Downsizing
Work Smart Not Hard
When Giants Learn To Dance
The Energetic Manager
How to Win Customers and
Keep Them for Life
The Service Edge**
and many more!

With *Executive Book Summaries*, you will:

1. Get ideas you can use immediately. Not buried in a pile of reading you'll never get to.

2. Bolster your business confidence. A "talking knowledge" of the latest books lets you respond intelligently.

3. Learn more, remember more. (According to a scientific study, the ideas in a summary are more easily remembered than the same ideas in a book.)

4. Slash hundreds of hours off your reading time. Get the "meat" of a book in minutes instead of hours!

5. Save money. To buy the 30 books that will be summarized next year, it would cost you about $742. And would you have time to read half of them?

There's nothing else like *Soundview's Executive Book Summaries*. The *Wall Street Journal* hails it as

"An inventive answer to what is becoming an increasingly irksome management problem: too much to read."

Special Introductory Offer 2 MONTHS FREE

Executives coast to coast, in every field, are discovering this unique time and money saving solution.

Try it now, risk free, before you decide. With this offer you get 2 months free (5 summaries) to evaluate for yourself, along with a one-year subscription at 28% savings. That's 35 summaries for a fraction of the cost of the original titles. You risk nothing. If you're not fully satisfied, you may cancel in your 2 month trial period and receive a full refund.

FREE Bonus

If you act now, you'll also receive a FREE bonus copy of *Skills for Success: The Experts Show The Way*— the book with hundreds of terrific ideas from past summaries. This handy reference tool is yours to keep even if you cancel.

So order now.

Call Toll Free 1-800-521-1227.
Outside U.S. Call 1-802-453-4062
Or complete coupon and mail today.

□ **YES,** send me **Executive Book Summaries** for 2 months plus one year (35 summaries) at only $69.50 (28% off the regular rate of $96). Also send my free copy of *Skills For Success: The Experts Show The Way* as a bonus for prompt response. I may cancel during the first two months and receive a full refund. Everything I have received is mine to keep regardless. [U.S. funds only.] [Outside U.S. & Canada $139]

Name _____

Company _____

Address _____

City/State/Zip _____

□ Check enclosed. Charge my:
  □ VISA   □ MasterCard   □ AMEX

Credit Card No. _____ Exp. Date ____

Signature _____

Mail to: Executive Book Summaries
5 Main Street, Dept. SVV060
Bristol, Vermont 05443

Or, call Toll Free **1-800-521-1227.**

©Copyright Executive Book Summaries, 1990.

FIGURE 8.1 *(Used with permission from Soundview Executive Book Summaries.)*

Here are some effective headlines that spell out benefits:

Speak a Foreign Language in
30 Days or Your Money Back.

This head for Berlitz Publications, Inc. makes a direct promise *and* supplies the guarantee.

"Quicken slashed my tax preparation
time and cost by 70%..."

The product is "Quicken," a financial software program, from a company called Intuit. The quote is from a business executive talking about how she has used the product. The implied benefit is that you too will save time and money.

For just $99, Hertz and the
American Express Card will
make the Car of the Year
yours for the weekend.

The Hertz ad talks about a luxury car as *Motor Trend*'s Car of the Year. The headline contains an almost complete offer.

How to Choose a Tax-Free Portfolio

This head for a mutual fund group uses two of the most effective headline words: *How to*. A how-to headline makes a promise. It says the ad (or the offer) will show you a way to do something, often for yourself. Another reason these words attract readers is that they're a favorite of editors who write headlines for articles. The reason many of us pick up magazines is to find out "how to" do something. If you're ever at a loss for a headline, try a how-to head, then give your first couple of paragraphs an instructional flavor. *How-to* has an almost magical attraction.

How to protect your computer and make it last longer

How to increase your purchasing power (credit card offer)

How to put your finish first (car care tips)

How to refund airlines' non-refundable ticket (Boardroom Books' *Book of Secrets*)

Don't forget motivators when you're looking for headline material. Fear is used frequently:

If this is your idea of
current financial news,
you're history.

In this ad for Dialog Information Services Inc., the headline is printed over a picture of a page of stock market quotations as they appear in a newspaper. The product is on-line computer stock information, which is more up-to-date than quotations in newspapers.

Some experts advise getting your product or company name in the headline because it fortifies your identity. For direct response, I favor focusing on your reader's concerns first and your product second. *How to Avoid a Woman's Worst Fear* is better than, *New Glopo Works Better than Any Other Ointment.* Phrase your headline in terms of what your product or service can do for readers. Tell your potential customers they can save money, improve their lives, save time, get recognition, or obtain some other benefit.

An effective headline is so important to your success that you need to remind yourself to stick with motivators or benefits and not catchy phrases or homemade slogans, no matter how much you may like them. I can preach this advice because I was reminded of the value of benefit headlines the hard way.

Several years ago I advertised business writing seminars that I conducted for companies and financial institutions. In one direct response ad I wrote for the seminars, I forgot about using benefits and making offers in the head. Instead, I stole the headline from a magazine article I wrote. The article was on business writing and the editor of the magazine had given it the heading "Great American Business Letters." I liked that headline so much that I used it on the ad.

It wasn't until later, when I hadn't received any responses, that I realized the headline was not advertising. I had been so enamored with the sound of the headline, I didn't look at it critically, with a proper dollars-and-cents, direct response, let's-get-results attitude. Later I substituted benefit-oriented headlines such as: How to get words on paper in half the time.

Headings on letters and brochures differ slightly from print ad heads in both layout and content. Some headings on letters are simply a list of benefits. The letter in Fig. 8.2 is in the form of a business memo titled *Service Authorization.* The benefits are numbered from 1 to 3 across the top of the page. Other letters have headlines that lead directly into the body, just as the Executive Book Summaries head leads you into the ad. Brochures, depending on their size and number of folds, have several headings. Sometimes one heading leads you to the next, other times each head is self-standing and related to the adjacent body copy. If a product has several different uses, for example, separate heads on different panels of a brochure might highlight different benefits related to the different uses. Chapter 9 has examples.

Here are two headlines from letters. They're not flashy or funny, but they promise solid benefits. A mailer for a secretaries' newsletter uses motivators from several levels of Maslow's hierarchy:

Money. Respect. Satisfaction.
If you're looking for more of the above
The Office Professional can help!

The *Financial Freedom Report* makes a promise in a headline then follows through in the balance of the letter:

FIVE *PROOFS* THAT
The Chicago Convention
WILL MAKE YOU MONEY
May 2–5—Schaumburg Marriott

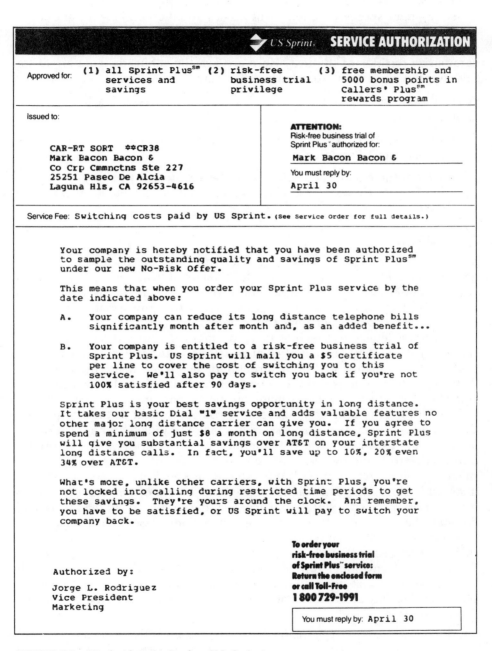

FIGURE 8.2 *(Used with permission from U.S. Sprint.)*

Subheadings—smaller headlines sprinkled throughout an ad, brochure, or letter—have special functions. They focus attention on benefits and other important points, and they work like subheadings in magazine articles to provide a break in long blocks of body type. In addition, they can be used to summarize sections of the text. Here are just the subheads from an ad for an educational product from Early Advantage.

A Head Start in Science for   Turn Your TV into a Teacher
Children Ages 7-12

Give Your Children What   Satisfaction Guaranteed
the Schools Aren't Providing

Just from these subheads, you should be able to tell what the product is (a Video Science Course for Children) and some of its benefits, including a guarantee.

LANGUAGE

Your headline usually sets the tone and leads into the body copy of your ad or mailer. The language you use depends on your audience, but in most cases it should be relaxed, simple, and direct. If you regularly write letters to friends or relatives, you have a good idea of the appropriate style. Good direct response copy is personal and friendly.

If business letters and memos make up most of your writing experience, try to forget about 50 percent of what you think "businesslike" writing should sound like. No matter who your target audience is, it's made up of people. And to sell to people you need to be friendly, relaxed, and convincing, not stuffy and official-sounding, as many business communications are.

The customarily inflated language of business can get in the way of your direct response message. Business clichés take the punch and appeal out of advertising: "Please be advised of the fact that we're undertaking to offer a new service to home owners relative to the subject of upkeep and potential monetary reductions in taxes." What does that say? Who knows, but doesn't it sound businesslike? This slightly exaggerated form of puffy business writing is precisely the style you should avoid in advertising. Avoid the formal and embrace the informal. Talk to your prospects as friends. Sound conversational.

If effective direct marketing is similar to an in-person sales presentation, then your language should be similar to spoken language. To capture the informal yet informational approach of a sales talk, and to help get the words flowing when you sit down to write, try writing the way you talk. Conversational writing has three advantages and one disadvantage. First the advantages and uses:

1. *It helps you find the right words when you're stumped.* The next time you can't find the right words—when you *know* what you're trying to say, but can't write it—say it. Say it aloud to someone. Chances are that 95 percent of the time the words you're looking for will come right out of your mouth. Then all you have to do is write them down quickly and continue your work.

While some people may think that *writer's block* can stall their writing, certainly *talker's block* does not exist. When you talk, you usually find the words you need. The reason is that you are far less inhibited when you speak than when you are trying to write something important. You may not phrase your idea perfectly the first time when you speak, but you usually get feedback from your listener that tells you whether you communicated or not. If you did not, you rephrase, explain, or expand until you see the light of recognition in your listener's eyes.

2. *Write your entire mailer by speaking it.* To give your writing that spoken quality, you can speak it. Use a tape recorder to write your whole message. You must first outline the advertising as noted above to give you prompts for your speaking, but the majority of the copy can be spoken, then simply transcribed to create the rough draft.

3. *Use the "spoken English" test.* If you ever wonder whether any of your direct response copy will be effective, or whether it sounds genuine, read it aloud. If it sounds like something you might say, then you've got a conversational ad.

Here's the Disadvantage. If everything you write is printed in the English you use when you speak, your advertising will be redundant, choppy, and too colloquial. Nearly everyone's spoken language is *too* casual for written communication. Therefore, in order to preserve the value of the three bits of good advice above, you must carefully edit your "spoken" advertising. Editing is your quality control, your chance to revise your initial ideas into a tight, persuasive package. Chapter 11 has an editing checklist to guide you.

Relaxed Writing

Just how casual should your language be? Are you worried that friendly language doesn't sound businesslike? Let's look at a couple of diverse examples to see what language is appropriate. You might think that a mailing from Chase Manhattan Bank aimed at an upscale audience and one from a catalog company selling novelty items would demonstrate completely different writing styles. You may find, however, as you study direct mail, that mailings often have more language similarities than differences. The following two samples share two important direct mail stylistic techniques: contractions (*aren't, you're, it's, you'll*) and personal pronouns.

A Lighter Side Company gift catalog explanation of a golf shirt embroidered with "I keep the score" says, "For duffers out there who aren't above kicking the ball or taking 3' gimmies. You know—the ones who keep their own score and always win, even when you're sure they took more swings..."

And a sample from a Chase Manhattan Bank DM letter says, "Even if you have a VISA or other card, it's time to move up to gold...you'll have a host of premium benefits at no extra cost."

In business writing, contractions and liberal use of personal pronouns are frequently frowned upon. In direct marketing they're required. If New York bankers use contractions and pronouns in their direct mail, you should be comfortable using these style relaxers for your small business too, without worrying about being too informal.

Pronouns help personalize and humanize your message and the pronouns *you* and *your* tell your reader who you're talking about. *You* is so important that it appears many times in the average direct mail letter. In one four-page direct mail letter I wrote recently, I used the words *you* and *your* more than 60 times. That sounds like overkill but it's not. Go back and read the first three paragraphs of Chapter 1. You'll find 19 *yous* and *yours*.

Short and Simple

Another way to make your language friendly and easy to read is to keep your sentences short and use simple, everyday words. Studies show that as the average number of words per sentence increases, reading comprehension decreases. You want your sentences relatively short, because they'll be inviting and because the reader will better understand and remember what you have to say.

Business practices, college composition classes, and other influences make some people think longer sentences sound more executive, more astute. In direct response advertising your purpose is to impress people not with your ability to write, but with the attributes of your product or service. The best writing style is unobtrusive; it shows no obvious effort. It is simply easy to read and understand.

Find out if your sentences are too long by simply averaging the word count. Pick a letter or something lengthy you've written and count the number of words. Then divide by the number of sentences to find your average. If you're in the 13- to 18-word range, your writing should be easy to read. If your average is below 12, then your sentences may be *too* simple and you may need some writing help. If your average is well beyond 20 words per sentence, keep that in mind and look for long sentences you can cut in two every time you edit your advertising.

Certainly sentence length is only one of many measures of readability, and an arbitrary one at that. I've read sentences of 200 words which were easy to follow, and I've been confused by 15-word sentences. Asking others to review your copy is another way of finding out whether your words are easy to grasp.

Jargon

Jargon may also work to restrict readability. People tend to use jargon without knowing it, because specialized language is just the way they talk or write. In advertising, it can be a plus or a minus.

Advantage   When you advertise in a trade or special interest publication or to a list of people who share some unique background, using technical language shows that you know what you're talking about. Techies in any field identify with jargon. It gives them a comfort level with the advertiser. Someone selling model trains to a list of enthusiasts could describe a locomotive as a 4–8–0 and the readers would know exactly what she was talking about.

Disadvantage Jargon becomes a detriment when it's used unintentionally with people who don't speak the specialized lingo. In that case it can not only confuse, it can also alienate. Think about the times a doctor, auto mechanic, or government employee used technical language you didn't understand. Did you think the jargon was used on purpose as a smoke screen? Usually use of confusing jargon is unintentional. We sometimes forget that not everyone knows that a 4–8–0 engine has four wheels up front, eight drive wheels, and no wheels under the cab. Whether the confusion is on purpose or unintentional, however, it's still confusion.

As with sentence length, correct use of jargon is something that is best monitored in the editing stage. Keep an eye out for terms and abbreviations your readers may not understand.

Modifiers

One stylistic element that should be used with caution is the adjective. You might expect advertising, especially direct mail, to use quantities of adjectives to hype products. To persuade people to act on your requests, however, you need more than just a string of *greats, fantastics,* and *spectaculars.* Far stronger than nonspecific adjectives are facts and specific details. Rather than saying your service is reliable, tell your readers how many years you've been in business, how many customers you've served, and how strong your guarantee is. Concrete information is stronger than generalities. Instead of saying you have a "large variety of styles and options" to choose from, say you have "23 different models and 7 different options, giving you 161 choices."

To get someone to respond immediately, you have to give him or her enough information to make a decision. The more particulars you can provide, the stronger your persuasion. Rather than say they make high-quality rugby shirts, Lands' End offers plenty of details:

> The fabric is a hefty 10.5 oz. 100% cotton jersey. Stands up to all kinds of grabbing, tugging, stretching. Prewashed too, so it never shrinks out of fit.
>
> The collar is strongly taped. The placket is made in one piece, so it has no weak point to tear. Special seams "give" instead of ripping out. Underarms are gusseted for easy moving comfort. Rubber buttons protect against contact bruises.
>
> Even the stitching in our shirts is "tough as the game." We use a special nylon/polyester thread that's five times stronger than cotton....

The word *quality* should be used sparingly. Rather than say you have a quality product, it's more convincing if you provide specific examples so the reader draws that conclusion himself.

Occasionally the details you need to include are not direct benefits, but specifics which show the extent, the depth, or a sample of what is offered for sale. In a Nightingale-Conant Corp. mailing selling a cassette series on business negotiation, the DM letter gave a taste of the program content by listing some intriguing myths and facts:

> Myth: Negotiation involves confrontation. In
> negotiations, somebody wins and somebody loses.
>
> Fact: A good negotiator will make sure the other
> guy feels *he* got a good deal. The good
> negotiator wants *both* sides to win.

Again, the details were communicated in simple, direct language.

The emphasis on specific details doesn't mean that direct mail *always* tells the complete story. Lead generation programs, also called two-step direct mail, usually provide readers with just enough information to make them want more. Another example of direct mail that does not tell the full story is advertising for business seminars. The brochures tell you just enough of the topics to interest you, but not enough to be useful. Typical seminar brochure copy says, "Learn the ten biggest mistakes most salesmen make and how you can avoid them," or "Find out how to use a simple idea that can double your productivity."

How Long?

Finally, at some point in the creative process, you start to worry about length. Is it too long? While your writing should be direct and free of unnecessary words, it does not necessarily have to be short. Since you want to do more than just make an impression on your reader, you've got to supply the facts, endorsements, benefits, and complete details that a person needs to make a decision. Direct response copy tends to be longer than other advertising. Take the Executive Book Summaries example in Fig. 8.1. About 85 percent of the ad is taken up with headlines and body copy, yet it is not too long. The ad skillfully blends many of the creative techniques mentioned so far.

The ad begins with a benefit headline and leads into a fear-oriented motivator. It provides concrete details along the way and speaks to the reader with the word *you*. The second column contains a list of five solid benefits *and* a testimonial. Subheads keep the type from looking too dull while they summarize the text and highlight benefits. In the third column is the complete offer, a call to action, an 800 number, and a coupon. The ad makes the complete sale.

Even if the ad were not as skillfully written, the length itself would not be a detriment, because the ad is selling a product to be *read*. Here again the advertising is aimed at prime prospects. People who are likely to read a long ad about books are precisely the people who are likely to be interested in the product.

One of the ways to decide on your length, for a direct mail package for example, is to select a standard format, as discussed in Chapter 9. Determine about how many manuscript pages it will take to fill the format, assuming a reasonable percentage of space for artwork.

Picking a format and length too early, however, can limit your creativity and perhaps reduce your persuasive punch. Suppose you're writing direct mail for your company's new product. You decide on an 8½″ × 14″ brochure, and after you've written just enough copy to fill it you get a great idea: Including a reproduction of your 15-point production control checklist would be a better way to demonstrate your high quality than just saying "high quality." Now what? Do you cut the brochure copy in half, eliminating some benefits to squeeze in the checklist?

Actually you have other, better options. You could print the checklist on another piece of paper and keep the brochure as you originally envisioned it. You could also enlarge the brochure to include the checklist. One of the flexibilities of direct mail is that you're not restricted to a specific size and number of inserts.

Other factors that affect the length of your copy are the complexity of your product or service and the action you want the reader to take. Notice how many things hinge on the requested action? If you're selling a well-known publication to a former subscriber, you don't need a long list of benefits. If you're trying to get someone just to send in a coupon for more information, you don't need page after page of advantages. On the other hand, if you want someone to write you out a check for a product he or she has never heard of, then you'd better take all the space you need to *sell*.

Imagine yourself reading a direct mail brochure about a product that interests you. How much are you going to read? When will you stop? You'll probably keep reading as long as you are interested and stop only when the copy becomes boring or you come to the end of the brochure. Direct response advertising does not have to be short and sweet. Interest is the key. Your readers will read what you have to say for as long as it interests them. You should be more concerned with keeping your material interesting and persuasive than in keeping it short.

POSTSCRIPTS....

Second-Best Way to Improve Writing

The best way to improve your direct response writing is to practice. The second-best way is to read good direct mail and start thinking of *direct response* when you think of advertising. When people with little advertising or direct marketing experience start to create direct response messages they sometimes pattern them after the advertising they're most familiar with, such as television commercials. Consumer TV ads, however, are examples of image advertising, where cleverness, mock cleverness, and repetition reign. In direct response you want your prospective customers activated, not amused or abused. To discover effective techniques and to start thinking in terms of direct mail, not conventional advertising, read good direct mail copy from such advertisers as *Reader's Digest*, the Bradford Exchange, Lands' End, Sears, Day-Timers, AT&T, and American Express.

Warning

Becoming direct response–oriented also means keeping an eye out for ideas you can appropriate to sell your product. I once received a package at work that was sealed with unusual-looking security tape. As soon as I saw it I thought it would be a great idea for a direct mailing. I haven't had occasion to use it yet; see if it can help you. It's guaranteed to get your mailer opened. Try this wording or modify it to suit your purposes.

WARNING WARNING This carton has been sealed with Pilfer-Proof Tape. If this seal is broken check contents before acceptance.

Guaranteed Free You

The above heading is not a syntactical error, it's an example of three of the most powerful words in direct mail. *You* is the most powerful word in English, followed closely by *free*. Actually you should use both to the best advantage. Work on your offer and your general copy strategy to see if you can use *free*. An informal survey of advertising creative people yields this list of the prime persuasive words: *special, unique, discover, money, how to, save, now, valuable, new, remarkable, only, limited, guaranteed, proven,* and *last chance*. (The word *free* must be used with some caution. See Chapter 10.)

Style Tips

As a review, when you're writing remember these style guidelines:

1. Write the way you talk, but once it's on paper, edit it carefully.
2. Use contractions.
3. Use personal pronouns, especially *you*, to personalize your message.
4. Favor short sentences.
5. Avoid jargon unless you're writing for a technical market.
6. Provide plenty of details. Use specific, tangible information and avoid superlatives and too many adjectives.

Be Wary of the Green

The environment continues to be a concern for everyone, and therefore marketers seem to be using every imaginable ecological tie-in for their products. Here are two reasons to be cautious when using environmental claims for your product or service.

First, in spite of some research to the contrary, it is not clear if consumers are willing to pay extra for environmentally safe products and, if so, how much they are willing to pay. If your major unique selling proposition or benefit is based on being environmentally sound, don't automatically expect consumers to willingly pay extra.

Second, the federal government and state legislatures are scrutinizing ecological product claims. Lawmakers are increasingly zeroing in on product claims such as *biodegradable, recyclable* and *ozone friendly* and requiring manufacturers to prove advertising claims. Some state legislatures have considered special legislation regarding product environmental claims.

How Many Cards?

A letter advertising a credit card protection service warns that "last year thousands of credit cards were lost or stolen." The statement was meant to evoke fear, but without an exact number it's a general warning, nothing specific. A small detail perhaps, but wouldn't "127,895 stolen credit cards" (or whatever the true figure is) make the statement more imperative and realistic?

9 SELECTING YOUR FORMAT

Writing Brochures, Broadsides, Inserts, Ads, Postcards, Self-Mailers, and More

> *Prospects for a new Cessna Citation business jet were surprised when we sent them live carrier pigeons, with an invitation to take a free ride in a Citation. The recipient was asked to release our carrier pigeon with his address tied to its leg. Some recipients ate the pigeons, but several returned alive, and at least one Citation was sold—for $600,000.*
>
> —David Ogilvy, *Ogilvy On Advertising*

Direct response advertising can take many forms. A mailing to executives in the movie and television industry, promoting Georgia as a prime location for filming, contained a large motion-picture film can filled with peanuts in the shell.

On a less elaborate scale, a small association mailed two hundred announcements of its nautical-themed educational conference in clear plastic flask-shaped bottles with corks for stoppers. Although they are relatively inexpensive stock items (sold complete with address labels for mailing), the bottles made a strong impression.

Other than postal regulations and your own good taste, there are few limitations on the types of mailings you can produce. You're free to make your format fit your marketing goals. Even within the limits of print advertising or radio, you still have considerable latitude in making a splash.

In spite of this variety of creative options, the majority of direct marketing uses but a few tested formats to generate business. But this works in your favor for two reasons. First, you can select and use the most effective direct mail and display advertising formats without having to invent and test your own. Second, when you want to boost your response with special customers, or when you have to present special promotions, you can deviate from the standard formats with something unique, guaranteed to attract every recipient's attention.

The suggestions from previous chapters for using advertising psychology and writing copy apply to all the formats that follow; however, each format requires slightly different treatment.

THE CLASSIC PACKAGE

The letter is the single most effective form of direct mail, also the most common. A letter is personal and flexible. It will sell just about any product or service. Since letters are the heart of direct mail, a separate chapter is devoted to writing and using letters.

The classic or traditional DM package is built around a letter and includes (1) an outer envelope; (2) a letter, often multipage; (3) a brochure; and (4) a postage-paid business reply card (BRC) or reply coupon with a business reply envelope (BRE). These fundamental ingredients are sometimes supplemented with other elements discussed later.

The classic package in Figure 9.1 shows an 11″ × 17″ two-fold brochure, a 4-page letter (printed on an 11″ × 17″ sheet of paper folded to produce four $8\frac{1}{2}$″ × 11″ pages), a reply card, and a BRE.

Within the four main ingredients of the classic package lies an array of possibilities you can use to get orders and promote your business. Brochures can be short one- or two- color flyers or large, glossy, full-color extravaganzas. Letters, too, can be any size and shape you wish. The letter–brochure–BRC format is so common in direct mail that people are accustomed to seeing the usual contents. Some readers who like pictures or are visually oriented go for your brochure first. Others are drawn to the personal aspects of a letter and will glance at it to see if the offer is of interest. The classic format gives you the space you need to create a complete selling package. Classic though it may be, the standard letter, brochure, and reply coupon is not the cheapest DM format, but it usually generates the most responses.

Reply Cards

Many experts see the response card as the most important element, not only in the classic package but in all direct mail. The typical business reply card has the postage-paid address on one side and the reply portion on the other. Business reply envelopes, also postage-paid, have the additional advantage of letting your customers enclose coupons, order forms, and checks. When you write a reply form or order blank, include the same ingredients as needed for a BRC. Chapter 15 explains how to obtain a business reply permit from the Postal Service.

If prospects decide to reply to your offer, they may throw the rest of your package away and save the BRC to fill out and return later. For this reason, your BRC or order form should contain all the necessary details of your offer (See Figure 9.2). It should sound as inviting, economical, and beneficial as the other statements of your offer, but it must be economical on words too; space on a card is limited. The best reply cards have the prospect's name and address already printed on them, but if you don't personalize the card, leave plenty of room for respondents to write their names, their addresses, and ordering information.

FIGURE 9.1 Ingredients of a direct mail classic package. (*Used with permission from Nightingale-Conant Corporation.*)

FIGURE 9.2   This response card contains the essence of the offer, including prices, options, and a guarantee. (© *United Communications Group, 11300 Rockville Pike, Suite 1100, Rockville MD 20852-3030 (301) 816-8950.*)

Since it should contain the essence of the offer, the BRC is sometimes the piece that prospective buyers read first, to find out what's for sale and how much. Remember this as you write the BRC. Consider writing the BRC first, in a way that makes the reader want to read on for more benefits and details.

Tests have shown that having "yes" and "no" boxes for prospects to check off will help response rates. If you have several different options from which your customers or prospects can choose, make the choices clear. Make the reply card easy to use. When you have someone sold, you don't want to confuse him when he's trying to say "yes."

Depending on your offer, your reply card should look valuable and sound important. If you're offering a discount with the BRC, then make it look like the valuable coupon that it is. Scroll borders can be used to dress up BRCs. You can also elevate your reply card and your offer by the name you give your BRC. Instead of simply calling it an order card or giving it no title at all, consider one of these, which have all been used successfully:

Acceptance Certificate

Private Reservation Notice

Membership Request Certificate

Special Reservation Application

Free Preview Certificate

Home Trial Certificate

Some order cards let the customer increase or "step up" an offer. Depending on your sales strategy, you may or may not mention the step-up offer in your letter, but do so on your card. It doesn't have to be a part of the main offer—just an additional box to check off on the card. While only a small percentage of your customers may use the step-up, every one is gravy, because it doesn't cost you anything to add the extra checkbox.

BRCs, or order forms placed in BREs, can include questions used to qualify prospects and gather data base information. Requiring a phone number on a lead generation response card—which some stockbrokers do, for example— tends to reduce the number of responses. Those who do respond, however, will be more serious prospects, who don't mind being called by a salesperson.

Many companies provide an 800 phone number in conjunction with a response form, giving readers an option. Those in a hurry will call. Those who want to write a check rather than use a credit card, or who want "more information" without fear of a sales pitch, will use the envelope. If your 800 number is on the order blank, it will be handy if your prospect throws the rest of your package away.

Brochures

Brochure is a fancy word for the flyer, circular, broadside, or other printed piece you put in the envelope next to your letter. I often use the word *brochure* in DM letters when referring the reader to the other material. The purpose of the other piece, whatever you call it, is to highlight your offer in a slightly different way than you do in your letter. You tell the story in pictures as well as words, or you supply more details. The brochure must provide sufficient benefits and specifications, and it should answer any questions prospects are likely to have.

If the purpose of your mailing is simply to generate a lead, the brochure doesn't have to have as many details. If you're trying to make a *sale* through the mail, you need to answer any questions that are likely to come up, because you won't get a chance to follow up. You won't even know when or why the sale was lost.

Brochures provide a change of pace. People reading a letter about a new type of wallet may quickly get bored with a description of its conveniences. They want to see what it looks like, so they turn to the brochure. If they like what they see, they may return to the letter to find out any special offers or details it may contain. In this way a brochure and a letter work in concert.

Often a brochure will have all the necessary details of the offer, but in a form different from the letter. The letter can talk about the all the accessories that come with a new power saw; the brochure can *show* the accessories and provide diagrams demonstrating how they work. When your letter talks about the reports and charts you provide to your financial counseling customers, your brochure should show samples. Brochures are especially valuable in highlighting benefits. The visuals in a brochure attract readers' eyes and lead them to your words, which should emphasize benefits.

Brochures also expand on topics too lengthy to be fully explained in letters. If a product has 22 uses, the brochure can list and explain every one of them; the letter may mention only a few.

The size of brochures varies, but here are some of the most common:

Size	Number of folds	Folded size
$8\frac{1}{2}'' \times 11''$	1	$5\frac{1}{2}'' \times 8\frac{1}{2}''$
$8\frac{1}{2}'' \times 11''$	2	$3\frac{2}{3}'' \times 8\frac{1}{2}''$
$8\frac{1}{2}'' \times 14''$	3	$3\frac{1}{2}'' \times 8\frac{1}{2}''$
$11'' \times 17''$	2	$5\frac{1}{2}'' \times 8\frac{1}{2}''$

Usually the brochure is the repository for the regulatory disclosures and any necessary substantiation of your claims. If your offer requires explanations of specific details, the brochure is the place to set them out. People are accustomed to legal disclosures (explained in the next chapter) and fine print, and they may read yours before ordering. As an incentive to write the fine print thoughtfully, pretend it's going to be set in large type. If your attorney has to write the fine print, see if you can rewrite it in everyday language and then have him or her review it for *content*, not language.

Copy in brochures is either a long, connected narrative or a collection of smaller articles. Which works best depends on what you're selling and what you have to say. A continuous narrative, illustrated with pictures, can carry a reader's interest, if the copy is benefit-oriented and written with the reader in mind. The longer the narrative, the more compelling the story must be to hold the reader. Resist the temptation to make the brochure a long, technical description of your product or service. Remember you're writing benefits for your reader, not a history of your R&D (no matter how proud of it you may be).

Most products and services have different components that lend themselves to separate illustrations and descriptions. Small boxes and sections of copy throughout a brochure appear to be easier to read than one long stretch of type. Here are a variety of elements that can create points of interest in a brochure:

Testimonials List them in one place or sprinkle them throughout the brochure.

Questions and Answers If your product or service does not lend itself to visuals, or if you want to save money on printing photographs, a *Q & A* section can make an attractive layout in a brochure. People enjoy reading this format. Make sure your questions hit motivations, not just product features. And make your questions sound natural, not contrived. "Why do I need one?" sounds more natural than "Why is the Acme Backyard Minesweeper such a pleasure to own and use?"

List of Benefits A long list, when highlighted by large numerals, also makes an attractive and impressive visual display that does not necessarily require photos or illustrations.

Guarantee A guarantee seems even stronger when it's printed in elaborate type, framed in a box, or adorned with a seal.

Models, Colors, Options Customer product choices can be pictured or described with words.

Benefit Tables, Comparisons Boxes listing benefits and features can help readers identify your product's advantages quickly. Boxes or grids can also be used to compare your product, benefit by benefit, with the competition or last year's model.

Call-outs Call-outs are descriptive labels arranged around a picture of the product and connected to the corresponding parts of the product using dotted lines or arrows. If you have a complex product, or even something as simple as a briefcase (see Figure 12.10), you can use call-outs to highlight technical features or advantages.

Some art directors like to design brochures with relatively plain covers that have scarcely more than a title or the name of the company on them. Brochures designed to sit in racks in banks can look this way, but your direct response brochures should give the reader a reason for looking inside. Fill your brochure covers with attractive artwork, tantalizing headlines, and benefits. Many DM brochures don't have covers per se, just opening panels that lure you into the meaty details inside. The outside panel on a brochure should contain a promise or an intriguing line that leads the reader inside. Headlines inside should follow up on the theme begun on the outside.

Sometimes you might want to give a brochure a plain cover to make it look like a passport, bank book, high school theme notebook, or other recognizable format. These "plain" fronts transplanted into direct mail packages are incongruous, and thus appealing.

The brochure in Figure 9.3 shows the opposite side of the Nightingale-Conant brochure from the classic package in Figure 9.1.

The size and quality of your brochure should be dictated by your marketing objectives as well as by your budget. Some topics, for example, benefit greatly from good-quality color photos. Selling food, travel destinations, and collectors' art will be easier with attractive, full-color photos. Direct mail is flexible, however, and if you're on a tight budget and can't afford color or photos, try words printed black on white.

Figure 9.4 shows part of a DM package that a small educational foundation has used successfully to sell Southwestern U.S. art tours costing more than $2,000. The mail packages use nothing more elaborate than typewritten itineraries printed in black. This particular package has a multipage itinerary and description of activities. Words, describing the vivid details of the tour, take the place of the photos. The foundation's director writes the copy himself in simple yet detail-filled language. "We will sit with these artists in their studios as they shape precious stones and metals into beautiful jewelry... discussing their views on the creative process," he says. An effective package *can* be created on a limited budget, and without artwork.

Occasionally a BRC will be attached to a brochure. This may complicate your printing or design stage, but it has one advantage for the respondent. If he saves the reply card, he may also save the brochure with its stronger sales message. The brochure in Figures 12.3 and 12.4 is actually a self-mailer, but it shows the design and location of an attached BRC.

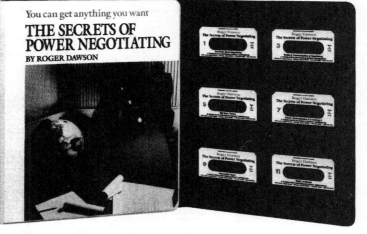

FIGURE 9.3 Here is the inside of the brochure shown folded in half in Figure 9.1 The copy provides concrete details, just enough to entice the reader to order. (*Used with permission from Nightingale-Conant Corporation.*)

ART AND ARCHAEOLOGY OF THE SOUTHWEST
A Special Field Seminar
Led by

Martha H

The arts of

today perhaps

century. Thr

jewelers, pot

range of work

innovation bu

origins. The

inspiration f

on the North

even cultural

centuries, ev

Crow Canyon

interpreters

on a 9-day fi

today's leadi

This seminar

We will sit w

precious ston

fire their po

tapestries fr

paintings of

the creative

and on occasi

maintain and

CROW CANYON ARCHAEOLOGICAL CENTER

BOARD OF DIRECTORS:
Raymond T. Duncan, Chairman
Albert L. Blum
Sally C. Duncan
John O. Lohre
Marianne O'Shaughnessy
Stuart Struever
William R. Thurston
Edward B. Wasson

CHAIRMAN'S COUNCIL:
Richard J. Anderson, Oak Brook, IL
Paul T. Bailey, Golden, CO
Richard & Mary Lyn Ballantine, Durango, CO
Seymour Bardes, Sands Point, NY
Mr. & Mrs. Yorke Bannard, Tucson, AZ
George Barter, Rosemont, NJ
Mr. & Mrs. George Beardsley, Denver, CO
Wendy Benjamin, Albuquerque, NM
Elizabeth H. Bennett, Chicago, IL
Mrs. Roland M. Boxler, Woodbridge, CT
Alan M. Bloom, Boulder, CO
Mr. & Mrs. Donald Britt, Bronx, NY
Lynn Godfrey Brown, Chicago, IL
Doris Cadoux, Scarsdale, NY
Katherine Carhart, New York, NY
Joyce Chelberg, Arlington Heights, IL
Edward Connors, Inglewood, CO
Marjorie Y. Crosby, Woodside, CA
Martha Lanman Cusick, Chicago, IL
Paul R. Duncan, LaGrange, IL
Mrs. Leonard S. Florsheim, Lake Forest, IL
Peggy V. Fossett, Chicago, IL
Donald A. Fredricks, Chicago, IL
David M. Gibson, Kansas City, MO
Dr. & Mrs. Farouk S. Idriss, Evanston, IL
C. Paul Johnson, Chicago, IL
Cary Knight, Chicago, IL
Mr. & Mrs. Raymond Kulla, Riverside, IL
Barbara Marcus, New York, NY
Charlotte Mittler, Mishawaka, IN
Herbert C. Paschen, Jr., Chicago, IL
Judith D. Prichard, Chicago, IL
Carly & Michael Searle, Chicago, IL
Howard M. Simpson, Peoria, IL
Darrell Skarsten, Burnsville, MN
Patricia Brown Specter, New York, NY
Russell Stoll, Colorado Springs, CO
Nancy & Les Sullivan, Winnetka, IL
Ellis J. Tallant, Englewood, CO
Nancy M. Todd, Denver, CO
Gomer W. Walters, Chicago, IL
Albert B. Wells, San Francisco, CA
Grant Wilkins, Littleton, CO
Gordon P. Wilson, Lake Forest, IL

March 6

Dear Friend of American Indian Art:

I am inviting a few long-time friends of North American Indian culture to join Martha Lanman Cusick (new married name is Martha Hopkins Struever) and myself on a very unusual field trip in June, September, and October.

Our journey through New Mexico and Arizona will be a unique opportunity to explore your interest in Indian art, by meeting prominent native artisans working in their own environment; by viewing expertly selected major collections; and by experiencing many of the complexities faced by any collector of American Indian Art today.

This field seminar is sponsored by Crow Canyon Archaeological Center, an independent research institute, with campus at Cortez, Colorado. One of Crow Canyon's goals is to provide special opportunities for interested individuals to meet living Native Americans still artistically expressing beliefs and skills handed down through generations. The Navajo and Pueblo peoples are among the very few cultures continuing to live and flourish in the same surroundings that were home for their ancestors hundreds of years ago.

I can think of no other opportunity that provides so intimate a view of southwestern Indian art today and in the past.

Participation is limited to 22 guests.

I hope you will join us in this very unusual field experience.

Sincerely,

Stuart Struever
Professor of Archaeology, Northwestern University (1964–1988) and
Founding Director, Crow Canyon Center

SS/bjg
Enclosure

1777 S. Harrison Street, P#1 . Denver, Colorado 80210 . Telephone: (303) 759-3303
DEDICATED TO ARCHAEOLOGICAL RESEARCH AND EDUCATION

FIGURE 9.4   You don't have to design fancy, colorful brochures to do a complete selling job in a direct mail package. This one-color letter and multipage itinerary sold an expensive tour of the Southwest U.S. (*Reprinted with permission from Crow Canyon Archaeological Center, Cortez, Colorado.*)

SELF-MAILERS

Advertising messages in envelopes get special attention. Since personal letters come in envelopes, and since every sealed envelope carries some mystery, envelopes are the preferred form for direct mail. You can tell immediately that mail without an envelope is advertising.

Since they're not usually sealed, and since they don't contain individualized letters, self-mailers are not quite as personal and don't involve the reader as much as a classic package does. In most cases, self-mailers have far less copy than direct mail in envelopes and thus fewer opportunities for strong written persuasion. Self-mailers have a variety of uses, however, and so do their envelopeless cousins: free-standing inserts (FSIs), statement stuffers, and package inserts.

Self-mailers cost less to produce than a classic package, but they are written in approximately the same style, to accomplish similar goals. Since they have no envelope, an address and postage are placed directly on the advertising piece. You unfold a self-mailer to see the message. The most simple (and cheapest) form of direct mail is a typewritten self-mailer photocopied on $8\frac{1}{2}'' \times 11''$ paper, folded twice, and stuck with an Avery label. Self-mailers may also be elaborate, full-color, multi-fold masterpieces printed on a large sheet of heavy, glossy paper. Chances are, yours will be somewhere in between.

Some self-mailers are much like brochures. They have appealing headlines on the two outside surfaces, which lead the reader inside to get the full message. The insides can contain details, testimonials, and many of the other weapons in your arsenal of persuasion (see Figure 12.3). Other self-mailers are akin to direct response print ads except that they have two headlines: one on the outside and one on the inside.

When folded for mailing, the self-mailer in Figure 9.5. has the headline "Some people think..." on one outside panel and the address label and postage on the other. The outside headline leads into the headlines on the three inside panels.

Another type of self-mailer, which tries to bridge the gap between the brochure and the classic package, contains elements from the latter. A letter will be printed on one part of the self-mailer, and other areas will include typical brochure copy. This hybrid self-mailer often has a BRC printed in one corner, perforated so that customers can simply tear it off to respond. The self-mailer in Figure 9.6 is a good example. It has a letter as a focal point on one side and a tear-off reply card across the bottom.

If you're not asking respondents to send you a check, a BRC makes a good addition to a self-mailer, because it's easy to use. The respondent doesn't have to find and address an envelope. A built-in BRC dictates that your self-mailer must be printed on paper that is at least the required thickness of a postcard.

The disadvantage of a self-mailer—that it is not as personal as a classic package—is offset by the instant impression it makes on everyone who receives it. It's like getting a billboard in the mail. The two outer panels can be designed to communicate a simple message and company image, whether the recipient wants to see it or not. Even if a self-mailer is not opened and read, potential customers can't help but see it and feel it.

Write your self-mailers the same way you do a classic package. If you include a portion that looks like a letter, make it sound like a letter and be sure to include a signature. The balance of the mailer should highlight the offer and include benefits. The coupon or BRC should contain the required elements.

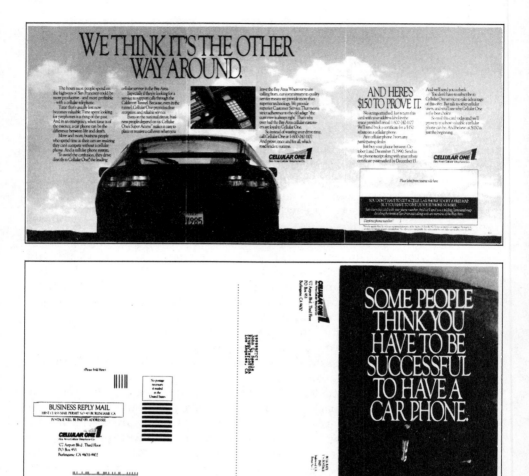

FIGURE 9.5   This self-mailer (front and back) is 18 by $8\frac{1}{4}$ inches and folds in thirds. Although it was produced in full-color, this size and format of self-mailer can be accomplished on a much smaller budget. It has a teaser head on the outside; complete details, including an offer of a $100 rebate and a free street map inside; plus a fold-over reply card. *(Used with permission from Bay Area Cellular Telephone Co.)*

Consider using a self-mailer when:

- You must save money, and awareness is as important as immediate sales.
- The cost savings may enable you to do a mailing when you can't afford a classic package.
- You only need a little copy to tell your story or sell your product.
- The self-mailer will be just one part of a DM campaign.
- You're advertising in a field, such as training seminars, which has successfully used self-mailers almost exclusively.

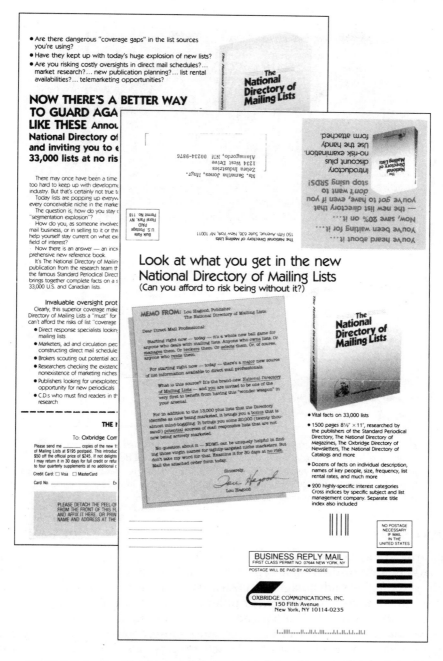

FIGURE 9.6 A self-mailer can include many of the elements of a classic package, such as a letter, brochure copy, and reply card. *(Reprinted with permission of Oxbridge Communications, Inc.)*

FIGURE 9.7 Two examples of using the "picture" postcard format. Although they both have an automotive slant, they're unrelated. The above (*Used with permission from Certified Federal Credit Union*) sells auto loans to credit union members; the other (on p. 137) was used in conjunction with a movie's exhibition on Pay-Per-View. (*Copyright 1990 Warner Bros. Inc. Used with permission.*)

POSTCARDS

Postcards are a standard format for vacationers writing to relatives and for the *response* side of direct marketing, but not too many advertisers use them as direct mail. The advantages of postcards are their shorter lead times and low production costs compared to other formats. Since they are relatively scarce in advertising, their uniqueness makes them stand out. With the right creative idea, a postcard can have the attention-grabbing power of a much larger or elaborate mailing piece. Like self-mailers, postcards have the power to create awareness-building impressions for your company or product.

Some advertisers treat postcards like small self-mailers, putting a headline on the address side and body copy with a second headline and artwork on the other side. I like to capitalize on the traditional format of a picture postcard. I put a picture or *short* headline on one side (the billboard side), and the message and address on the other.

FIGURE 9.7 *(Continued)*

If you copy the picture postcard format, your billboard side should contain a strong benefit headline or offer, an intriguing photo or illustration, or both. You might even try a mock vacation postcard with a photo of a vacation destination. On the flip side, your message must be brief. Be sure to write about customer benefits.

Two postcards that use one complete side for the "picture" and put the address and message on the other side are illustrated in Figure 9.7. To add an even more personal touch, try using handwriting for your message. Don't hand-write each card—just use neat handwriting for the original. As to the size, the only reason to stick to a small format is to qualify for the first-class postcard rate, which covers cards $4\frac{1}{4}'' \times 6''$ or smaller. One of the two cards in Figure 9.7 is eight inches wide, and the other is slightly wider than that.

It's difficult to do a complete selling job with a postcard, so applications are limited. Cards can be useful for building traffic and getting people to call an 800 number for more information. Postcards can also add impact to a series mailing. Use cards to remind people about a previous mailing or tease them about an upcoming one.

Postcards can also carry an immediacy that letters and envelopes don't have. Try a card that looks as if it were produced on short notice, or a card that's just like the ones you buy at the post office. Give your reader a deadline

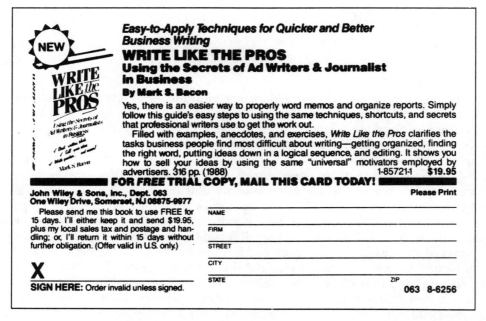

FIGURE 9.8 The two panels above show the front and back of a card-pack card offering the direct sale of a book *(Copyright 1988 John Wiley & Sons. Used with permission.)* The card on p. 139 is an offer of more information.*(Copyright 1991 Used with permission.)*

Earn $4,000 Per Month From Your Home With A Computer !

Start part-time with potential earnings of $10,000 or more per month. This is a proven turn key business an individual or couple can run. If you purchase our software and business program, we will give you the computer and printer. If you already own a computer, you may receive a discount. You do not need to own, or know how to run, a computer — we will provide free, home office training. Complete financing is available.

FREE CBS 286 Computer

Find out how other couples, and individuals like yourself, are getting rich!
To receive a free cassette and color literature,
Call toll-free: or return this card:

1-800-343-8014, ext. 380
(in Indiana: 317-758-4415)   *Or Write:*
Computer Business Services, Inc.
CBC Plaza, Ste. 380
Sheridan, IN 46069

Name Mr./Ms. _____
                              (please print)
Address _____
City _____
State/Zip _____

FIGURE 9.8   *(Continued)*

to act on a late-breaking offer, unexpected shipment, or the last few seats at a seminar.

CARD PACKS

When writing a post card for a card pack, the best place to start is with the card pack itself. Review previous packs and you will get a sample of good and bad ideas. You'll also see the types of offers your card will be sandwiched between.

As with other small direct response formats, you have to be succinct. Write a benefit headline and tie it into action-oriented copy that quickly reveals the offer. Here's one medium in which the design controls the amount of copy. Don't overwrite and then compensate by making the type smaller. Cards in many decks have type that is just too small to be read comfortably.

If you use a photo of your product, make it simple and easy to recognize. To save space, you can have customers put their names and addresses on the upper left corner of the address side of the card.

Use some of the strong, universal motivators in your headline and lead. Try to work in some of the proven headline words, such as *free* and *how to*. Take your time to hone the copy to its finest edge and to make the head and offer as irresistible as possible. The medium seems so simple that the tendency is to spend little time creating the message. Since the space is so limited, however, you may need to spend more time on a persuasive message. Sell your offer in 150 words or less.

In card packs, two-step offers work best. When your words are limited, it's easier to sell free information. As you can see from the examples in Figure 9.8, however, there are some items, such as books, that can be sold through this medium.

In deck cards and other media where the space is limited, remember to sell your offer, not your product, if the two are different. A card gives you enough space to sell a free trial, or sample, but don't use copy that reminds readers of your ultimate intentions.

FREE-STANDING INSERTS

Free-standing inserts (FSI's) come in so many sizes and shapes that it's impossible to identify a standard format. A simple $8\frac{1}{2}'' \times 11''$, two-sided circular may be the most common for small businesses. An $11'' \times 17''$ format can also be used to advantage, whereas many retailers and package goods sellers usually favor larger-format multipage booklets. FSIs in Sunday newspapers tend to be more elaborate, filled with many store coupons. Inserts in neighborhood advertising publications and co-op mailings are often smaller.

Depending on the size of your FSI, you might want to pattern it after another DM format. Coupon-size co-op mailings require card deck–style prose, while larger FSIs, such as those in newspapers, may be patterned after self-mailers.

Many small-business FSIs are comparable to the old-style broadside, and many are amateurishly written and produced. To stand out from the pack, study the guidelines for good design in Chapter 12 and write your FSI as if it were a self-mailer. Retail FSIs often use coupons. If you do too, sell your offer first and everything else second.

CATALOGS

Catalog copy is full of advice, fashion and decorating ideas, and hundreds of interesting tidbits. Truth is, I'm a catalog junkie. I read catalogs the way some people read magazines. I look for bargains and for creative direct marketing ideas I can use.

Start reading catalogs and you may find not only a variety of small technical ideas for describing merchandise or generating orders, but also advertising layout and merchandising possibilities. For example, notice that effective catalogs are slightly "busy": Each page is not usually devoted to one item but to several. Energy almost comes off the pages at you, there are so many things to see and read. The copy and the design should combine to intrigue, tempt, and impress you. But most of all, of course, the copy should make you respond.

Catalogs are often set aside to be read in detail later. People browse through them. If they have sufficient points of interest, created by both the words and the layout of pages, catalogs can sell many things at once. Selling too many different products at the same time is something to avoid with other direct mail or direct response formats.

When writing for a catalog, create headlines that stress unique benefits and product advantages. If a standard product is being offered in a new color, or if features have been added, highlight the changes. Catalog copy needs to make the complete sale, so it should answer questions and work with the illustrations to describe the product fully. To promote additional sales, catalog copy often explains different ways a product can be used and suggests accessories or complementary products.

Consider giving your catalog a personality. No matter what you're selling, you can build rapport with customers and make reading a little more inviting by carrying a theme throughout the book or by using personal pronouns to make the narrative copy almost a dialog with customers. Your catalog theme can easily relate to the category of merchandise or services you offer. If you deal with antiques, your copy can be delicate and precise, almost with a rhetorical patina. If you have a sports-oriented product or service, your copy can sound like sports stories in a newspaper.

The *Comfortably Yours* catalog is aimed at an older audience and carries products to make life a little easier. The copy for nearly every item sounds like things a concerned, helpful salesperson or even a friend might say.

> During a recent trip to Europe, I noticed almost every cab driver sitting on a wooden beaded car seat. Out of curiosity, I purchased one and put it in my own car. It's wonderful! The beads lift me off the cold seat in winter and allow air to flow beneath me in summer. My tired muscles are gently massaged while I drive. I'm sure you will love yours as much as I do mine.[1]

Comfortably Yours and other catalogs carry a letter from the publisher on one of the first pages. The letter is another way of emphasizing your catalog's personality and yours. It lets you tell something about yourself and your company. You can explain your philosophy of customer service and reassure readers that they're making a wise decision to shop with you. Some catalogs carry letters-to-the-editor sections, which go beyond the usual testimonials to include questions and sometimes even complaints.

Other important stock elements in a catalog include details of your warranty and your policies on such things as shipping methods and charges, returns, credit, availability of stock, and rain checks.

While catalogs have longer life than other direct mail, they often lack immediacy. That can be improved using coupons and some of the urgency devices mentioned in the next chapter. In a small specialty catalog, you can place one blanket deadline on everything which gives the catalog a limited shelf life. Another way to add immediacy is with limited-time sales offers. Print a notice on the cover, saying that customers can take $X off any order above a certain amount. Then supply a time limit on the offer. You can imprint the deadline on the back of the catalog near the mailing address.

Another way to offer sales merchandise is to set aside a "sale" section of your catalog. These can be discontinued lines, odd sizes, or any other leftover merchandise. Provide a deadline or make the sale subject to existing stock.

PRINT ADS

Writing a convincing print advertisement for a magazine or newspaper is as challenging an assignment as there is in direct marketing. You must start with an irresistible headline that connects to the lead, the first few paragraphs of the ad. From there, benefits encourage the reader onward, with emotions used to motivate. The language is almost as personal as that of a letter.

Your offer and your audience help you mold the strategy that goes into the copy. You write to your prime prospects, using what you know about the readers. Use the publication's demographics to help you make decisions on jargon, choice of benefits, and other variables. For example, if you're running an ad in a sewing magazine, you don't have to sell people on the benefits of doing their own sewing, just on the benefits of your particular product. The demographic knowledge helps you use your limited space wisely.

Think of a print ad as a condensed direct mail package. You need to cover all the important points—appealing head, enticing lead, multiple benefits, illustrations if applicable, guarantee, and response device—but in a smaller package. That's one of the reasons you should not use a print ad as a mailer. Even an excellent direct response ad can be improved on in a mailer. The message becomes more personal and you have all the space you need to give the complete story.

The Most Important Ingredients

The headline and lead are critical. Only a small percentage of people will get beyond the head and the lead—but they're your prime prospects, so you must write just to them. Who are they and what will keep them reading? What benefits or advantages are they looking for? Here are two very different examples of writing directly to chief prospects, from two direct response ads for business training.

The Harvard Business School identifies its prospects in its headline and talks to them:

> In January, 120 busy executives who run their own companies will break away to the Harvard Business School.
>
> If you own and manage a $3 to $100 million company, this program is for you.[2]

The lengthy ad, which is run in the *Wall Street Journal,* continues with detailed information about the type of instruction offered and the high level of participants—all are company chief executive officers (CEOs). It uses praise and exclusivity by saying the program is "designed to exploit your company's greatest competitive advantage . . . you." The copy makes the program sound like hard work, something this target group usually thrives on.

Here's a different direct response ad, from *Popular Mechanics,* aimed at a different market:

Make up to $26.00 an hour
Be your own boss – Start your own money-making business

> Hundreds of Foley-Belsaw trained men have
> succeeded in this fascinating and highly profitable field....[3]

This is an ad for locksmith training. It says that there is an increasing need for locksmiths, and it emphasizes cash profits and extra income. The target audience, which includes people who may have dreamed of working for themselves, will be interested in self-employment at $26 per hour. Thus, both Harvard and the Foley-Belsaw Institute identify target audiences and aim motivating messages via direct response ads in specialized publications.

Here's a review of more headlines:

Free Corporate Jet Operating Cost Audit

There's the magic word, *free*. Even though this is an ad aimed at chief financial officers (CFOs) and other corporate officers, a free offer has appeal. The free audit gives a flight operations management company a chance to demonstrate to potential clients how they can reduce company costs.

First in the field of bicycle vacations.

This unimaginative, ineffective headline for a bicycle touring company is aimed at families. The copy that goes with it is filled with benefits. It's too bad none of the benefits were used in the headline. The head doesn't give you a reason to read on, and the ad doesn't explain what "First in the field" means.

Increase Income and Save Taxes With The Pomona Plan

Here's a benefit headline selling donations to Pomona College. The private college asks you to transfer your financial assets to them, after which you will receive income for the rest of your life. (When you die, the college owns the assets.) The use of benefits makes giving up your personal assets sound more attractive than taking a bicycle vacation. Body copy mentions savings on three levels of taxes.

Do You Know These Little-Known
Natural Health Tips And Cures?

This ad for a health book offers you a glimpse at things most people don't know. Your curiosity is aroused. The writer is sharing some exclusive information with you.

Many ads begin with a problem, sometimes tied to fear. "How to get more sales leads." "How to save time in the kitchen after a busy day." "How to help the kids get better grades." "How to make life more exciting." The answer to these problems leads the reader to the benefits which will help him avoid the fearsome consequences. Can you identify the products (and solutions they bring) connected to these two direct response headlines: "Did you make this mistake in writing your will?" "Are your feet killing you?"

In the problem/fear/solution format, you solve the problem with benefits and then add a testimonial, a recap of benefits, and the all-important call to action. The reader may never look at your ad again and will never be more ready to buy than at the moment he's finished reading it; therefore, give him a nudge. Offer an incentive and make it as easy to order as possible.

Whether you elect to build the ad around a problem and solution or to use some other format, your copy should become more convincing, encouraging, and urgent as you go along. You build one grabber on top of another and lead to the call for action.

Another way to organize an ad is to compartmentalize each necessary element. Following the lead, which summarizes the offer, you have a list of benefits and product advantages, then a series of endorsements set off in a box. The coupon and copy above it constitute another compartment. If you're selling several products or services, or several versions of one product, you could have one section for each—almost several ads in one. Be careful, however, of trying to sell too much at once. The same goes for direct mail.

Content

Should all direct response ads be filled with copy and look like direct response ads? Not necessarily. If you have a simple product and you're advertising to a market that understands the value of it, then you may not have to have a copy-heavy ad. If you're not trying to make a one-step sale with an ad, it might look like a conventional ad, except that it should have an 800 phone number, coupon, or company address displayed prominently at the bottom.

Having a prominent coupon gives your ad a direct response look, but that's not undesirable. When people look at it they recognize that here is an ad they can use to buy something or send away for free information. It gets readers primed for action.

Figure 9.9 is a direct response ad with a conventional look to it. The original size of this half-page magazine ad is about 5" × 7". The headline is what I would call soft-sell. The benefit is there, but it's implied. Since the purpose of the ad is to generate leads rather than to make a complete sale, the copy can be light and to the point. The artwork of the business calendar emphasizes the point. Maintaining health, reducing stress and worry, and even getting ahead on the job are the motivators at work here.

Depending on your purpose, you may not need to buy a full page or even a half page. If you want to sell an inexpensive item to build a house list, or if you're just offering an information brochure or free catalog, a small-space ad can do the job for you. To generate leads and build lists, direct marketers traditionally use $\frac{1}{6}$ page ads, generally about $2\frac{1}{4}$ inches by $4\frac{1}{2}$ or 5 inches. The mail-order sections of many magazines are filled with such ads. Figure 12.7 is an example of a simplified lead generation ad. It's a $\frac{1}{3}$-page ad, but the design could be reduced to a smaller space.

Although small-space ads are a favorite for generating leads and building lists, they can be used to sell moderately priced products, as Figure 9.10 shows. The $\frac{1}{6}$-page Kryptonite ad has the look of a conventional ad and even uses a play on words in the headline. But the word play doesn't distract from the product—it helps emphasize a benefit. Notice the ad has a guarantee, the benefit of possible insurance rate savings, color selections, and ordering information.

The people who need exercise the most have the least time to exercise.

The busier you are, the more tired you get. The more tired you get, the more stressed-out you feel. The more stressed-out you feel, the more your job performance suffers.

It's a vicious cycle, unless you exercise regularly. And fitness experts agree that no form of exercise is more effective at raising stamina than cross-country skiing.

NordicTrack® duplicates the cross-country skiing motion to provide a better cardiovascular workout than bikes, rowers and treadmills.

With only three, 20-minute workouts per week, you'll feel stronger, more alert and less stressed-out.

So call NordicTrack. Because by the looks of your schedule, time isn't on your side.

```
┌─────────────────────────────────┐
│    Free Brochure & Video.       │
│  Call Toll Free 1-800-328-5888. │
│     In Canada 1-800-433-9582.   │
│  □ Please send me a free brochure. │
│  □ Also a free video tape □ VHS □ BETA │
│  Name_____  │
│  Street_____  │
│  City_____State___Zip____  │
│  Phone (   )_____  │
│  141 Jonathan Blvd. N. Chaska, MN 55318 │
│  430D0                          │
└─────────────────────────────────┘
```

NordicTrack
A CML COMPANY

FIGURE 9.9 Unlike the copy-heavy ad in Figure 8.1, this ad is clean and simple. The difference is that this ad is just asking for a request for more information, not an order. *(Used with permission from Nordic Track.)*

The video computer training ad (Figure 9.10) comes from a newspaper, and the headings are designed to look like news. With no illustrations, the ad is packed with words, but it's not too cramped until the bottom. Notice all the elements squeezed into the small space, including an endorsement and two product levels. Speed is the major benefit, sold in the headings and body copy. I particularly like the line, "for people with *absolutely no computer experience* (and no time to study)."

As Figure 9.10 shows, small ads don't necessarily have to have a coupon. To save space, an ordering address can serve the purpose. You can also put a bold dotted line around the entire ad to get across the idea that you have a direct response offer.

BROADCAST

Radio ads can have the fastest turnaround of any direct response format. If you have a station announcer read your copy live, you can write the commercial one day and have it on the air the next.

The language you use in radio (or TV) commercials should be closer to the way you talk than the language in other advertising: Your words will be spoken. Use short sentences, avoid words which may tongue-tie an announcer, and don't worry about repeating yourself a little, especially when you're giving

FIGURE 9.10 Moderately priced products can be sold through small-space ads as these two successful examples demonstrate. (*Kryptonite ad © 1990 M.T.V.C., Inc. All rights reserved.*)

your phone number. People can't reread the benefits in your commercial, so restating a benefit is not a fault.

When you write direct mail or print ads, you can use samples of what others have done to get ideas or understand techniques. With radio you can do the same thing, but you need to do more than listen. Record some local direct response ads and transcribe them. Read them aloud and see if they are easy for you to say. Notice the length of sentences and the vocabulary used.

In writing your own commercials, refer to any print or mail advertising you've written as a guide for using benefits. Use benefits similar to those you have already decided on for your other advertising. Start off with a promise, a statement of a common problem, or some other typical direct response beginning. Mention benefits for listeners (you can use the word *you* to talk directly to them) and conclude with a call to action.

A 60-second commercial will take up about about three quarters of a page of double-spaced typing (see Figure 9.11). It's not much time to make a sale. Although you can use a variety of sound effects and music, your best bet is to stick with a straight, single-announcer spot. Once you are more experienced writing for broadcast, you can experiment with different techniques.

In your script, help the announcer by providing phonetic spelling for any unusual words. Read the script yourself aloud to see if there are any places where the announcer might change the meaning by changing word emphasis. If so, use underlining to make it clear which words you want emphasized. Reading the script aloud should also tell you if your sentences are too long to be read comfortably in one breath.

Writing for television can be many times more complex, because you must consider the visual message as well. If you are contemplating TV, you should get some professional help. That does not mean you have to hire an expensive ad agency. Your station's account executive may be able to recommend a local production company. Alternatively, a freelance TV writer or producer may be able to put together the production team you need.

POSTSCRIPTS....

Marketing with Newsletters

Are newsletters a form of direct marketing? They can be, but often they are not. Due in part to desktop publishing technology, newsletters are proliferating. Many firms write newsletters and fill them with pictures, articles about their companies, and even news of their industries. When people mail these to clients or prospects, they mistakenly think they're doing direct mail marketing.

Newsy newsletters may be valuable for public relations, but unless you provide an offer and a means of response, don't expect your newsletter to sell for you. There is value in keeping your name in front of your customers or potential customers, but why not at least make your newsletter pay for itself by using it to sell? Include a coupon in each issue, which lets your readers reorder or, at least, request information on a new product. This would also give you a

Knight Protective Industries

:60 Radio Commercial
Home Protection Tip #1

Anncr:

The following Home Protection Tip is brought to you by Knight
Protective Industries--makers of the ultimate home security
system.

Your home is an easy break-in target if all sliding glass
doors have not been secured with at least a dowel or steel rod,
cut to fit the door channel or track, so the door cannot slide
open. An inside, pin-type lock is even better.

Also, two or three screws in the overhead track will make it
a lot tougher for a thief to simply lift the door right out of the
track for easy entry. Turn the screws so the door just clears
them when it slides.

This home protection tip, and literally hundreds more, are
now available without cost or obligation to all Southern
California homeowners. Call Knight Protective Industries at
1-800-388-7730 for your own personal copy of Knight's 32-page
guide, "Protecting Your Home and Family." It includes well over
250 easy steps you can take to protect your home and family
against loss due to burglary, intruders, fire, earthquakes, and
emergencies.

That's 1-800-388-7730 for the safest call you'll ever make.
1-800-388-7730.

FIGURE 9.11 Direct response radio commercial written to be read by one announcer. (*Used with permission from Knight Protective Industries.*)

way to *measure* the effectiveness of your publication. Chapter 12 offers some valuable typographical suggestions that can help make your newsletter look better, and Chapter 17 has ideas for using newsletters to keep customers happy, and keep them buying.

Make a Call to Action

Asking for the order is the ultimate, necessary step in person-to-person sales, a step that some people forget. In direct response advertising the term is *call to action*. The final paragraph of your ad, or the last words before the signature in your DM letter, should tell your readers what to do. Tell them to take advantage of the offer, order right away, come in, or call for information. In a small-space ad, the call to action can be a sentence that directs the reader to the address or phone number. In a letter, you can summarize the benefits, explain why now is a good time to order, and then show the reader what to do.

What's Funny?

Humor is an element of advertising that many people like to use. When used correctly, it can grab attention and even generate separate publicity. A bank in San Francisco offered bonus interest to savers who brought in their old toasters. This switch on the old bank premium caught attention and helped boost deposits by $13 million.

The bank's "Toast Busters" campaign is a rare exception. Humor is often used imprecisely. What is funny to one person may not be funny to someone else. Using humor is a risk. The greater the potential for laughter or amusement, the greater the possibility of distracting from the offer or even offending someone.

Light humor and slight wordplays, such as in the Kryptonite ad, are the safest. If someone isn't amused, at least he's not offended, and the sales message is still clear.

10 BUILDING URGENCY, HEEDING REGULATIONS

Getting a Response from Everyone Except the FTC

So safe, so pure it has been used to filter the air in leading hospitals.

—1953 ad for Kent cigarettes' Micronite filter

No matter what format you select for your advertising, you must focus on getting action. Inertia is the main enemy. To overcome the human tendency to procrastinate, direct marketing practitioners have created an array of urgency devices to get people to respond.

While you're building urgency in your advertising, you must also consider the legal and regulatory requirements governing such things as contests, advertising claims, and guarantees. To say the same thing more positively, you should be careful that your desire to boost responses doesn't eclipse the need to act responsibly. This chapter provides suggestions.

The federal organization with primary responsibility for regulating advertising, including direct marketing, is the Federal Trade Commission (FTC), the watchdog agency mentioned in Chapter 7.

The FTC was created by Congress in 1914 to promote free and fair trade through the prohibition of unfair methods of competition. In 1938 the power of the FTC was increased, with passage of the Wheeler–Lea amendments to Section 5 of the FTC Act. These amendments gave the FTC consumer protection powers by prohibiting "unfair or deceptive acts or practices in commerce." As a government body, run by five commissioners appointed by the President, the FTC is subject to political changes in Washington, D.C. When Ronald Reagan was president, for example, FTC actions reflected a more pro-business orientation than under previous presidents.

Although it has a variety of investigative and enforcement methods, the FTC must rely in part on the voluntary cooperation of advertisers. The scope of advertising in the United States is so vast the FTC can't possibly monitor all commercials and ads. In fact, it monitors very few and investigates when it receives complaints. It can issue cease-and-desist orders or ask-for-consent orders, in which an advertiser volunteers to modify or cease some promotional practice.

One way the FTC promotes cooperation is by publishing industry guides, which contain specific requirements and policies regarding advertising claims, guarantees, mail-order fulfillment practices, and other subjects. Next to getting advice from legal counsel, reading the FTC guides is one of the best ways to ensure regulatory compliance. Some of the information in this chapter is summarized from FTC guides. Appendix B tells you how to get copies for yourself.

In addition to the FTC, both state and local governments regulate advertising and promotion directly and indirectly. State attorneys general and local district attorneys can and do institute court proceedings against advertisers who violate state and local ordinances. Often prosecutions are reserved for flagrant fraud, repeated bait-and-switch techniques, or other intentional transgressions. This does not mean, however, that a careless or negligent mistake on your part cannot find you in court.

Most states have recently passed legislation similar to the FTC Act to prevent deceptive and unfair practices. The typical state law authorizes investigations, cease-and-desist orders, and court injunctions to halt unfair promotional practices.[1]

The main purposes in advertising regulation are to help maintain fair competition among businesses and to provide reasonable protection for consumers. While some areas of advertising are riddled with fine points of law, old fashioned honesty and common sense are your best guides for avoiding many of the deceptive practices that regulators look for.

CONTESTS AND PREMIUMS

Contests and premiums seem to bring out the worst in some direct marketers. In the past, misleading and deceptive contests have brought intense scrutiny from legislative bodies and punitive action from the FTC and other authorities. Yet contests continue to be a popular response booster for marketers aiming at all demographic levels. As with many direct marketing techniques, you can dress up or dress down a contest.

A variety of upscale and business magazines get results by offering premiums for new subscribers. In business-to-business direct marketing, unsolicited gifts are common to get prospects' attention. Follow-up gifts or premiums are commonly offered in exchange for a response or an order.

If you think greed is not an effective motivator, conduct a contest and see. Direct marketing professionals know that sweepstakes (*sweeps*) work. They may not like them very much. They may not want to advise you about them, but they know they work. DM veterans may eschew sweeps because they smack of junk mail, because they are time-consuming to administer, and because they usually require legal advice. But they do increase responses.

Anyone who reluctantly (or eagerly) uses sweeps will discover additional drawbacks. The responses received are often not as high-quality as those you would have generated with a simple good offer. Contest players may be players, not serious customers. In addition, if you use a sweepstakes to boost initial response, what are you going to do to maintain that excitement and level of interest in the back end? Have another contest? A direct marketing executive who spent years working on major magazine subscription campaigns calls them the "sweepstakes wars" and the "premium wars."

So, knowing all this, use contests with caution. One way to improve the quality of contest-related responses is to emphasize your product or underlying offer. In a lead generation campaign, however, if you emphasize your product and reduce the focus on the contest, you're working to reduce your total responses.

Even knowing in advance that a sweepstakes will increase your response, it may be difficult to evaluate whether the increase will be enough to justify the cost of the prizes. Here's where a test mailing can help. But if you can't afford to test, you can at least track responses carefully and compare results with previous and subsequent noncontest mailings. You can also work backwards by adding in the cost of a contest, then determining how large a response you need to justify the additional cost. Response increases of 30 percent or more are not unusual with some sweepstakes offers. (That's a 30 percent increase, not an increase *to* 30 percent.)

Sweeps or contests pose a variety of legal challenges to the inexperienced. They are regulated, and sometimes prohibited, by different levels of government. As a first step, you must make sure that you're not running a lottery. Lotteries are prohibited by criminal statutes in many states, and once you mail a lottery promotion, you're in violation of federal (postal) regulations.

Many financial, DM, or retail marketing directors know the rudiments of keeping a legitimate promotional contest from becoming a lottery. A lottery is composed of three necessary elements: consideration, chance, and prizes. Eliminate at least one of those factors, and you no longer have a lottery. Normally, eliminating consideration is the easiest. *Consideration* is a legal term meaning your customer has to buy, or otherwise provide value in order to receive a chance in the contest. Be careful: Consideration is not limited to money or a purchase. Requiring customers to be present to win a drawing may be construed as consideration.[2]

FTC Sweepstakes Guidelines

FTC investigation into sweepstakes over the years has found a variety of deceptive practices, including ending a contest before all prizes are awarded; advertising large prizes out of proportion to their availability; programming when, during the run of a contest, most of the prizes would be won; and artificially manipulating which retail outlets in a chain would give out the most winning coupons.

Currently the FTC has adopted guides to contests only for the gasoline- and food-retailing industries, but some of the suggestions are appropriate for most sweeps. Here are a few considerations, based on past FTC policies and the honesty/common sense approach.

Randomness The FTC has approved the use of computers to select random winning numbers in a contest. You should somehow ensure that no one can influence the selection of winners.

Disclosure Giving people information they can use to determine whether they wish to participate in the contest is the FTC's underlying reason for disclosures, but you should provide complete contest rules as well as the odds of winning. When you don't know the odds ahead of time, explain that the odds depend on the number of entries, but that you expect X number of responses.

Awarding all prizes: You may be able to construct a contest in which you are not legally required to distribute all prizes, but it's easier, safer, and a moral obligation to give away everything you advertise.

Don't discourage "no" answers Some contests, particularly those sponsored by publishers, ask that a "yes" or "no" answer to the offer accompany each contest entry. Even people who respond with a "no" show responsiveness and should not be ignored in future mailings. Furthermore, of course, they should have an equal chance of winning.[3]

Common sense will help you with contests, but if you're planning an elaborate sweepstakes, requirements can be so complex that you may want to get help. Special consulting firms experienced in administering sweepstakes are available to manage a contest for you, but you must factor in the firm's fees to determine the practicality of the promotion. Such firms often advertise in direct marketing trade publications.

Premiums

Offering *early bird* prizes or premiums can successfully boost responses. If you're having a sweepstakes, you can offer an additional drawing for prospects who respond by a certain date. Or, as a general incentive, you can offer a premium to the first X number of people who respond to an offer.

Two schools of thought exist about the selection of premiums. One school, which I'll call the "thoughtful marketing directors," advises you to select premiums that are related to your product or service. It seems more logical for publishers to give away books or magazines, office supply companies to give away office equipment, and banks to offer bonus interest. The other school of thought, the "peerless promoters," suggests giving away what's hot. For years and years, pocket calculators were the premium everyone gave away. Today radios and portable compact disc players are popular, but they are not as universal as the calculators used to be.

When you offer something for free, obviously the buyer expects it to be free and expects to pay no more than the regular price for the product that includes the premium. According to the FTC guide regarding the term "free," the terms and conditions you attach to premiums should be printed in close proximity to the statement of your free offer. You may mention the term "free offer" on the outside of an envelope or in a DM letter, for example, but when you specify the item to be given away, you should consider that as a trigger term requiring an explanation of conditions. For example, if you mention a "free offer" on the outside of a mailing, you should refer readers to your brochure, where you explain the premium and the conditions readers must meet in order to obtain it.[4]

The FTC guide also says, "So that a 'free' offer will be special and meaningful, a single size of a product or a single kind of service should not be advertised with a 'free' offer in a trade area for more than 6 months in any 12-month period. At least 30 days should elapse before another such offer is promoted."

When offering something for free, you obviously must not increase the price of the other item or reduce its value to cover the "cost" of the free premium. Additionally, accepting a free item or a trial should not obligate someone to pay for return shipping if he decides not to keep the item.[5]

PRICING

When establishing your prices, you have many business factors to consider, such as raw material costs, competition, customer acquisition costs, salaries, and overhead. In direct marketing, you also need to consider price as an urgency device. Your prices are not always the deciding factor in your direct marketing success, but the dollar figures you select and the way you explain them certainly affect your results.

Plateau pricing is one of the oldest techniques in selling and one that still works. The idea is to make your price appear to be low by setting it just under a monetary plateau: $9.95 rather than $10, $49.95 rather than $50. You may already know the important plateaus, depending on your product and market. If not, testing may be in order. In mail order, for example, advertisers are sometimes surprised by how much they can increase the price of their products without a significant drop in orders.

In setting your prices, it's as important not to price something too low as too high. For example, it's likely you could sell almost as many $9.95 cat boxes as you could ones selling for $7.95 or $8.95, because all three prices are perceived as about the same: under $10. Just how high that philosophy goes depends on your product and market. For an upscale market, you might sell as many $39.95 items as ones costing $36.95, because the two prices are perceived to be similar. Testing or research may also tell you at what level an item ceases to be an impulse buy. Oil companies and department stores that use statement stuffers for mail-order selling usually know where the impulse pricing level is for their markets and products. Notice that many of the items offered for sale through stuffers are in the impulse category.

This does not mean that you should set your prices *too* high. That can be ruinous. You may price yourself out of the market, and if your prices are significantly above manufacturers' suggested prices, you have to use a notice to that effect in some jurisdictions.

The way you state or explain your price can be as important as the price itself: *Just $4 per month, billed annually.* Isn't that the cheapest 48 bucks you ever saw? And just in case customers multiply the $4 by 12, the total is under the $50 plateau. Here's another, from the Chevron Travel Club: "...you'd expect to pay at least $5 a month for the insurance and road service alone. Yet you can receive all 13 benefits for as little as $3 a month—10 cents a day!"

Whenever possible, it's a good idea to express the price in more than one way so that buyers get a better idea of what they're getting for their money. Publications often cite the cost per week, per month, or per issue. The obvious purpose is to break the total down into smaller, cheaper bites. If your product or service is aimed at a family of four, you can state your per-person price at 25 percent of the total. If your product consists of several components, explain the price of each.

Even if you have a service to offer, you can still provide a breakdown of your price. You can show how much each stage of the work costs. You can charge by the hour or day, or use some other benchmark. When I sell in-house business writing seminars to companies, I offer the price broken down per person.

In some cases, consultants and other professionals may be better off *not* citing an hourly or daily rate. It may be worth thousands of dollars to a customer for you to perform a particular job, but if your client perceives that it doesn't take you very long to provide the service, you may lose a sale. If you're writing to companies, offering your services to create manuals of policies and procedures, for instance, it's better to quote a price for a completed job, rather than to say you charge $100 per hour. Better still, don't mention costs at all in a lead generation mailing unless your price can be instantly recognized as a unique selling proposition by your readers. Overall, it's best to state a service in terms of the customer's problems you solve rather than the specific duties you perform. That's just good benefits selling again.

Another way (in addition to all the "sale" offers listed in Chapter 2) of making a price sound like a bargain is to compare the cost of buying the product or service some other way. In my seminar promotion, I show how the price per person is far less than the cost of sending the same people to outside commercial seminars. To avoid deceptive practices, when you compare your prices to some other prices, you need to explain the nature of the other prices and stand ready to substantiate those other prices as well.

The FTC's *Guides Against Deceptive Pricing* says that in order for you to offer something at a reduced or sale price, it must have been offered for sale at the previous, higher price for "a substantial period of time, in the recent, regular course of [your] business." You do not necessarily have to have sold any merchandise at the previous price, but it must have been openly available for sale.

The FTC booklet on pricing also warns against comparison pricing that implies that your price for something is lower than the generally prevailing price in your trade area, when, in fact, only a few small outlets charge a higher price.

As should be obvious, you can't artificially inflate the price of a product or service or lessen its value, then reduce the price (perhaps back to what it was originally) and offer it on special sale. Be careful not to reduce a price insignificantly, such as 2 to 3 percent, and then advertise a big sale or price reduction, without mentioning the specific amount of the reduction.

In addition to legal considerations, an exceedingly low price can sometimes work against you from a marketing standpoint. To counter the unbelievability factor, provide concrete, specific reasons why your price is low and your offer genuine.

You don't need to write an explanation for every low price, but if you ever need to explain a drastically reduced price, the following example may help. Here is one of the best, most convincing explanations of a low price I've ever read. A DAK Industries, Inc. eight-page self-mailer, advertising $773 worth of name-brand software for $49.90, carries this explanation:

> This unparalleled bribe is a two-pronged attack. Bribe Reason 1: Word-Star wants to expand their customer base and to ferret out both new and current users.
>
> So, they've given DAK factory-authorized permission to offer WordStar 5.0 as part of this amazing $49.90 bribe.
>
> WordStar has over 2,000,000 users (legal and otherwise), who use Word-Star's older, outdated, outmoded versions...
>
> Take my bribe and you can unleash this world-class word processor (and 2 other powerful programs) on all your business and home projects.
>
> It's just part of your bribe for $49.90. And with your name in my computer, I can offer WordStar add-ons and even program upgrades in the future.
>
> Bribe Reason 2: In the mail-order business, it's expensive (and time-consuming) searching for active computer owners. I have to mail hundreds of catalogs just to get an order. So it can end up costing me over $20 per name.
>
> So, it's a gamble. I'm betting you can be bribed by this amazing offer. And, I'm wagering you'll be so thrilled by all the power you'll command with this $49.90 bribe that you'll buy from me again and again in the future. But be careful.
>
> CAUTION!!! If you plan to take this bribe and run, let me warn you about 2 things. 1) I'm going to inundate you with LOTS of future computer catalogs. And 2) I'll keep tempting you with incredible offers like this bribe.[6]

This DAK mailer also makes use of another technique mentioned earlier: It makes the offer more believable because it tells the reader what the seller stands to gain.

ADDITIONAL LEGAL ISSUES

Review your advertising—what is said and what is omitted—to guard against deception. To assist your review, here are six advertising standards, offered by direct marketing attorney Robert Posch, which are helpful in understanding how authorities will determine the meaning of your advertising.

1. Who is your audience? The nature of your audience will be a factor in determining whether your advertisement is deceptive. Advertisements directed at vulnerable groups, such as children, who are often governed by appearances and general impressions, receive closer scrutiny than others.

2. Your advertisement will be viewed in its entirety. A total net impression governs here.

3. Literal truth will not save your advertisement, if it is misleading when read in the the context of the entire advertisement. Here you must avoid deception by half-truth or the failure to disclose material facts.

4. An advertisement may be found false and deceptive if any one of two possible meanings is false.

5. Expressions of subjective opinion (*puffery*) are not actionable unless they convey the impression of factual representations or relate to material terms.

6. You have a continuing obligation to make sure all your material claims are substantiated, such as test results, price claims, and endorsements.[7]

Use Tax

For decades states have eyed mail-order sales as a potential source of new tax revenue. In 1967 and again in 1992, U.S. Supreme Court rulings have supported mail-order merchants' claims that they should not have to collect sales or use tax for mail-order purchases, except in states where they maintain offices. Thus if your company is located in Virginia and you sell craft supplies to someone in Ohio, you need not collect an Ohio use tax.

The most recent Supreme Court decision overturned a ruling from the North Dakota Supreme Court. The lower court had said the Quill Corporation, an Illinois-based office supply company, was required to pay the state's use tax on sales to its residents. In the Quill case, the U.S. Supreme Court left it up to Congress to pass a law subjecting out-of-state sales to in-state taxes. Several states are still trying to find ways to get their hands on the additional revenue out-of-state taxes would yield, but fortunately mail-order firms and their trade association lobbyists are, for now, a stronger influence in Washington. If you sell via mail order outside your state, the imposition of use taxes on those transactions is a threat, but not a certainty.

Comparative Advertising

Using comparative ads calls for caution lest you put yourself at legal risk. First, however, you have to decide whether you *should* use comparative advertising. Naming your competitor, so one argument goes, gives him prominence. All your reader may remember from your ad is the other guy's name. Theoretically, I believe you should not give any of your advertising space over to your competitors. Practically speaking, however, I've done it many times, advertising the advantages of credit unions over specific banks, for example. This is a standing issue among experienced advertising people, with strong arguments on both sides.

Try this rule: Only use comparative advertising if you have a distinct and easily recognizable unique selling proposition that your competitor does not have. Two corollaries follow: (1) Don't advertise minor differences or even major differences that require extensive explanation. (2) Obtain substantiation for your comparison claims *before* you advertise them.

Recently, firms have used a 1946 federal statute, the Lanham Trademark Act, to sue advertisers who use comparative ads. Courts have permitted companies that claim their products have been misrepresented to sue under Section 43(a) of this act. In one case in particular, a U.S. District Court awarded a $40 million judgment to U-Haul International, which claimed that a competitor, Jartran Corporation, violated the Lanham Act and engaged in unfair competition. The court said that Jartran used a promotional rental rate and compared it, in an ad, to U-Haul's regular rate.[8]

Although the FTC seems to encourage comparative advertising, because it promotes a full exchange of information that consumers can use, make certain, when you compare yourself, that you can prove all of your comparisons. You may have to.

Warranties

Although the FTC does not require one, a written warranty is helpful in establishing credibility in direct marketing. If you decide to offer a written (express) warranty, you must then comply with the provisions of the Magnuson–Moss Warranty Act. According to the act, if you specify your warranty as "full" (as opposed to "limited"), you must provide a range of services to customers including the following:

- Fixing or replacing a defective product within a reasonable time.
- Providing a refund or replacement if the product cannot be or is not repaired after a reasonable number of attempts.
- Honoring the warranty for anyone owning the product during the warranty period.
- Paying the cost of returning the product.

The FTC rules require that if a written warranty is offered on consumer products costing more than $15, the warranty be available to consumers before they buy. Mail-order companies must include a statement of the warranty in their advertising or say that they will provide a copy to customers who request it.

Time limits and other limitations on warranties must be clearly and conspicuously stated. The term *lifetime,* when used in a warranty, is open to several interpretations. The lifetime of an automobile muffler, for example, might be as long as the original purchaser owns a car, as long as the car itself lasts, or as long as the purchaser lives. To avoid confusion or deception, the FTC guides advise clearly specifying which "lifetime" is intended.

Further details on warranty requirements are explained in the FTC's *Businessperson's Guide to Federal Warranty Law.* This booklet advises you to investigate the Uniform Commercial Code and your state law's regulation of warranties.

Bait and Switch

Bait advertising is defined by the FTC as alluring but insincere advertising for merchandise the advertiser does not intend to sell. The purpose of the "bait" ad is to switch customers to something else, usually at a higher price.

To determine if your advertising is bona fide, the FTC will consider, among other things, refusal to take orders for the advertised merchandise, or a sales plan that discourages salespeople from selling the advertised product.

Step-up offers, mentioned earlier, are not necessarily a bait-and-switch practice. Offering someone a choice between a one-year subscription and one of a longer duration will usually not be considered deceptive if both are equally available to the consumer.

MORE URGENCY DEVICES

Deadlines

Deadlines will increase your responses. If you have no deadline, potential customers are free to procrastinate forever. And they will. With a deadline, it's now or never. DM beginners always seem to worry about the "never" portion of that last statement. They think that if they omit a deadline, they will avoid losing business from that guy who waited until the day *after* the deadline and then didn't order. In truth, that guy is *still* waiting. And he'll continue to wait until you give him a reason to act now.

Deadlines will not just increase your responses *by* a certain date—they'll increase your total responses, period. The strategy is to make the deadline long enough to give everyone a chance to act, but short enough to give customers a feeling of urgency. Forever is not urgent. Neither is two months.

The problem with deadlines is that they are often artificial and sound that way. People wonder why they have to order by a certain deadline. The way you answer that question will dictate how believable and urgent your deadline will be. Here are several levels of deadlines, ranging from the weakest to the strongest.

1. *Act now. Do it today.* This is better than nothing, but it hardly gets people out of their chairs.
2. *Please respond by Nov. 9.* A specific, yet unexplained, deadline is stronger but lacks credibility. If you can't cite a specific date because of uncertainties in mailing, say, "Please respond within two weeks" or "by the end of the month."
3. *Charter membership requests will be honored only until April 3.* Special charter-member or advance-notice offers build the urgency. To avoid deceptive practices, make certain your offer is limited.
4. *Prices will be going up June 1.* Whether you're reacting to cost increases, inflation, or just changing your pricing structure, this deadline packs a monetary punch. (Be sure you can substantiate it, too.)

5. *Governor Whipsnade needs your maximum contribution by Oct. 28 so that we can keep his commercials on the air until election day.* A deadline over which you have no control, such as a holiday, an election date, or a tax deadline, is the strongest yet. The urgency is universally understood and you need only remind.

If you're a mail-order marketer or telemarketer, you too have deadlines. The FTC's mail-order rule gives you a deadline for shipping merchandise or notifying customers of a delay. For details, see Chapter 17.

Involvement Techniques

Direct response is an interactive form of advertising. It seeks to get the reader involved, ultimately in ordering but also in almost anything that will keep his attention. Headlines are written with promises that pose questions or with half-told tales. The purpose is to draw the reader into the advertising and make him a part of it. When your advertising gets your prospects to *do something,* you've accomplished an important first step toward the sale.

Tokens, stamps, and scratch-off cards are some ways to get readers involved, but these devices are often expensive to produce. Another way to involve your readers is to ask them to select a prize they would like to win in your contest. To make that choice, a reader pauses and thinks about your contest offer—exactly what you want him to do, right?

Quizzes can be used to involve your readers and make them think. Make your questions relate to your service or product, but don't ask self-serving questions, such as, "Which company is dedicated to serving all your copier supply needs?"

Use your imagination to think of ways to involve your readers with your product. One of the most intriguing involvement devices I've seen was a packet of litmus paper mailed with a small bar of Dove® soap. Instructions told you to wet your current soap bar and the sample of the Dove beauty bar. Then you were to apply a piece of litmus paper to each. According to the instructions, if the paper turned blue or green, it meant that your current soap was alkaline. The paper would not change color with Dove, you were told, because Dove was nonalkaline.

A chemical company used a similar technique in a mailing to chemists. In one advertising package, the company sent samples of its chemical product and a sample of a competitor's. Chemists were invited to check out the advertising claims themselves. As a test, the company sent out similar advertising packages that contained the same claims, but without the do-it-yourself samples. The mailing with the samples generated a one-third greater response.

A direct response ad for gourmet mail-order coffee had a flap over the top portion of the ad and instructions to the reader to open it. Opening the flap uncovered a picture showing the top of a coffee container; the ad made the reader appear to open a package of coffee.

Direct mail lets you send samples of your product or service. Some mail-order clothing merchants send fabric swatches. Package goods manufacturers mail small, sample-size boxes of their products. Direct marketers have mailed plastic phonograph records, cassette tapes, and tickets to events.

What can you mail that will give your reader a sample of your offer? Lumpy packages invite your potential customers to open them. Some marketers have used $1 bills as attention getters in mailings, but I think a 50-cent piece (are there any in circulation these days?) or a quarter will have greater appeal, because they can be *felt* through the envelope. The National Pen Company mails a sample pen in their envelopes, and small paperback books have even been mailed in fund-raising campaigns.

POSTSCRIPTS....

Regulatory Updates

Trade associations can be excellent sources of legal and regulatory information about advertising and promotion in your particular profession or industry. Their advice can sometimes be worth the membership fees. Some associations offer legal/regulatory seminars and publications. If you don't have access to a trade association, you can get help on advertising through independent regulatory update services. (See Appendix B.)

One Reason for Legal Review

Legal/regulatory compliance can be tricky sometimes. Consider the word "only." As discussed in Chapter 7, it is a key ingredient in unique selling propositions. But the word can have extended implications. When you say your product is the *only* one to have certain attributes, you are, in effect, doing comparison advertising by comparing your product to all others. Lawsuits have been based on this point.

Guidance from Newspapers

Most newspapers have guidelines for the acceptability of advertising. Some are more discriminating than others. Some newspapers, including the *New York Times,* publish their guidelines, which may include discussion of substantiation of claims, appeals to minors, mail-order responsiveness, and other subjects. While many papers will include a summary of requirements with their rate cards and advertising materials, it's a good idea to discuss the subject with your newspaper account executive. Many newspapers, such as the *Los Angeles Times,* for example, require all direct marketers to list a street address in advertising, in addition to post office boxes. They also may ask to see samples of direct mail products before advertising runs.

Watch Your Asterisk

Qualifers often take the oomph out of advertising and asterisks are the universal symbol of a qualified statement in direct response. Avoid them whenever you can. Often you can provide the substantiation or qualifications you need without resorting to the asterisk. If you have to use an asterisk to provide a legal qualification of some claim, perhaps the claim is not as strong and persuasive as you thought.

11 THE POWER OF LETTERS

Direct, Person-to-Person Communication

...cleverness must give way to clarity and "show biz" to the business of being understood.

—Stan Rapp and Tom Collins
The Great Marketing Turnaround

A letter is the most persuasive, personal, and effective form of direct mail marketing and at the same time the least complicated for you to produce. To promote your product or service, just write a letter to prospective customers and tell them about it. It's that simple.

With a letter, you're using a format that has been tested by the millions over decades. It's the medium that every company uses, regardless of its size. Carefully written and printed, your letter will get results.

Letters are so effective that you should use them in more than just classic packages. As we've seen, letters can be incorporated into self-mailers and catalogs. Try them in brochures and other printed formats. In a brochure or other printed medium, a letter becomes a focus of attention. It is perceived as more personal or individual than the copy around it, so the letter can set a tone, introduce a product or idea, and direct readers' attention to other parts of the advertising. Never mail a brochure or a booklet by itself in an envelope. Add a letter, even a short, simple one, and watch your responses increase.

WRITTEN CONVENTIONS

The persuasive strength of a letter lies in its outward simplicity and its individuality. It's simple communication, not splashy advertising. Next to the human voice, a letter is the most personal way to communicate. Even people who rarely if ever receive personal letters recognize the intimacy letters embody. Although they are an imitation, advertising letters possess many of the same qualities as personal letters.

The first lesson in writing direct mail letters is that a letter is a communication from one person to another. To make your letter carry all the weight it can, you should write it to one person. Even if your letter is going to be read (you hope) by thousands or tens of thousands of people, it must be written to just one. By focusing on one person, rather than a group or an entire market, your words will take on a singular quality which gives letters the personal touches they must have.

When you know that each copy of your letter will be personalized with an individual's name and address, it may be easier to remember that you're writing to one person. Even the letters that will not be personalized must begin with singular salutations. If you're writing to a group of dog owners, you don't begin with, "To all dog owners" or even "Dear Dog Owners." You say, "Dear Dog Owner." Focusing on one reader, rather than thousands, encourages you to say

You'll avoid the distressing feeling of watching your dog scratch when you use Fido Shampoo

rather than

Everyone will avoid...

or, worse,

All of you dog owners will...

Writing to one person will change your language in many other subtle ways, making it more friendly, more realistic.

Of course, your reader probably knows she's not the only person receiving the letter. And she knows that her name and address at the top doesn't signify a special message just for her. All the same, writing letters to individuals rather than groups gets results. Much of the communication we receive today at work and at home is impersonal, sometimes intentionally so. A thoughtfully written letter, even an advertising letter, can present a welcome contrast to officious memos, dry newsletters, and emotionless circulars.

In line with this technique, you should never mention that your message is not an individual letter. People apologize for photocopying the messages they send out with their Christmas cards: "I'm so sorry I couldn't write individually to everyone this year, but we've been so busy..." Don't copy this technique in your direct mail. It attracts attention to the nonsingular nature of your letter. An effective direct mail letter ignores the fact that it is a mass-produced computer marvel and focuses on its message.

Another convention of direct mail letters is to speak to the reader, directly and as soon as possible. Brochures, conventional ads, and most other promotional communications begin with claims, facts, or prices. In a DM letter, the sooner you can use the magic word "you" the better.

Finally, don't hide your personality. While "you" is stronger than "I", you can still refer to yourself in a letter. Remember a letter is a communication between *two* people. The price explanation from the DAK mailer in Chapter 10 is so strong because it's obvious the writer is speaking directly to the reader. Some colloquial language, seemingly off-the-cuff comments, and persuasion on a gut level are all acceptable when you want to sound like you.

VISUAL CONVENTIONS

If a direct mail letter must sound like a real letter, it must indeed look like one too—or close to one anyway. Some direct marketers use large headlines in non–typewriter style type to attract attention at the top of a letter. The Rodale Press letter in Figure 11.1 carries the headline idea to extreme. The letter itself doesn't begin until the very bottom, but it continues for five more pages.

Figure 11.2 shows by description and layout some of the conventions used to make a DM letter look authentic. When you study the direct mail you receive at home and at work, you'll see a variety of styles of letters. The ones that stick close to the form of a standard business letter are preferred.

If you want to emphasize something in your letter, you have several choices. Rather than print the type in a different color, which detracts from the look of a hand-typed letter, just underline it with a different color so that it looks like you underlined it with a felt pen. Handwritten margin notes can also be effective, when used sparingly, to point out a benefit or other important point.

Indented paragraphs, double spacing between paragraphs, and unjustified right margins make your letter look slightly more friendly, informal, and easier to read. To make the illusion of an individual letter complete, be sure to include a signature. If you write margin notes or underline any words, sign the letter using the same pen (and handwriting).

HOW TO BEGIN

As with any other direct response writing, you should begin the creative process by focusing on your purpose. A typical DM letter should (1) attract attention and lead the reader into the text of the message, (2) explain benefits clearly, (3) overcome objections, and (4) initiate action.

The headline and the lead are the most important parts. More than just attract attention, the beginning must grab the interest of good prospects and set the tone for the balance of the letter. Leads that arouse without informing fail to bridge the gap from the reader's attention to his wants and needs. If you have a strong offer, that alone can make an effective beginning.

The first paragraph should be no more than a few lines. Short paragraphs at the beginning draw readers in. By the time they've finished reading the first three paragraphs, not only should your readers have had their interest aroused, but they should also have been given enough benefits or information on the offer that they want to continue reading. You can't tease them along for long.

What should your lead say? Here are five ways to begin a direct mail letter. One of these leads should fit any selling situation you face.

1. *Present the offer clearly and attractively.* When people open your DM package and look at your letter, they're looking for an offer. By giving it to them in the first few lines, you'll get the attention of interested prospects. In subsequent paragraphs you may have to expand your offer statement to include all the necessary details, because the lead should be free of lengthy

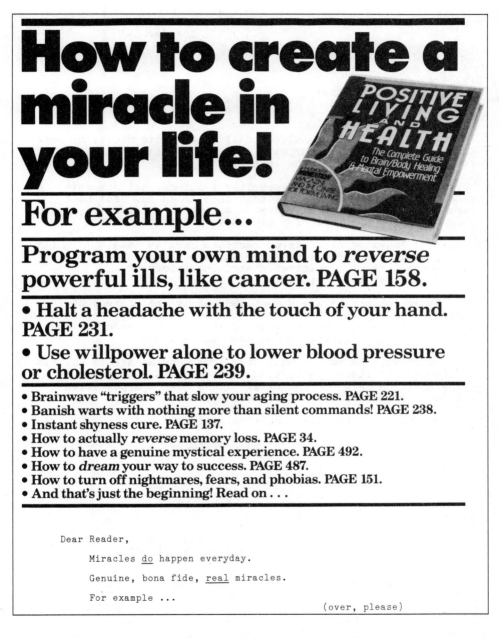

How to create a miracle in your life!

For example...

Program your own mind to *reverse* powerful ills, like cancer. PAGE 158.

• **Halt a headache with the touch of your hand. PAGE 231.**

• **Use willpower alone to lower blood pressure or cholesterol. PAGE 239.**

• Brainwave "triggers" that slow your aging process. PAGE 221.
• Banish warts with nothing more than silent commands! PAGE 238.
• Instant shyness cure. PAGE 137.
• How to actually *reverse* memory loss. PAGE 34.
• How to have a genuine mystical experience. PAGE 492.
• How to *dream* your way to success. PAGE 487.
• How to turn off nightmares, fears, and phobias. PAGE 151.
• And that's just the beginning! Read on . . .

```
Dear Reader,
        Miracles do happen everyday.
        Genuine, bona fide, real miracles.
        For example ...
                                        (over, please)
```

FIGURE 11.1 Version of direct mail letter with large, elaborate headlines. The letter continued for five more pages. *(Copyright 1990 Rodale Press Inc. Used with permission.)*

Tuesday

Douglas Smith
123 Snap Lane
Centerville, CA.   98981

Dear Mr. Smith,

First paragraphs in direct mail letters are short, no more
than three lines. The purpose is to grab attention and lead the
reader into the body of the letter.

Letters are set in a typewriter typeface, not something
fancy that reminds the reader that this is an ad. For best
results use black type on white or off-white stationery. Again,
this simulates the look of a genuine, individual letter.

      Indented or centered sections such as this
      are permitted because they attract the eye to
      one part of the letter containing important
      information or benefits.

Paragraph breaks are determined not by the content of the
sentences as much as by the need to make the letter look inviting.
Long paragraphs discourage readers. Short ones encourage them.
Don't make any paragraph longer than seven lines.

Other ways to make a DM letter look genuine are to use single
spacing and to indent paragraphs. Avoid justifying your
paragraphs. A ragged right margin looks like a typewritten
message, not a computerized advertisement.

Remember to end with a call to action.

          Sincerely,

          Steven Clark

P.S. Here's a must. Postscripts give you a chance to emphasize
      your offer, a deadline, or a significant benefit.

FIGURE 11.2   Letter showing visual conventions of direct mail.

explanations or qualifiers. Examples:

With this letter comes your special RSVP invitation to sample our custom lawn care package at a newly reduced rate.

—A nursery offer

You could turn the equity in your apartments into cash, lots of it...and borrow at a fixed rate of only 11.5% amortized over 30 years, due in 15 years.

—Ja-Va Inc.

I'd like to offer you an opportunity to experience one of our most popular cruises to Tahiti or the Caribbean—at a generously reduced fare.

—Windstar Sail Cruises

2. *State the strongest benefit.* Hit your readers with the biggest reason why they should buy from you. Whether your main benefit is exclusivity, saving money, or staying healthful, tell your readers what they will gain.

I think you're going to be really surprised when you unwrap the free gifts I've reserved exclusively for you.

—Chevron Travel Club

Prove these benefits for yourself...

—Increase your work output by as much as 20–40% or more

—Know everything you must do each day, in order of importance

—Day-Timers, Inc.

Beginning today you can take steps to protect yourself and your family against disability that could cut off your salary and keep you out of work.

—Sanders & Assoc.

3. *Use personal or inside information.* Here is where your database can tell you what to say. What do you know about your customers or potential customers that you can use to attract their attention and show them you have something valuable specifically for them? Are you mailing just to people you know? Computer owners? State employees? People who have bought saddles and other equestrian equipment through the mail?

Living in Shaker Heights separates you from the average homeowner. You enjoy an elite, affluent, more pleasurable lifestyle. Your home is a point of pride.

—Home owner mailing

Because you know me, I thought you'd want to hear directly from me—The Publisher—about this amazing new venture and why it's important to you.

—Linda Kay, the Brainstormer

4. *Use praise or fear immediately.* These two motivators make good beginnings because they can be tied into your offer easily.

Because of your distinguished position in the business world you have been selected to....
A credit card offer

After booting up your system, do you ever feel like you're lost in an electronic publishing jungle—with no way out?

Relax. Now you can slice right through the mountains of documentation....
—United Communications Group

The good news is that almost half of all Americans who get cancer can be cured.

The bad news is that the cost of treating cancer is unbelievably high.
—Mutual of Omaha

5. *Ask a question.* Ask a stimulating, engaging question that someone just can't avoid answering or at least thinking about. The question might cause the reader to consider its ramifications. Ultimately, the question must lead the reader to your offer and benefits. Asking a question can be effective, but it's tricky. You don't want to ask a question the reader can quickly answer with a "no" as he crumples your letter and aims for the waste basket.

If money were no object, would you own the Encyclopedia Britannica?

Will you help me feed at least one hungry person this Thanksgiving season?
—Los Angeles Mission

How close are you to becoming financially secure?
—Rick Ulivi,
Integrated Resources

Suppose that twenty-five years ago the Chairman of IBM had offered you stock in his company and guaranteed to buy it back any time during the first year for the full price you paid....
—The Bradford Exchange

One other type of lead that you will notice as you read direct mail is the story lead. The letter begins with a narrative so interesting that it draws you in to read further. In a few paragraphs the writer shows you how the story relates to the offer, and by then you're supposed to be spellbound. In the hands of careful, skilled copywriters this technique can draw a considerable response. But not just any story will do. It must be compelling, striking, dramatic, and filled with human interest. The most common hazard for beginners is the tendency to start a letter with a rambling, unrelated story. Here's an example:

"Here's an illustration of an executive who might be very much like yourself. This person decided he simply could not afford to spend the time necessary to examine all the vendors who came his way with products and services for sale. Sometimes it seemed that everyone had a special bargain, yet if he had taken the time to check out everyone, he would never have gotten any work done.

"Does this sound familiar? When you receive too much information it can bog down your decision-making process, giving you even less time to consider changes that we've all got to make no matter what type of business we're in. In many industries, well-known names can provide some guidance in the idea of examining and deciding on ways to facilitate decision making, but when you have a limited amount of time and...."

Where is this example going? Does it suggest a product or service? Do you want to read on? Stick with the five tested leads. They will help you to keep focused. And no matter which of the five you choose, by the middle of the first page you should have mentioned, or strongly implied, the details of your offer.

ORGANIZING A LETTER

Although they appear unstructured on a page, DM letters are organized around a few points of emphasis. Here, in order of importance, are the parts of a letter with suggestions on how to use them.

Headline and Lead.   The headline, if you use one, and the first few paragraphs, attract the most attention.

Boxed Introduction.   Instead of a headline, some copywriters begin a letter with a short paragraph or headline-like statement enclosed in a box at the top of the letter. It goes below the company name on the letterhead and above the address and salutation.

Postscript.   Readership studies show that after the head and lead, the P.S. has the highest readership of any other part of a letter. Therefore, do not use it for "oh-by-the-way" copy. Use the postscript to emphasize one of your strongest benefits, a deadline, or some other critically important element of your offer.

Postscripts are read so consistently because they stand out. All the other paragraphs of a letter seem lumped together, but the P.S. stands alone in the white space beyond the signature. You should probably write the P.S. *before* you write the body of the letter, because people will read it in that order too.

Indented Paragraphs.   One of the few other ways to emphasize something in the body of a letter is to box it or float it in the center of the page by indenting both sides. See the third paragraph in Figure 11.2. I've often used an indented paragraph at about the middle of the first page to state the offer. Like other forms of emphasis, use this sparingly. If you only indent one or two paragraphs in the whole letter, they'll stand out. If nearly every other paragraph is indented, nothing will be emphasized.

Conclusion, Call to Action. People often look at the end of the letter to see what you want them to do. Sum up the benefits and tell the reader how to respond.

ESSENCE OF COPYWRITING

I sometimes look at writing direct mail letters as a mental game of cat and mouse. Your purpose is to snare the reader's interest even though his defenses—sales resistance and skepticism—are up. He knows your purpose and he knows that the "personalized" letter is not just for him. He also knows that you know all this too. But if you have something that interests the reader, he'll read on in spite of his skepticism, with his sales resistance *somewhat* in abeyance. If you succeed in persuading him that your product or service would be beneficial, you've only accomplished half your objective. The second half is to overcome apathy and generate a response. To accomplish this, you have to do more than show him the benefits; you will have to make him want the product. Here's where the emotional or motivational link is essential. It provides the impetus, the drive over the inertia hurdle.

In some cases, you are not selling products, or even benefits, but dreams. Dreams of vacations, security for the family, happiness, status, and other needs can all contribute to emotional connections to a sale. While emotions are responsible for a big portion of the sale, you need to supply technical information and the practical benefits—for either business buyers or consumers—so that they have reasons to justify their emotional decisions.

Although all letters are supposed to be sincere and personal, some DM letters appeal to the reader with such an honest-sounding folksiness that the reader no longer thinks of the writer or narrator as a salesperson. When that happens, the reader is more open to make emotional or benefit-oriented connections to the product. Some people seem to know just how much of their personality to put on paper.

Professor Struever's letter in Chapter 9 (Figure 9.4) is so sincere-sounding that it has no hint of a contrived or professionally written appeal. No professional copywriter would have the guts to use up a portion of the all-important lead with a clarification of a person's name. Professor Struever did, because the person is his wife. His letter is unassuming while having a strong appeal to exclusivity. Sincerity or honesty in your language or persuasive approach can often give your letter just the disarming personal touch it needs to be effective.

Question: How long should letters be? Answer: Long enough to make the sale. In other words, it depends. As with other types of direct response writing, it depends on the complexity of the product, the response required, and the demographics of the audience. Business letters tend to be short, consumer letters longer. Four-page letters used to be almost a requirement for most consumer packages, one or two for business. Although long letters (four or more pages) still test well for major mailers, and many direct mail authors still advise long letters, I suggest that you take a close look at the makeup of your target audience before you write. Cover the necessary points in your letter, but keep the interest of your readers in mind at all times.

ENVELOPE TEASERS

First the negative aspects: Most envelope teasers are a guarantee that nothing but advertising lurks inside. This can be particularly ticklish in business mailing, where you want your envelope to get out of the mail room and past the secretary. If poorly constructed, teasers can cause unrealistic expectations, which result in disappointed, possibly angry readers.

Now the positives: Teasers broadcast a message recipients can't avoid. Teasers also lead the reader inside, getting her to look for something specific. For people who might only be mildly interested in looking inside, the teaser teases them and gets them to peek.

Although the balance seems to lean toward teasers, in some instances you might want to leave that envelope blank. If you have a continuing relationship with a customer, your blank envelope might contain a statement, a personal letter, or some other nonpromotional message. Chances are, it will get opened. This is absolutely true in the financial world. If you receive something from your financial institution, you will likely open it even if you're sure it's advertising, because it just might have something to do with your account or your money.

Fidelity Investments nearly bludgeons its investors with direct mail, yet in spite of the barrage, it's impossible to throw an envelope away without checking inside.

An envelope with nothing but a two-line return address intrigues the recipient, because no one knows who the message is from. Bulk rate postage might be a tip-off, but you can reduce the tell-tale signs of third-class mail with precanceled stamps, metering, and laser addressing.

When you do decide to tease, what do you say? One type of teaser, which used to be popular, was designed to make the recipient think the envelope did not contain advertising. These teasers mentioned taxes, used phrases such as "official notification," or otherwise made the package look like something from the bank or the government. You need to be cautious with official-looking envelopes and teasers. Legislation approved by Congress in 1990 requires official-looking mailing pieces to contain disclaimers saying they are not government documents.

The purpose of a teaser is to tease, not to give away the whole story. Occasionally, your offer is so strong that you want to tell your reader on the envelope. If you can, phrase the offer in a way that leaves out one detail or promises a gift or additional benefit, which is disclosed inside. The words *free and how to* and the other attractive headline words work well in teasers. You want to do everything you can to tempt the reader inside, but don't promise anything you can't deliver.

Try to avoid asking your reader to buy your product on the envelope. Remember, to get your reader's interest, you don't first ask him to buy—you show him the benefits you have to offer. When the teaser is used to ask someone to buy, that spoils the illusion that the purpose of the contents are solely to benefit the recipient.

Here's a supposedly intellectual teaser:

How to avoid being hoisted by your own petard.*

This contrived teaser was written for effect. What effect, I'm not sure. The majority of recipients probably don't know what *petard* means and probably don't care. Rather than be drawn inside, the reader may have been insulted. Maybe the writer knows what petard is, but the reader doesn't (but is sure he doesn't have one and doesn't worry about being hoisted by it). The asterisk further weakens the statement.

Here are some almost universal teasers I've collected. They don't refer to a specific offer, but most require an explanation inside:

The unexpected is inside.

Suppose I knocked on your door.

Dated offer, open at once.

The favor of a reply is requested.

Reading time: $3\frac{1}{2}$ minutes.

This last one, and similar approaches, have started showing up on business mail. It tells a busy person she need only invest a couple of hundred seconds to decide if the enclosed is for her or not. Of course there's nothing that prohibits the reader from spending more time, if the copy keeps her attention.

LIFT LETTERS

The *lift letter* is often used to address skepticism in the open. Lift letters are the small, personal notes in direct mail packages designed to "lift" or boost responses. They have labels such as, "Read this if you decided not to take advantage of this offer." Lift letters diffuse skepticism and sales resistance with copy such as, "Frankly this offer sounds so good, I wouldn't believe it either. But I know it's genuine because . . . "

Dear Possible Member,

There are a lot of things in life it's wise to be skeptical about.

But this offer is the real thing.

You can buy four books, for $1 each (plus shipping and handling), read them, then add them to your library. You never have to buy another book from us again. (Of course, I'd rather you did buy, but there's nothing that says you have to.)

Nothing typifies the purpose of a lift letter better than these first three paragraphs from a Book of the Month Club lift letter. Lift letters should be short and printed on note size paper, such as 6 × 8 inches. They should be signed by a person other than the one who signed the main letter, preferably a higher authority. Lift letters should reassure the potential buyer that all is well and say, in essence, that the offer is genuine.

Some direct marketing pros today say that lift letters don't work in business mailings and are ineffective in some types of consumer mail. I have seen lift letters help boost business mail response, however, and lift letters are so inexpensive to produce that they need only lift response slightly to cover their costs.

PROFESSIONAL EDITOR'S CHECKLIST

No professional copywriters are satisfied with their first drafts. They always revise and rewrite, yet many do-it-yourselfers, entrepreneurs, and others expect to be able to write the perfect direct mail letter the first time. Writing a draft of a DM letter, or any piece of direct mail, is just the first step. Editing, revising, and rewriting will make it something worth mailing. Read through your copy and see how your words flow. Is the meaning clear? If anything is open to interpretation, revise it until it says precisely what you intend. First drafts sometimes just form an outline for the following versions. Don't hesitate to rewrite.

Even though direct marketing is copy-oriented advertising, concise writing is still mandatory. The competition for a person's time today demands that direct response copy be lean and clear. Remember, people read advertising voluntarily.

Don't confuse editing with proofreading; they're two different steps. Editing is part of writing. In the editing stage you can, and often do, make major revisions. Editing is done to strengthen the selling power of your words, clarify any possible misunderstandings, and add anything necessary. You may edit and rewrite several times. The words you're reading now were revised five times *before* being submitted to an editor for more work.

Proofreading is the work you do when your writing is done. You check the spelling, look for typos, make sure your prices are correct, and review for correct capitalization and punctuation. Proofing is best done by someone else. When you proofread something you've written, you read it as you meant to say it, not as it actually appears on the page.

Twenty Ways to Improve Your Copy

Here is a list of things to remember when you're editing:

1. Focus on the offer. A successful conventional advertising technique is to make the product the hero. Keep in mind that your offer is the reason you're advertising, so concentrate on it. Be sure the offer is clear and obvious.

2. Avoid stylized writing. The purpose of your style is to communicate the offer. If your language is too cute, clever, or humorous, it can detract from your offer.

3. Write concisely. You can make your writing more concise and forceful in hundreds of ways. Eliminating *of*-phrases is one good way. "Become a member of the club and increase your level of participation by ordering just 25 of the units." Removing the *ofs* in the preceding sentence makes it shorter and more forceful: "Become a club member and increase your participation by ordering just 25 units."

4. Write to *one* person.

5. Reread your first paragraph to be sure it grabs the reader's attention.

6. Use *you* and other personal pronouns. Make sure your letter speaks directly to the reader.

7. Use contractions, simple language, and other techniques to sound friendly and slightly informal.

8. Chose specific, concrete language and avoid generalities, especially when referring to benefits, product advantages, and specifications.

9. Remember, if you have a two-step offer or if you're just offering more information or a free trial, sell the offer and not your product. Focus on the benefits of your trial period, not of buying the product or service.

10. Use neuter, singular salutations when you don't personalize a letter. Say "Dear Refrigeration Executive." Male salutations unnecessarily risk alienating women.

11. Tell your readers what you want them to do. Make it crystal clear.

12. Avoid jargon when writing to people who are not technically oriented. You may understand the technical language of your business, but your customers don't. Jargon is acceptable—indeed preferred—when you're appealing to members of a particular group or industry. Your use of *their* jargon tells them you know what you're doing.

13. Use short paragraphs. None over seven lines in a letter.

14. Write your message for the District Attorney. In other words, assume your message will receive regulatory scrutiny. Check for trigger terms, which require disclosures, and questionable product or service claims. Provide substantiation when necessary, and be sure you clarify which products are covered by your warranty. Are you offering something for free? Is it free? Double check any "sale" pricing. When in doubt, obtain a legal review.

15. Don't overdo attention-getters. Use these devices sparingly: <u>underlining</u>, **boldface**, ALL CAPS, exclamation points!

16. Be sure your letter flows smoothly. One way to find out is to read it aloud and listen to your words.

17. State your prices in more than one way. Give your reader a practical way of grasping your price—so much, for example, per unit, per hour, or per edition.

18. Check the reply card to be sure it contains the whole offer.

19. Check to see whether there is a deadline or other urgency device.

20. Have someone else read it.

POSTSCRIPTS....

Proofread Carefully

Watch out for typos and grammatical errors. Some people may care. Example: I got a letter from a company that offered low-cost keypunching of mailing labels and data base information through facilities located overseas. The letter stressed that the work would be supervised by college graduates who speak English—except they spelled it *english*. The next sentence said, "This group of employees *are* ..." It should have been *is*. If this is an example of the work the company does–and I suspect it's a good example–I will be sure never to use their services.

Miscellaneous Tips

Never end a page of a direct mail letter with the end of a sentence. Give readers an additional reason to turn the page. Don't let the reader think you're finished. Sometimes I play around with the typesetting so that each page ends in the middle of a provocative-sounding statement: "You can save even more money if you ..."

Frankly can be a disarming word in a DM letter, but use it conservatively. If you say it too often, people will wonder if you're telling the truth at other times.

Write your letter *exactly* as you would if it were an individual letter. To emphasize the individual sound of your message, say, "*I've* enclosed," rather than something impersonal such as, "enclosed is."

Remember that your letter is the central element to any direct mail package in which it's contained. People look to the letter for direction. Refer them to the other pieces.

Real letters are dated. If you are confident enough of your production and mailing schedule that you can print a realistic date on your letter, do so, even if it's only the month and year. Keep in mind the range of delivery times for third class. One way to add authenticity to a third-class mailing is to write a day of the week in the corner of your letter where the date usually goes. No matter when the letter is received, the reader can imagine it was written *last* "Wednesday."

More About Salutations

If you don't personalize letters (you can personalize the reply card instead), use a salutation that tells the reader you have something in common with him or otherwise lets him know he's special. Some examples: Dear IBM-PC User, Dear Cruise Enthusiast, Dear Mystery Lover, Dear Fellow Republican, Dear WGBS Viewer, Dear Fellow Space Enthusiast, Dear Friend and Customer, Dear RV'er, Dear Conservationist, Dear Country Music Lover.

When personalizing salutations, using just first names is risky. You may sound friendly, but to some people it will be too friendly. You want to sound personal, but let's face it, you're not on a first-name basis with everyone on your list. If you're unsure of gender, you can use the first and last name, e.g. Dear Pat Wilson.

A veterinarian used to write letters to my dog. It certainly attracted my attention when I got a letter addressed to "Duke." Or was that "Duke Bacon"? I think the letters used to advise him to tell me he needed a booster shot.

Short, Compelling Story

Charity fund-raising letters are the exception to the rule about not beginning a letter with a story. Successful fund-raising letters often begin with a poignant story about an orphaned child, a handicapped person, or someone afflicted with a disease.

If you plan to write such a DM letter, keep your story short. By the third paragraph or so, tell the reader how he can help. And don't forget guilt as a motivator.

Using AIDA

Here's another standard way of organizing a DM letter. The AIDA formula stands for *A*ttention, *I*nterest, *D*esire, *A*ction. You open with an attention-getting statement that relates to your offer or product. Next, you interest your reader in the offer by using benefits. Then you build up the reader's desire to act by answering any questions, countering objections, and providing incentives. Finally, you finish with a call to action, telling the reader exactly what you want him to do.

12 DESIGNING DIRECT MARKETING

How to Attract Readers' Eyes

Art is not an end to itself, but a means of addressing humanity.

—M. P. Moussorgsky

Until recently most direct response advertising was designed by graphic artists who worked with pencils, pens, and rubber cement to draw and paste up finished artwork. Today, with the necessary software and accessories, you can do it all yourself on your computer.

With about a $4,000 to $5,000 investment in computer desktop publishing (DTP), you can do the layout, set the type, and design the finished artwork for all your direct mail and print advertising. If you already have a relatively new Macintosh™ or IBM-compatible personal computer, you'll need to spend even less. Desktop publishing software, a high-resolution monitor, a mouse, a scanner for transferring images onto your hard disk, and a laser printer are the basic ingredients for your computer design center.

Although you can use these tools to start producing layouts and even finished artwork, they are only half of what you need. The convenience of desktop publishing has given small business a variety of new, low-cost options. It has also spawned unappealing, ill-designed advertising. In some respects, the power of DTP needs to be used with restraint. Just because you *can* use six different typefaces in one brochure doesn't mean you should.

This chapter focuses on design principles, the other half of what you need to create direct response advertising that's appealing and easy to read. You may choose to do it all yourself, you can have your artwork prepared by a designer, or you can share the work. This chapter will help you, no matter which method you choose. Included are terms and concepts you'll need to know if you work with a graphic arts professional.

ART, START TO FINISH

Let's start the review of direct marketing design with a brief look at the procedures and terminology involved when you start with an idea and finish up with a completed ad or brochure. This is a synopsis of the design steps for a brochure, from a designer's viewpoint.

Assuming a designer has been given approved copy, he or she first brainstorms to get layout ideas. Usually this brainstorming is done on paper with a pencil. A designer may sketch out several ideas for placement of the design elements, such as body copy, headlines, borders, and artwork. If artwork, such as photographs or drawings, has not been provided, the designer reviews the copy to see how best to illustrate the benefits mentioned.

These preliminary designs may be sketched on paper or drawn on a computer screen. The first-stage drawing is called a *thumbnail* (sketch) and may look like glorified doodling, but it's done to get ideas and arrange the design elements in different ways. The next step is a *rough*. It's usually more detailed than a thumbnail, but it just shows general locations for the pictures and copy. It also shows the number of pages, the format of the brochure, and how it will be folded. A rough will also include a sketchy idea of what the brochure cover will look like.

A designer may show roughs to a client or may select the best idea and do a more elaborate drawing. Clients rarely see thumbnails; such an incomplete drawing provides so little information that it's difficult for many people to visualize what the finished product will look like. If you do the designs yourself, you should use the thumbnail and rough steps to experiment and refine your ideas.

The next stage in the design is a comprehensive layout, called a *comp*. The amount of detail in a comp varies. At minimum, a comp will be a full-size layout, drawn with colored markers to show the approximate ink and paper colors to be used. With computer assistance, a comp may also include reproduction of some or all of the major headlines and artwork. In hand-drawn comps, space for headlines is indicated, but not all the words are written in. The comp is designed to give you a good idea of what the final printed brochure will look like.

Using the comp as a guide, the designer then creates the finished artwork, called a *mechanical,* which includes all photos or illustrations, headline and body type, and other design elements. A photocopy of the mechanical will give you a black-and-white version of exactly what the brochure will look like. Final proofreading is done on the mechanical.

Once a mechanical is approved and ready, it's sent to the printer, either by a data link or by in-person delivery of the artwork mounted on cardboard. Further stages in production are reviewed in Chapter 16. Now comes a look at each component of a design.

PHOTOS AND ILLUSTRATIONS

As examples in preceding chapters have shown, you can create effective direct mail and print advertising without photos and with minimal, if any, illustrations. Today, however, visual elements to attract the eye are so important that you should use artwork whenever you can afford it. Photographs help sell products better than drawings, but drawings are sometimes easier to obtain and use. If you take a photograph of a person to use in your advertising, you should obtain that person's permission in writing with a form called a *model release*.

People Are a Must

People are a necessary ingredient in many photos. Recently, when I was selling my car, I looked through a local magazine-format automobile advertising publication. Each page contained about ten pictures of used autos for sale. After skimming through a few pages I noticed how barren and uninteresting the cars looked. At first I thought it was the poor quality of the photography. Then I realized there were no people in any of the photos. The photos were lifeless.

If possible, have people in your photos doing something, not just looking at or pointing to your product. People using your product in real-life settings is best. Before-and-after pictures work well in ads for services. In general, you should use artwork that demonstrates benefits. If lightness or portability is a benefit of your product, show someone carrying it.

Photos attract more attention than other visual elements. When you skim through a magazine, for example, as you turn each page, your eye is drawn to the photographs, whether they're in an ad or illustrating an article. To take full advantage of the attention-grabbing power of photos, you must use captions. Captions on photos (and illustrations and graphs) have the highest readership of any copy in just about any printed medium. People look at photos and then naturally read the captions for an explanation. Don't assume that people will read body copy to find out what a photo is about. In fact, the purpose of photos and captions is to get people to read the body copy, after they're naturally drawn to the captions.

Since more people will read your captions than anything else, fill them with benefits. Captions in direct mail or print advertising don't serve the same purpose as captions with news photos. You don't describe the picture; you describe the benefits of your offer first, and relate the benefits to the photo second.

There are a couple of exceptions:

- In some simple print ads that have one photo and one block of copy, headlines or, occasionally, body copy may function as a caption.

- In some brochures, designers will use artwork as a mere design element. For instance, a drawing of a palm tree in the corner of a travel brochure doesn't have to have a caption. (If it did though, it would have higher readership than the body copy.)

Where to Find Art

You can obtain illustrations or photos three ways: Do them yourself, hire a professional, or buy stock artwork. Depending on the use, no one option is always best. Buying what is called *clip art* is cheaper than hiring a pro. Clip art is available either in books you can clip from—hence the name—or on computer disks. With clip art, you buy a book or disk and have free use of the material thereafter. The variety of clip art available today lets you create attractive, if not unique, layouts for next to nothing. You have seen many stock cartoons and illustrations from clip books without knowing it.

An incredible array of stock color and black-and-white photos is also available, but use is more restricted and prices higher. Stock photo suppliers' charges are based on the quantity of your printing, the type of printed piece the photo will appear in, and the purpose of the material—information, sales, or other use.

Here's an example: A company paid $360 for a stock black-and-white photo, which was used on the cover of a 10,000-circulation catalog. Since the photo had people in it, the cost was higher than for stock scenic and still-life photos. Although stock pictures without people are cheaper, you can probably find a photographer to do inexpensive local still-life shots for about the same price you would pay for a stock photo. See Appendix A for information on hiring photographers.

TYPOGRAPHY

Your words are the key to selling, and the way your words are set in type dictates how easy (or difficult) it will be for your prospects and customers to read them. Some aspects of typography are subtle and have to be taken on faith, others are, or should be, obvious.

To most people, all type is pretty much the same. As long as the words are readable, most people don't notice typography. As you're reading these lines right now, you're more aware of the words and the meaning than of the shape and arrangement of the letters forming the words. And that's precisely how it should be with direct response advertising! Readability should be the primary goal of type selection. Problems arise when designers, either professional graphic artists or do-it-yourself desktop publishers, select unusual typographical images for their effects rather than for their contribution to reading ease.

Types of Type

Type is classified in several ways. To begin with, most of the thousands of typefaces available come from one of two groups: serif and sans-serif. The word serif refers to the small lines or feet which project from the vertical strokes of a letter. Next, type has a weight and a style. *Weight* refers to the thickness of the strokes and ranges from thin to ultra boldface. *Styles* include condensed, italic, and standard (called book). Finally, type has a *size,* measured in *points*. A point is $1/72$ of an inch; therefore 36-point type is $\frac{1}{2}$ inch high, and 12-point type is $\frac{1}{6}$ of an inch (see Figure 12.1).

You can further organize type, as used in advertising, into headline type and body type. The difference is simply in size. Headlines, or *heads,* are set in larger, sometimes bolder type, to attract attention. The purpose is to make the reader read the headline first. Body type, which contains the body of your message, is set in a smaller, yet still highly readable typeface.

Serif type looks like this because each letter has little projections at the end of the strokes.

Copy in 14-point Times type looks like this.

You can see this 10-point Times is smaller.

Here's 12-point Times Condensed,

and this is Times Italic.

Some sans-serif typefaces, such as this 12-point Avant Garde, have a more modern look.

Here's Avant Garde in bold.

FIGURE 12.1

Leading refers to the amount of space that is inserted between lines of type. The lines of type you're reading now are separated from each other by two points. This is 12-point Helvetica Condensed. Twelve-point type with two-point leading is often referred to as 12 on 14.

FIGURE 12.2

Space between lines of type is another variable. To make type easy to read, lines should not be too close together. For the average body type, there should be one or two points of space between them called *leading* (pronounced "ledding—orginally it consisted of strips of lead between lines of metal type). This space keeps the *descenders* of letters (such as the bottoms of *y*'s and *g*'s) on one line from hitting capital letters and the *ascenders* (the tops) of other letters on the line below. See Figure 12.2.

Now for some guidelines, using this new jargon. Use no more than three typefaces on the same side of a page. You might use a large size of one typeface for a headline, a second typeface for the body copy and, perhaps, a third face for a coupon or other element on the page. In Figure 12.3, for example, a serif typeface called Clearface is used almost exclusively. The main headline is set in 36-point Clearface Heavy. The body copy is set in 12-point Clearface Regular, and the intermediate headlines, called subheads, are set in 18-point Clearface Heavy. (These sizes are obviously smaller in this figure, because the self-mailer has been reduced to fit in this book.) Notice the typeface used for the hospital's name in the lower corner of the coupon.

Now There's A Better Way:

The Saint Joseph Hospital Physician Referral Service.

Good Advice From Caring Professionals. And It's Free!

For your employees, choosing a physician is one of the most important decisions they'll ever make. It's also a decision that's important to you as their employer. You want to be sure they receive the best possible care.

Because a healthy employee is more productive. And proper care also helps reduce your medical costs in the long run.

Most people turn to a friend or acquaintance for advice in choosing a physician, but wouldn't it be better to get a referral from Orange County's leading healthcare facility for over 50 years...Saint Joseph Hospital?

The Number To Call Before An Emergency: (714) 633-DOCS

We've set up a free physician referral line to help your employees find the kind of medical help they're looking for...a family doctor, OB/GYN or other specialist. A doctor who is located close to their home or work and accepts their health insurance plan. The time to act is now... before an illness or emergency arises and they're left without a choice.

The Right Book To Go By When Choosing A Doctor.

We can also provide you with free copies of our Physician Referral Directory. It contains the names, addresses, telephone numbers and specialties of the finest physicians in Orange County.

Best of all, these doctors are all affiliated with Saint Joseph Hospital. That means your employees will receive the finest medical care, not only from the physicians they select, but also from the entire staff of Orange County's most complete medical facility should they ever need to be hospitalized.

Don't Put It Off!

Quality healthcare is one of the most important benefits you can provide to your employees. Our corporate relations staff is ready to meet with you and explain our services in more detail. They'll tell you about our free health risk appraisals and our many other health education services like employee cholesterol and pulmonary screenings. Just complete the attached postage-paid reply card and return it to us today or call (714) 771-8024.

☐ Please forward _____ Physician Referral Directories.

☐ I'm also interested in your employee health programs and cholesterol screening services.

Company Name _____

Contact Person _____

Address _____

City _____ State _____ Zip _____

Phone (___) _____ * of Employees _____

Health Insurance Offered: ☐ Indemnity ☐ HMO ☐ PPO

Name of Insurance carrier(s): _____

SAINT JOSEPH HOSPITAL

The health of your employees is as important to you as it is to them. Let us show you how to get the best. Call **(714) 771-8024** or mail this card today for more information.

FIGURE 12.3 The inside of this inexpensive self-mailer created for a hospital combines a readable typeface, attractive illustrations, and a reply card at the bottom. Size of the original was $8\frac{1}{2} \times 14$ inches. (*Reprinted with permission from Saint Joseph Hospital.*)

FIGURE 12.4 The outside of the self-mailer in Figure 12.3 contains an eye-catching headline and illustration on one panel, the address on another panel, and the front of the business reply card (BRC) on the third panel.

WHICH HEADLINE IS EASIER TO READ? ACCORDING
TO READERSHIP STUDIES, HEADINGS WHICH USE ALL
CAPITAL LETTERS SLOW READERS DOWN.

The Shape of Upper and Lower Case Letters in Headlines
Makes Them Easier to Read.

FIGURE 12.5

Had some of the headlines been set in this modern sans-serif type, it would have been distracting. Used just once in the corner of the brochure, it helps identify the corporate name.

Desktop publishing makes using different typefaces and weights as easy as clicking a mouse, but when you mix too many typefaces on the same page, it becomes a jumble. Words set in different typefaces sometimes fight each other for attention or are not perceived as a cohesive unit communicating a single message. If readers ever start noticing different typefaces, that will be a further distraction.

Capitals

The next rule is violated by nearly everyone, including the highest-paid designers in the country, but the rule will ensure the readability of your headlines (and body copy for that matter). The rule is simple: Never use ALL CAPITAL LETTERS for more than about four words in a row. See Figure 12.5.

Capital letters are harder to read than a mixture of upper and lower case. The generally uniform shape of capital letters, and the reduction of leading between lines (because capital letters have no descenders), simply make the eye work harder to bring the message to your brain. What? No all-capital headlines? Yes, you do see examples of all-cap headlines everywhere, including this book. My only explanation is that designers must think all-caps attract more attention or are more aesthetically pleasing in some designs.

Figure 12.6 shows some of the other options you can choose if you want to make your message more difficult to read. Reverse type can be effective, but only if used sparingly to attract attention. In choosing type, keep it simple. Select upper and lower case letters, with black type on a light background. Furthermore, I suggest you use serif type for body copy. Serif type is what we're all used to reading in magazines, newspapers, and books.

A couple of other good ideas are evident in the hospital mailer (Figure 12.3). First, notice that the body type is not *justified:* The lines of type end unevenly. By comparison, the type in this book is justified: It has an even right margin. *Ragged right* is the terminology for this unjustified type, and it makes reading just a little bit easier.

IF YOU WANT A HEADLINE TO STAND OUT, MAKE IT BIGGER. DON'T SET IT IN ALL-CAPS. WHATEVER YOU DO, DO NOT SET BODY COPY IN ALL-CAPITAL LETTERS. RATHER THAN CALL ATTENTION TO YOUR WORDS AND GAIN READERS, YOU ACTUALLY DISCOURAGE READERS BECAUSE ALL-CAP TEXTS MAKE READERS WORK HARDER. COPY LOOKS UNINVITING.

Even worse than setting body copy in all capitals is the occasional practice of setting it in reverse type such as this. Reverse type sometimes attracts attention, but like all-caps it inhibits reading. WHEN YOU COMBINE REVERSE AND ALL-CAPS YOU MAKE READING BODY COPY ALMOST IMPOSSIBLE. *HOWEVER, JUST WHEN YOU THOUGHT IT COULDN'T BE MORE DIFFICULT, someone gets the idea to use italic type in reverse. I once received a brochure that had two entire panels printed in reverse, including one paragraph in reverse italics. The brochure came from a communications association too!*

FIGURE 12.6

The second good idea here is to select for the headline a type size that is significantly larger than the body copy—in this case, three times as large. The main headline attracts attention and acts as a visual beginning for the page. Another way to make headlines and subheads stand out is to print them in a different color from the body copy. The headlines in the hospital mailer were printed in blue and the body copy in black.

LAYOUT BALANCE

Photos or illustrations, type, and open space are the three main building blocks of an advertising layout, whether it be an ad, brochure, or some other format. The way you arrange and balance the components on a page will determine how you attract a reader's attention and how easy it will be for him to obtain all the information you have.

In the past, the design of direct response print ads and a sizable chunk of direct mail could best be called *busy:* Nearly every available space had type squeezed into it. Illustrations, if any, were small and limited to a picture of the product or, sometimes, the person selling it. Crowded designs can add an urgency to direct response advertising. Some busy, copy-heavy mail order ads generate their own excitement. Ads for investments and money-making propositions lend themselves to busy layouts that look as if they are filled with important, valuable details.

Use of White Space

While busy designs are desirable in some applications, a balanced layout, with the open, airy look of conventional advertising, is better suited to the variety of direct marketing materials a typical small business produces. The biggest difference between the two layout styles, and indeed between advertising that is attractive and advertising that is unappealing, is not so much the use of type or photos, but the use of open space, called *white space* in design lingo. The ad for the book summaries in Figure 8.1 is copy-heavy, yet it uses white space to keep from being too crowded. The type is set ragged right to add white space between columns. Subheadings add more white space because each subheading is essentially surrounded by a little empty space.

White space does not represent, as some people may think, the designer's failure to fill every square inch of advertising space. White space attracts attention by providing a contrast to the type and artwork it surrounds. Even a small ad can use white space to good advantage. The Kryptonite ad in Figure 9.10 uses white space as a contrast for the headline and the upper portion of the product photo. The headline here is in all capital letters, but it's not too difficult to read, because each word is on a different line, thus creating white space.

You can give yourself a design education just by reviewing direct mail brochures and direct response ads and seeing how white space is used.

Endless variations exist for the use of type and artwork. Contrast, harmony, proportion, emphasis, and other concepts can be considered. The levels of sophistication increase when color printing is added to the formula. Several general principles and suggestions, however, should be enough to help you get started in creating your own layouts or in evaluating the work of free-lance designers. The rest of this section discusses some basics.

Five Elements

In a direct response ad, there are usually five main elements: central headline, photo or illustration, body copy, company logo, and coupon. In a vertical format, the elements are usually arranged with the artwork or the headline at the top, followed by the body copy and the coupon. The Peachtree Windows ad in Figure 12.7 is arranged in traditional art–head–body–coupon order. This arrangement leads the eye from the artwork, which attracts initial attention, to the head, then to the short body copy, and then to the response device.

Obviously, the five elements of an ad can be juggled around. The ad for Ansett Airlines, (Figure 12.8) attracts attention primarily with the Australia-shaped coupon, which also serves as the main artwork. Even though this ad deviates from the traditional order, its design is still effective, in part because of its liberal use of white space.

In the NordicTrack ad (Figure 9.9), the five elements are arranged in a horizontal pattern, but the eye is still directed to the elements in approximately the same order as in the Peachtree ad. You tend to read from the headline, to the artwork of the appointment book, to the body copy and the coupon. When you're just starting out in advertising, it's easiest to create effective, eye-catching ads if you work with the five elements in approximately the traditional order.

Providing an eye path is one goal of a balanced layout. No matter where you place your central focus, such as across the top or across the bottom in a wide brochure, you should consider arranging the elements to lead the reader through your story. In some cases, your layout can direct the reader with numbered instructions. An imaginative brochure layout can simplify an otherwise complicated-sounding procedure for ordering a product. Each step can be labeled with a large numeral and arranged in list fashion.

When the copy comes before the layout, you should look at the copy and ask yourself how you can make it inviting, valuable, and easy to read. Large blocks of copy, as in a brochure, can be lightened up, first with white space, and second with photos, line drawings, graphs, and any other visual elements which help explain or expand on the written words.

The hospital self-mailer (Figure 12.3) looks more copy-heavy in its reduced form here than the original 8 1/2" × 14" mailer does. Nevertheless, it uses small line drawings and white space to balance the type, and it provides a simple downward eye path: from the main head to the body type and illustrations, down to the response device. The eye path on this mailer actually starts with the teaser headline and illustration on the outside. (Figure 12.4.)

Grid Designs

One common way of creating an effective layout balance is to use a grid that divides the page with equally-spaced horizontal and vertical lines, creating a checkerboard. The lines are used to align copy, headlines, art, and even white space. The vertical lines form columns, as in newspapers.

The NordicTrack ad could have been designed on a layout grid with four vertical columns. Two of those columns are nearly filled up with the illustration. The other two hold body copy, coupon, and logo. The headline travels along a horizontal line and is flush with the left and right edges of the imaginary columns.

We'd Like To Put 600 Windows And Doors In Your Mailbox.

When you buy a Peachtree Door or Window, you get the industry's most innovative designs, most advanced materials and longest warranty.* Just mail in the coupon, give us a call, or stop by and see all the Peachtree products in decorated settings.

Peachtree Planning Center

PEACHTREE
DOORS AND WINDOWS

Free Brochure

For a comprehensive brochure on the broadest line of windows and doors, give us a call or just mail in the coupon below.

I plan to: ☐ build ☐ remodel ☐ replace

Name:_____

Address:_____

City:_____State:_____Zip:_____

Mail To:
(Dealer Name and Address)
Or Call:
(Dealer Phone)

---

*Ask for complete warranty details at your Peachtree Planning Center

FIGURE 12.8 Unconventional in placement and shape, this coupon stands out. Adding another layer of design complexity, the ad features the silhouette of people in a light background screen. (*Used with permission from Ansett Airlines*).

In some designs the checkerboard squares are small; in others they're larger. Sometimes many of the imaginary squares are left open for white space. Look at the inside of the cellular telephone self-mailer (Figure 9.5) and see if you can imagine a grid as the basis for the design. Imagine that the page is divided by six vertical lines, which match up with the six columns of type, and about four horizontal lines. Some of the resulting squares are empty, some contain type, and the rest contain artwork.

Newsletter design is even more regimented by columns. Each separate article begins with a headline, and the copy is often divided with subheadings.

FIGURE 12.7 Designed as a $\frac{1}{3}$ page lead generation ad, this layout (on p. 188) uses an illustration, headline, body copy, and coupon in traditional order. (*Used with permission. ©1990 Peachtree Doors, Inc.*)

FIGURE 12.9 A sofa-shaped coupon helps add interest in this advertisement. Notice the unusual typeface for the company name. *(Copyright 1990 Stanley Steemer International, Inc. Used with permission.)*

Most of the general suggestions for typography apply to newsletters too. If the format closely resembles a newspaper, that adds to the urgency and immediacy of the copy.

Coupons

Coupons are usually at the bottom or the bottom right corner of ads, to make it easier for the reader to clip and mail them. In this location, the coupon is where people expect it, and it's at the end of the eye path. In the book summaries ad (Figure 8.1), the coupon is at the bottom of column three, at the end of the narrative.

The Ansett Airline coupon (Figure 12.8) is the exception, but a worthwhile one. The coupon visually communicates the essence of the offer: The shape tells you it's for Australian travel, the dotted border tells you it's asking for a direct response, and the "25% off" means a money-saving offer. The Stanley Steemer ad (Figure 12.9) has a coupon at the bottom, but the shape is slightly unusual. It visually communicates the idea of a discount on sofa cleaning.

In direct mail, many coupons are rectangular business reply cards (BRCs). Self-mailers and some brochures may have attached coupons or BRCs. As a design element, the coupon can be integrated into the brochure, or it can stand out to call attention to the idea that action is requested.

OTHER DESIGN ELEMENTS

Although not strictly a design element, paper is an important factor in the effectiveness of printed material. The paper you choose for your direct mail carries a strong message to the reader. Flimsy, inexpensive paper communicates a message through the finger tips even before the recipient has read a word. Conversely, heavy textured stock can convey an image of high quality, regardless of the product or offer.

Through your selection of paper, discussed in more detail in Chapter 16, you control the feel of your mailing pieces, the quality of the artwork reproduction, and, of course, the weight, which may have an effect on postage costs. Consider the selection of paper as a consequential decision in the creative process.

Here are some of many possibilities:

- Newsprint paper can be used to convey a feeling of immediacy, especially if you print something that looks as if it came from a newspaper. Newsprint can communicate frugality, because it's obviously inexpensive paper, whereas a light bond paper might simply convey cheapness.
- Heavy, shiny, coated stock carries a rich, formal look and feel.
- Heavy weight, rough-surfaced, speckled paper communicates high quality too, but without pretension.
- Colored paper can add excitement if it's bright, or inject a somber or refined tone if dark or dull colors are used.
- A manila envelope gives an entirely different message from that of a textured, sparkling white one.

Graphic Artists' Tools

To highlight or balance a layout, here are some other design elements you can use and their technical definitions:

Bleed   A bleed is any portion of a design that runs off the edge of the page. The photo at the top of an ad might bleed off the top and sides, but the bottom of the ad might have the body copy surrounded with white space. If the outside of your brochure is completely covered with ink, it's a full bleed.

FIGURE 12.10   One of the best ways to get people to read about the individual benefits of your product is with *call-outs*. In this portion of an ad for Boyt attaché cases, artwork and copy are combined to provide many points of interest in the layout. Call-outs can be effective in getting people interested in direct mail brochures. (*Used with permission.*)

Box   A box is simply a line or *rule* around a block of type or a photo. This design technique makes one area stand out from another. A coupon is a form of box.

Dot Pattern (also called a screen)   In order to print photos and some drawings, artwork is converted into a pattern of tiny dots. Look at a printed photo under a magnifying glass and you'll see the dots. The number of dots used indicates how clear and sharp the photo will appear. The number of dots per inch is referred to as lines per inch. An 85-line dot pattern, will produce a fairly grainy photo, while a 150- or 200-line screen shows minute details. A reproduction of a photo using a dot pattern is called a *halftone*.

Reverse   This refers to white type, not only on a dark or black background, but sometimes "reversed out" of a photograph. The visual effect is that of letters printed on a photo, but in fact it is the paper color (usually white) that shows through the photo where ink is not applied to the paper.

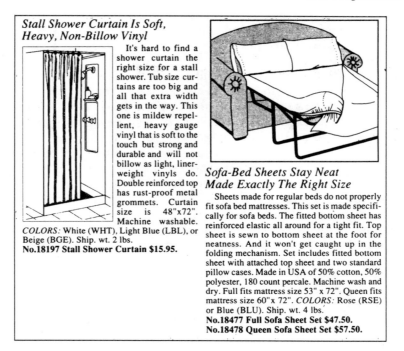

Stall Shower Curtain Is Soft, Heavy, Non-Billow Vinyl

It's hard to find a shower curtain the right size for a stall shower. Tub size curtains are too big and all that extra width gets in the way. This one is mildew repellent, heavy gauge vinyl that is soft to the touch but strong and durable and will not billow as light, liner-weight vinyls do. Double reinforced top has rust-proof metal grommets. Curtain size is 48"x72". Machine washable.

COLORS: White (WHT), Light Blue (LBL), or Beige (BGE). Ship. wt. 2 lbs.
No.18197 Stall Shower Curtain $15.95.

Sofa-Bed Sheets Stay Neat Made Exactly The Right Size

Sheets made for regular beds do not properly fit sofa bed mattresses. This set is made specifically for sofa beds. The fitted bottom sheet has reinforced elastic all around for a tight fit. Top sheet is sewn to bottom sheet at the foot for neatness. And it won't get caught up in the folding mechanism. Set includes fitted bottom sheet with attached top sheet and two standard pillow cases. Made in USA of 50% cotton, 50% polyester, 180 count percale. Machine wash and dry. Full fits mattress size 53" x 72". Queen fits mattress size 60"x 72". COLORS: Rose (RSE) or Blue (BLU). Ship. wt. 4 lbs.
No.18477 Full Sofa Sheet Set $47.50.
No.18478 Queen Sofa Sheet Set $57.50.

FIGURE 12.11 Catalogs don't have to be lavish and colorful to be successful. Here are examples of illustrations from the black and white catalog of the Vermont Country Store. (*Used with permission.*)

Screen This term refers not only to a dot pattern, but also to an overlay of light color used to highlight all or a portion of a page. A screened block of color can highlight material, much like a box. Screens are measured in percentages with a 10 percent screen being a light overlay and a 100 percent screen being a solid block of color.

Logos

One design technique that small business can learn from big business is use of a unified visual image. J. C. Penney, a retail chain which is also one of the top three leading mail-order sellers in the United States, presents essentially one graphic image to the public on all its advertising including direct mail, print advertising, and even in-store point-of-purchase displays. By using the same company logo, similar design principles, and even the same typeface for ads, the company establishes one image and reinforces it at every opportunity.

Small businesses need to make even greater use of every bit of advertising, because they do not have vast media budgets that allow them to plaster their names all over magazines, newspapers, television, and direct mail. Each ad or piece of direct mail is an opportunity for a small business to reinforce one central company image or theme. This principle has been used in conventional advertising for years, but only recently have direct marketers begun to tap into the benefits.

One primary way to maintain a unified image is through a logo. No more personal, potentially controversial, or unnecessarily complicated design issue faces a small business executive than creating a logo. While some start-up companies sink thousands into professional logo development—sometimes without deciding on a satisfactory symbol—you may not need one, at least just yet. You can simply have the name of your company set in a unique or attractive typeface. Even a simple sans-serif face can be effective. Use your name in that typeface every place you would use a logo.

The reason the selection of a logo can be so disruptive to a company is that everyone, regardless of his or her background, will give you an opinion on a logo design. On the surface, developing a logo seems just a matter of personal taste. Quite the contrary: Designing an effective, flexible, and unique logo is a challenge even for an experienced designer.

Some day, when you have a little advertising money left over, you can hire an independent designer to come up with a logo for you. Remember that the fewer people you include in the decision process, the better. I know of a company that spent thousands of dollars on professional design work, then adopted a logo that a member of the board of directors drew on a napkin.

Whether you have a professional logo or use your company name in a typeface you select, use that image every place your name appears. In addition to your advertising, remember to use it on checks, letterhead, newsletters, business cards, shipping labels, invoices, memo forms, order blanks, postcards, signs, name badges, fax cover sheets, and anything else you can think of.

POSTSCRIPTS....

Return Address Label

If you want your mailing to have the outward appearance of a personal letter, try using a plain envelope with a small return address sticker that has just your name (not your company name) and your address. These return address labels, like the kind you receive free in charity solicitations, are often used by people for their personal mail. This idea has not been overused by direct marketers yet, so it should be effective in getting your envelopes opened.

Ransom Note

When you mix too many typefaces on the same page, your message can look like a ransom note, the kind movie gangsters make by cutting out words from magazines and pasting them on paper.

The only time that might work is when you want something to look like a ransom note. That typographical hodgepodge is exactly the effect the Book of the Month Club wanted when it used a ransom note–style headline in an award-winning mailer for mystery books. "We have what you're looking for so do exactly as we say..." the copy said.

Fitting Copy

When you're writing advertising copy, it's helpful to have an idea of how much space your words will take up. Some computer programs may help you with that, but here's a general guideline. One full page of typing, double spaced, using pica size type, equals about one column of type on a standard magazine page.

13 CAMPAIGNS AND CASES

. . . .

Putting It All Together

> *When I say "our kind," I mean people who like pizza. Our kind eat 90 acres of pizza a day.*
>
> —L. M. Boyd

When Steve and Linda Green took over an aging Domino's Pizza franchise in Buffalo, New York, in the mid-1980s, they added a new ingredient that made sales soar. They didn't experiment with cheese or add spicier pepperoni; their recipe for success was data base marketing.

They developed their data base; segmented customers; created special offers for different groups; sent out attractive, targeted messages; then analyzed the results and modified their plans as necessary. Through use of a data base, the Greens brought such an efficiency to pizza marketing that they're now conducting direct marketing programs for pizza stores, and other small retailers, all over the country.

Developing a single direct mailing, not to mention an ongoing direct marketing campaign, requires combining a variety of disciplines, but the process is not unmanageable. For some small businesses, data base marketing can be relatively simple yet deliver powerful results.

PLANNING A CAMPAIGN

Once you understand the main concepts that we've been covering so far, you need to apply them to your situation. Doing that requires you to focus simultaneously on implementing broad campaign ideas and on keeping an eye on many details. Through examples and suggestions, this chapter shows you how to combine the direct marketing concepts to form a campaign. You'll see how you can make money with effective use of the three direct marketing elements: lists, offers, and creative work. For checklists to help you handle the many production steps that make up direct response advertising, see Chapter 16.

So far I've used the term *strategy* rather broadly, but now it's time to get more technical. Short-term marketing decisions and actions constitute *tactics*, whereas strategy is concerned with longer-term planning. When you combine many of the tactics, such as list selection, media buying, and creating offers, you have a strategy, which often dictates the scope of a campaign: a coordinated advertising effort aimed at accomplishing a stated objective. Usually the term *campaign* refers to more than just one mailing or one ad, and it covers planning, follow-up, and promotional support.

No matter how simple or complex, a campaign must be planned every step of the way. The planning is not glamorous, but once it's done, you can move on to the less tedious work of creating your ads or devising your media buy. Because it is an extension of your business plan, a campaign strategy should be aimed at accomplishing a specific and measurable goal. To ensure success, the strategy and the goal should be in writing.

• •

Steps for Waging a Successful Campaign

1. Evaluate resources.
2. Review the business plan, identify problems, and set goals.
3. Conduct research as necessary.
4. Set a budget.
5. Assign tasks.
6. Develop a time line and production schedule.
7. Select media.
8. Integrate direct marketing with sales, PR, and other media.
9. Plan order fulfillment and lead follow-up.
10. Create the advertising.
11. Buy space and lists; conduct mailing.
12. Follow up on leads and orders.
13. Analyze results.

• •

Planning and Goal Setting

The resources you have available may or may not be a final determinant of your goals, but you need to take into account your staff work load and the amount of staff time you'll need, not only for researching and creating the advertising, but also for responding to the new business you'll generate.

You can identify your campaign goals in many ways, but whatever method you choose should be quantifiable. "Increasing business" and even "generating more high-end sales" are not adequate goals, because they are not measurable. Most small business marketing advisors tell you to have measurable goals, but when you try to measure conventional advertising, you can only judge by trends and total sales figures. You may not know exactly what worked or didn't work. With the accountability of direct marketing, your goals are even more important, because you should be able to discern the specific tactics that helped you accomplish the goal. Then you can repeat the success.

Even if you simply pick an arbitrary sales volume or response level, you'll have something to work toward, a specific objective you and your employees can focus on. In many cases, of course, you will have past marketing results, industry averages, or other research to guide you in developing goals. Set your sights high, but make your goals attainable.

Communicating campaign goals clearly to all staff may be even more important than communicating company objectives, although both are vital. The smaller your firm, the more you may assume that everyone knows where you're going. But if the president, owner, or marketing manager does not clearly identify the advertising goals and strategies, employees may be working in different directions.

Your planning should also consider past marketing problems. Such challenges as an excessively high percentage of incorrect addresses in your house list, customer complaints about slow order processing, or a rapidly growing competitor should be addressed in a written campaign strategy.

Budgeting

Setting an annual advertising budget is viewed by some business owners and marketing managers as a curse. Setting a budget for individual campaigns is not much more attractive. Often, arbitrary limits are set, based on available funds. Ideally, your goals should dictate the budget; allot the money necessary to accomplish the goals. Keeping an eye on your available capital also helps keep goals reasonable, but the processes of budgeting and goal setting often alternate between chickens and eggs. Which comes first?

When I'm selling an advertising budget to a client or boss, I present the amount of money as an investment. In some cases you advertise just to stay in business, but if you have confidence in your plan, you should be able to see the profits at the end of the campaign and treat them as dividends on the advertising investment. Mail-order direct marketing allows you to be even more specific. Expected sales percentages give you monetary goals you can use to establish a budget and thus a profit margin. Viewed as an investment, the job of budgeting for advertising is not so onerous.

When I was marketing director at Orange County Federal Credit Union, there were several stock methods financial institution marketing managers used for determining, or perhaps justifying, an annual budget. Some people advocated spending a certain number of dollars per customer or member per year. Others preferred to set the budget using a percentage of assets or a percentage of gross income. Some marketing directors increased the previous year's budget by a hefty amount and then hoped the president or board of directors wouldn't axe too much.

There are various budgeting formulas in different industries. The main purpose of a stock formula should be to justify or compare a budget you prepare based on your actual anticipated needs. Set up a proposed budget first, then compare it to industry benchmarks and see where it falls. To find benchmark figures for your field, consult a trade association, trade journals, or colleagues.

Establishing a budget for a specific campaign can be more mechanical and precise, because you can set list sizes, numbers of publications, and sizes of ads. If you add together your estimates for the cost of each ad or mailing, you arrive at a campaign budget figure; adding the campaigns together gives you an annual budget.

If you're just starting out in direct marketing, you don't have the costs of past campaigns to tell you how much you might have to spend, so you will have to obtain rate cards, printing estimates, media directories, and other sources to help you identify what your expected costs will be. When you add up all the costs, you'll come up with a cost per thousand (CP/M) for each medium you use.

Assigning Tasks

Effective corporate managers delegate; owners or small business presidents often try to do everything themselves. The more you delegate, the more time you have for planning and analysis. Remember, if you have few employees you can still divide up the work and assign tasks to freelancers, agencies, brokers, and other outside help. Make sure everyone knows what he or she is responsible for and how each task is important to the entire campaign. Set deadlines and follow them up.

Setting the Timing

A schedule is essential. Everyone must know what needs to be accomplished and by what deadline for each step of production. At the direct marketing agency Krupp Taylor, Executive Creative Director Craig Walker says he insists on a written creative plan, which everyone follows through to completion. See Chapter 16 for a sample time schedule.

Selecting Media

Although Chapter 3 covered the subject in detail, the next chapter, on business-to-business direct marketing, provides additional suggestions on selecting and buying media.

Integrating the Campaign

Technically, direct marketing doesn't require complex, integrated campaigns to be effective. One direct response ad, carefully created and placed in the right publications, can yield money-making results even if the reader has never seen the company name or product before. For a small business, however, image and cumulative effects of advertising and public relations may be important, especially if direct marketing is not your only form of advertising and mail order not your only source of income.

A small business campaign should include as many ways to gain exposure and make sales as possible. "Integrated campaign" almost sounds redundant, because when you decide on a goal for a campaign, you should pursue that goal every way you can. Every contact an employee has with a customer is an opportunity to communicate your promotional message. Every piece of routine mail you send a customer is a chance to include a response device. If you can afford to reach your target group with more than one publication or medium, do it. With advertising space and postage costs increasing, you should never miss an opportunity to promote.

The concept of unity through consistent advertising design, discussed in Chapter 12, applies to campaigns. If you have a particular way of phrasing your offer, a unique logo for a contest, or a campaign theme, repetition of those elements will help you multiply your impressions and responses.

Publicity can add another dimension to a campaign and can actually generate direct responses. Select the media for your publicity the same way you do for advertising. You want your publicity to reach the same audience. Many trade publications have special sections for new product stories and photos. Some give preference to advertisers for such features, but you should send all your publicity to all publications and stations in your industry and geographical area, regardless of where you advertise.

To receive favorable responses from editors, news releases should contain news. Here are some standard occasions for issuing news releases: introducing a new product or service; opening a new business; staff additions or promotions; industry awards or recognition; acquisition of a new, large client or contract; and charitable contributions.

Beyond these routine stories, you should think about human interest or feature story possibilities. Do you have an unusual product or service? Have you solved a business or industry problem that has plagued others? Is there anything about you, your business, or your employees that is out of the ordinary? The point of a feature story idea is to interest an editor in writing about your company because the story would intrigue many readers. Read industry publications and local newspapers to identify the different types of feature stories they use.

Serving Customers or Clients, Fulfilling Orders

Before the first label is applied to the first envelope in a direct response campaign, you should be ready to answer your first replies. Orders and leads are valuable only if you respond to them soon. That's common sense, but I know of companies that collect reply cards until someone has "time to deal with the hassle." Usually that happens in larger companies, where employees don't know the value of each new prospect.

These campaign steps are general guides. Depending on your experience, you may need to spend more time on some steps than on others. For a look at typical direct marketing applications, and to review principles discussed so far, here are some examples.

PIZZA MARKETING

"The demographics of people who eat pizza are pretty similar to people who breathe oxygen," says Steve Green, president of Green Marketing Resources in Oxford, MS. "Everybody eats pizza."

But not everybody markets pizza the same way, even though a pizza store that delivers is an ideal candidate for precisely targeted direct marketing. Using a data base and targeted messages, the Greens tripled the volume of their Buffalo store in a few months. They ultimately moved south for warmer weather and established a data base marketing firm for small business.

The Greens' pizza marketing approach is elegant simplicity. Recency and frequency, they discovered, are the most useful ways to predict customers' pizza buying behavior. "People who have bought pizza from you before are more likely to buy from you again," says Linda Green.

Demographics and other factors have a place in some data base marketing, says Steve, but with pizza a record of past purchases is just about all they need. The other critical pieces of data are provided by each customer who orders pizza: a name and address. Thus, every Domino's Pizza franchise has the raw data necessary to conduct an effective direct marketing campaign.

The Greens established their marketing firm to take the raw material and create successful marketing programs for individual pizza store owners. The owners are usually so involved in operations, says Steve, that they don't give marketing much attention.

Here's how the pizza-pitching program works: A pizza store provides Green Marketing Resources with names and addresses of their customers for the past three months, organized by order dates. This information is put into a computer, analyzed for frequency, and sorted by addresses. All of a store's customers are segmented into one of three categories: (1) current, established customers; (2) new customers; and (3) fading customers. For direct marketing purposes, a fourth category is added for noncustomers within the trade area.

With its customers identified, the pizza store can then select specific marketing messages for each group. Green Marketing develops postcards, other uncomplicated mailing pieces, and door hangers for placing on doorknobs of local residents. The marketing materials are geared to:

Encourage established customers

Welcome new customers and provide incentives for repeat business

Bring fading customers back or find out why they're not ordering

Attract new customers

Steve likens data base marketing to politics. "A politician doesn't give the same speech to every audience he speaks to," says Green. "He modifies his message depending on the people he's addressing."

The philosophy of traditional advertising, including traditional pizza advertising, treats everyone the same, creating inefficiencies and making it difficult to predict long-term results accurately. Pizza store marketing typically consists of mass-mailing a discount flyer or running a coupon ad in a local paper. Everyone receives the same message. Established customers, who would probably buy anyway at full price, get a discount, whereas new customers may order, but they receive no individual follow-up to keep buying. Fading customers probably look for someone else's coupon.

Mass advertising, says Linda, can generate a one-time boost in sales, sometimes to the detriment of the store because it gets jammed with more orders than it can handle. New customers get a poor introduction. Some pizza store owners are afraid of direct mail, she says, because they associate it with untargeted mass mailings, which can overload their capacity.

A second drawback to mass advertising is explained in a marketing package that Green Marketing provides its clients. Discount advertising can bring in a wave of new customers to a pizza store, but without a tracking mechanism the owner has no way of knowing whether the business is coming from new customers or old ones. Temporarily bolstered by mass advertising, business can be going up in the short term even while established customers are fading away—a portent of long-term decline. The Greens' tracking system lets an owner identify buying trends and conduct segmented advertising when and where it's needed the most.

Figure 13.1 shows one of the many mail advertising materials Green Marketing Resources has produced. This 12-page new-customer kit contains a welcoming message, nutrition information, coupons, and interesting statistics about Domino's pizzas. Figure 13.2 shows the inside of a one-fold postcard used with fading customers.

Several times I've mentioned the disadvantages of emphasizing low prices to gain new customers. It's often hard to retain low-price buyers without continuous specials. In general pizza marketing, price (aside from Domino's swift delivery) seems to be the focus of advertising. Here again the Greens' strategy departs from the norm. Their aim is to reduce the need to provide deep discounts to existing, satisfied customers. In addition, clients of Green Marketing Resources are counseled against using too high a discount for any market segment.

"Some owners are willing to give a pizza away for free, just to have a new customer try them," says Linda. She advises against this tactic and offers

FIGURE 13.1 This is the cover of a 12-page booklet which new Domino's customers receive. It's the first in a series of direct marketing pieces Green Marketing Resources aims at pizza buyers. (*Reprinted with permission*).

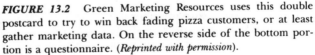

FIGURE 13.2 Green Marketing Resources uses this double postcard to try to win back fading pizza customers, or at least gather marketing data. On the reverse side of the bottom portion is a questionnaire. (*Reprinted with permission*).

specific campaign strategies that attract more new customers while saving money for the store owner.

As a pizza store advertises and gains new business, the staff records customer names and addresses and continues to forward them to Green Marketing Resources to update the data base. The segmented nature of the data base allows store owners to test different offers with different groups to find the optimum appeal.

With help, store owners also prospect for new business. Using lists from Polk, R.R. Donnelley and others, the marketing agency helps owners plan and conduct targeted marketing among people who have not ordered before.

Originally Green Marketing Resources served only Domino's franchises. Now they offer their services to any pizza store that is not in the same trade area as an existing pizza store client. Using custom tracking software that Steve developed, Green Marketing has expanded to provide similar data base marketing services to other small businesses as well, such as video stores.

"Data base marketing really gives the small businessman an advantage over national firms," Steve says, "because he knows his customers."

Points to Remember:

1. Knowing many things about your customers will help you, but avoid gathering more information than you need. Depending on your business, you don't have to collect complex demographics. The three main DM list criteria—recency, frequency, and monetary—may be all you need.

2. There's no substitute for accurate customer records.

3. Segmenting your market lets you tailor your offers and your creative work to gain maximum results with minimum cost.

4. With the right list and the right offer, a straightforward, inexpensive creative package will sell. Postcards sell pizzas by the thousands.

5. If the direct marketing idea of reselling existing customers as economically as possible sounds like common sense and logic, it is. Not everyone in business, however, uses common sense or logic.

CREDIT UNIONS' VALUABLE HOUSE LISTS

At the credit union I worked for, our house list was our biggest marketing asset and greatest limitation. Credit unions (CUs) are not open to the public but only to members of specific groups. Although some credit unions have been permitted to expand membership eligibility requirements, the majority of credit unions are still based around employment by the same company or organization. Since credit unions are closed organizations with limited membership, service is usually more personal than banks', and members are more satisfied than bank customers.

Limited by law from advertising membership services to the general public, I had to focus most of my credit union marketing efforts on existing members. Because of their membership link to the credit union, members responded in remarkably high numbers to our offers of new services and accounts. Our response percentages were sometimes more than double the corresponding responses that banks were getting when they advertised similar accounts and services to the general public.

Our list was a major difference. When the credit union promoted credit cards by mail, for example, our list of satisfied members (coupled with an interest rate offer banks couldn't match) brought double-digit responses.

Credit union members didn't need to be sold on the concept or soundness of the credit union. They knew who we were. Our primary marketing goal was simply to sell additional products and services to people who already knew and trusted us. It sounds simple, and in some respects it was, but the same opportunities are open to you no matter what your business is, once you establish a customer base and carefully maintain your house list.

Credit unions, like any other business, need to add constantly to their customer base, but CUs' opportunities are limited. At Orange County Federal, the membership base included people who worked for the County of Orange, California. All county employees were eligible to join. One of the ways we reached eligible non-members was through promotional material we were occasionally permitted to have inserted in employee pay envelopes.

Later, when I left the credit union and started working for myself, one of the clients I wrote for was Lockheed Federal Credit Union (FCU), which serves employees of the Lockheed Aircraft Co. At Lockheed FCU, where the membership list contained between 35,000 and 40,000 loyal members, the marketing director's plans included expanding to serve more family members. Credit unions are permitted to serve the families of members. In other words, if a person belongs to a credit union, his or her immediate relatives are also permitted to join.

In Lockheed Federal Credit Union's case, this meant that thousands of relatives of members were eligible to join, but the credit union didn't know who they were. The credit union's only connection to this group was through their regular members, so that's how the campaign was targeted.

The idea was to send a mailing to credit union members, but actually aim the package at the members' families. The mailing package we ultimately used was developed through the creative steps outlined in previous chapters.

I worked with designer Don Markofski, whose agency, Don Markofski and Associates, serves many credit unions. We brainstormed for ideas. At each target household, our package would be addressed to one person but aimed at relatives in the house. The letter should be addressed to the credit union member, we thought, but it should tell the member to pass the package along to other members of the family.

That pass-along request might work, we thought, but we wanted something extra. We visualized someone bringing in the mail at the typical credit union member's home, and that helped us come up with several more ideas.

On the outside of the envelope we put a large routing list, like those seen on office memos. This one, however, directed the recipient to "Route to: sisters, brothers, children, grandparents" and other family members. Our next step was to decide that we would make the mailing package so unusual that even if the credit union member didn't pass it along immediately, it would attract the attention of any family member who might see it being opened or see it lying around at home.

The "brochure" which accompanied the letter was a brightly colored, 22" × 28" poster filled with a list of 104 reasons to join Lockheed Federal Credit Union (see Figure 13.3). Since we didn't know the specific needs of all the ultimate readers, we decided to focus on all the credit union's advantages rather than on just one or two. If you have a long list of benefits, you can sometimes use the list itself as the focal point: To avoid fragmented, disjointed copy, which can happen if you try to sell too many things at once, simply highlight the number of benefits itself as if it were the one major customer benefit.

45. Save money when you borrow for a sports car.

46. (People never get tired of saving money on new & used car loans.)

47. Save money when you borrow for a 4-wheel drive.

48. Save money when you borrow for a van conversion.

·times off, too.

an add a turret, t home

8 years,

the Skunk

locations arour

66. Auto and hom

67. Our checking a checking accou Lockheed Fede Which makes r

68.♦92. Two doze to visit your m (Lockheed Fed from Titusville, California).

93. If you're near c specialists in e

Lockheed Federal Credit Union presents 104 reasons to join.

s in the country, ervice. But ke you feel like a

checking

npare that to

credit union as

d has an IRA, heed Federal

art OLIE system

49. Low rates on car loans and speedy service are just part of the special treatment when you borrow. Our Kelley Blue

Book Service can help you decide the value of your old car... and a new car discount buying service is available.

50. You could apply for an RV loan like Bud and Phyllis Gerding did. Bud's now retired and they're on the road enjoying their credit union membership.

51. Automobile mechanical breakdown insurance – with no deductible – is available at **substantial** savings over the cost of extended warranties at car dealers.

94. Here are some don't spend o
• Loans to fc
• Oil or energ
• TV comme
• Endorseme
• Stagecoach

95. For a nice, saf twenty five mi

96. Joint checking

97. Or you could h

98. Manage your r Select maturiti

FIGURE 13.3   This reduction shows the center of the 22″ × 28″ poster for Lockheed Federal Credit Union. The headline was the focus of attention and the 104 reasons for joining were spread out around it. The mailing drew about a 10 percent response from people other than those to whom it was addressed. (*Reprinted with permission from Lockheed Federal Credit Union.*)

24. You can talk to our computer over the phone. Our state-of-the-art QUE system allows you to make transactions automatically from any touch-tone phone, 24 hours, 7 days a week.

25. If stretching every month to cover a bank's high payments and fees is torturing your budget, relax. You can join us. Our low rates and helpful employees can eliminate the strain.

26. A car loan can put you in a Lamborgini.

27. Our VISA Card at a restaurant will pay for fettucini.

28. You can get money from your checking account at 3:17 a.m. on a Saturday at one of our Instant Tellers. (Money is also available at 11:27 p.m. on Monday, at 6:03 on Thursday and at thousands of other popular times.)

29. Things we don't do are important reasons too! Here are a few: We don't charge prepayment penalties on loans like they do at many banks.

FIGURE 13.4 A few of the 104 reasons from the Lockheed Federal Credit Union poster shows the tone of the copy: light humor designed to highlight benefits and uses. (*Reprinted with permission from Lockheed Federal Credit Union.*)

To give the poster even more appeal, we used humor. Light humor, sometimes aimed at banks, was sprinkled throughout the poster and highlighted with cartoons. While nothing was intended to make the readers roll on the floor laughing, nothing would have offended anyone either. I used mostly "safe" puns, rhymes, and other wordplays. The humor was not used just for laughs, but to emphasize specific member benefits (see Figure 13.4.)

The combination of humor, the long list, and a colorful—yellow and purple—poster seemed appealing enough to get family members to see and read it. To make sure, we put the poster in a $9'' \times 12''$ envelope, which was almost mandated anyway by the size of the poster. (We didn't want to fold it too many times, and a mailing tube would have been too expensive). To put more excitement on the envelope, we added the 104-reasons slogan in purple ink and a cartoon with caption on the envelope back.

The results surprised the credit union and kept the staff busy answering the 4,000 people who responded by either calling or returning the BRC.

Points to Remember:

1. Never forget the value of your house list. This program's success was tied to the good relationship between the credit union and its primary members.

2. With ingenuity, you can sometimes appeal to people other than those addressed on your envelopes.

3. Humor does work, but the earlier caution remains: Use it at your own risk. So much alleged humor today, especially the sitcom variety, is put-down comedy. Insults and negative comments may draw noise from a TV show's laugh track, but they can also offend. The purpose of humor is to draw attention to benefits.

4. Give yourself enough time for planning and brainstorming. One idea can lead to another, and, as with this mailing, just one "concept" or idea may not be enough to accomplish your goal.

LANDING NEW ACCOUNTS

The self-mailer illustrated in Figures 13.5 and 13.6 packs a wallop. Except for being reduced to fit in this book, what you see is exactly how the direct mail piece looked when it was sent out. The stark silhouette of the jet fighter, coupled with the boastful, dynamic, and enticing headline, makes it difficult to look at the outside without unfolding the flaps to see what it's all about.

The printing is all black on white, without even any shades of gray or screened areas. This simplicity saves money in the design and printing stages, and yet it contributes to, rather than detracts from, the impact. In today's colorful world, some black-and-white direct mail advertising stands out by contrast, as does the occasional use of black-and-white in TV commercials.

This simple yet successful business-to-business program, based on fundamental direct marketing principles, yielded new business for Visual Dynamics, a firm that produces corporate audiovisual (A/V) programs.

The program was conducted by Greg Smith and Partners, a Southern California advertising agency owned by Victor Productions, also the parent company of Visual Dynamics. The objectives of the program were simple, explains Greg Smith, agency president. Since the best way to sell an A/V production is to dazzle prospective buyers with a sample show, the goal was to get prospects to sit and watch one of Visual Dynamics' multi-projector programs.

The mailing list was a combination of Visual Dynamics' house list and two rental lists of subscribers to *AdWeek/West* and *Sales and Marketing Management* magazines. They used subscribers only from California and further narrowed the outside lists by selecting executives and managers in sales, advertising, marketing, and related fields. After a merge/purge among the house list and the two outside ones, labels were created. The mailers were addressed to people by name and title.

They decided on the one-color, self-mailer format, says Smith, to save money. Although they used all-cap headlines, the copy and artwork work well together to emphasize the offer and make it sound unusual. The copy says the show will include 25 different programs. That sounds time-consuming, but it's also evidence that the presentation will be varied and filled with good ideas the viewers can use. The ultimate product, a stock/customized corporate A/V program, is mentioned, but the mailer highlights the drama and adventure of the special program.

WATCH US LAND AN F-18 IN A HOTEL ROOM.

FIGURE 13.5 Imagine receiving this in the mail so that the message on the bottom panel was all you saw. Could you resist the temptation to open it? (The mailer folds in thirds, so only the address and headline panels show on the outside.)(*Copyright 1990 Visual Dynamics. Reprinted with permission.*)

AND GET BLOWN AWAY BY OUR SAMPLING OF MULTI-IMAGE, MOTIVATIONAL PRESENTATIONS.

Come to Visual Dynamics' Multi-Image Festival and preview multi-image presentations like *Breaking Away*–featuring flight footage of pilots from the famous Top Gun school. This five part, wide screen package uses 15 projectors and projected video to thrill and inspire audiences to reach for greater heights through dedication and teamwork.

HIGH-BUDGET PRODUCTIONS INEXPENSIVELY CUSTOMIZED FOR YOUR MEETING.

You'll preview state-of-the-art, rentable, multi-projector shows–ideal for motivating, entertaining and adding sizzle to your meeting or presentation.

Each show can be customized for your needs. Amidst the theme images and motivational message, slots exist for slides of your firm–people, products and achievements.

And transition points throughout the presentation allow you to tie the theme into your company's meeting or presentation.

With their striking photography and music, these productions originally cost hundreds of thousands of dollars to produce but can be quickly and inexpensively customized for your group.

SAMPLE A WIDE RANGE OF THEMES AND MOTIVATIONAL MESSAGES.

Come to one of our Los Angeles or Orange County showings and experience the latest in multi-image presentations. See 25 different presentations like:

Sharing The Vision. A wide screen package celebrating the individual's contribution to the organization's vision. With its awesome panoramas and powerful soundtrack, this is one of our most popular shows.

Engineering The Future. Using bold graphics and an uplifting musical score, this presentation shows audiences how individual effort can influence tomorrow's world.

Year In Review. A high energy presentation of world events mixed with your company's highlights in the past year.

Great Imposters. A comical and satirical puppet production. Great for meeting breaks.

I'M COMING IN FOR A LANDING.

Save me a seat at the following air show.

LOS ANGELES 11/27 at the Biltmore.
☐ 10AM–NOON ☐ 1:30PM–3:30PM

ORANGE COUNTY 11/29 at the Four Seasons Hotel in Newport Beach.
☐ 10AM–NOON ☐ 1:30PM–3:30PM

NAME: _____

TITLE: _____

COMPANY: _____

ADDRESS: _____

CITY: _____ STATE: _____ ZIP: _____

BUS. PHONE: _____

MULTI-IMAGE FESTIVAL– TOUCHING DOWN IN HOTELS NEAR YOU.

LOS ANGELES Tuesday, November 27 at the Biltmore (Emerald Room), 506 South Grand Avenue, Los Angeles 90071. Two showings: 10AM–Noon and 1:30 PM–3:30.

ORANGE COUNTY Thursday, November 29 at the Four Seasons Hotel, 690 Newport Center Drive, Newport Beach 92660. Two showings: 10AM–Noon and 1:30PM–3:30.

FIGURE 13.6 The inside panels of the Visual Dynamics self-mailer carry out the theme started on the outside. (*Copyright 1990 Visual Dynamics. Reprinted with permission.*)

Was the black-and-white self-mailer enough to generate profitable results? Ten thousand mailers were sent out, generating a total of 176 reservations at the four showings. The 1.76 percent response was especially good, says Smith, considering every person who responded agreed to attend and sit through a two-hour program.

Visual Dynamics account representatives were involved in making the program a success. They called respondents before the program to remind them, and they were present at the hotel presentations to hand out sales literature and answer questions. After the programs, they scheduled follow-up meetings with the prospects to provide more information and close sales. With a product as complex as a corporate audio/visual production the sales process can be long, but in this case an inexpensive mailer made the program take off.

Points to Remember:

1. Simple, inexpensive design and printing can be effective. A design such as this could easily be done on a desktop publishing system.
2. White space is an important element in a dramatic design. Both sides of the mailer have plenty of white space to add to readability.
3. Not only should you sell the offer, but you should also dramatize it wherever possible.
4. Even with a classic piece of direct mail, in business-to-business direct marketing it's the follow-up work that ultimately yields the results.

POSTSCRIPTS....
CU House Lists

Credit union membership lists are usually not available to rent. You may find compiled lists of credit union members, but they're not membership lists from individual CUs, just lists of people who say they belong to a credit union. Lists of credit union offices are available through many compilers and through the National Credit Union Administration, the federal regulatory agency.

While you can't buy a CU house list, many CUs do modified versions of co-ops and offer insurance, travel, discount buying, and other services through outside vendors. If you would like to do business with credit union members, you should contact some large credit unions in your area. Ask the director of marketing or the manager of the CU's "service corporation" about making your products or services available to members via direct response advertising.

A 40/7 Rule?

Steve Green reports their research shows that 40 percent of a typical pizza store's business comes from 7 percent of the store's service area. Variations of the 80/20 rule are prevalent in many businesses. A careful look at your data base should tell you who your most valuable customers are and how much of your business they're responsible for.

14 BUSINESS-TO-BUSINESS DIRECT MARKETING

Prospecting, Selling, and Creating Awareness

With consumer direct marketing, you send a customer a mailer and he responds by ordering a pizza.

In business marketing, your goals are different. You want to get the corporate pizza buyer to see a salesperson, who will demonstrate the stringiness of your mozzarella and your abundance of olives. You may also have to show how your pizza contributes to a company's bottom line, and you want to give the corporate pizza buyer a list of strong benefits she can use to explain to the boss why she bought your pizza.

This cheesy example is meant to point out the biggest difference between business-to-business direct marketing and its consumer counterpart: Lead generation is the main goal of business direct marketing. No matter how you slice it, however, the two forms of direct marketing have more similarities than differences.

If business-to-business is your niche, this chapter gives you a good summary. Most of the principles and techniques discussed elsewhere in this book also apply to business marketing and are not repeated here. We concentrate on ways to modify basic direct marketing techniques to appeal to business buyers.

BUSINESS-TO-BUSINESS GOALS

Another difference between business-to-business (B-T-B) and consumer direct marketing is in the size of the target audiences. Most business marketers sell to a small select group of companies and typically mail to lists that range from a few hundred names to rarely more than 20,000. Even a list of 20,000 may represent only a few thousand companies, if several people at each company are targeted.

With shorter lists and higher average dollar amounts per sale, B-T-B marketers can afford to spend more money per prospect. Direct mail CP/Ms are often higher in business mailing. A cost of $1,000 to $1,500/M or higher would be expensive for a mass consumer mailing, but for a short business list, in which one order might yield thousands of dollars in profit, the CP/M is not unrealistic.

The psychology of B-T-B direct response advertising is slightly different too. You must take into consideration that the person who reads your ad or direct mail may be neither the ultimate user of your product nor the final authority on whether the company can spend the money. In addition to persuading with personal motivators, you need to provide solid business benefits the buyer can use to get his or her boss's approval or to justify a purchase.

Company buyers tend to be more practical and less prone to impulse buying than consumers are. On the other hand, since they are not spending their own money, business people can often be persuaded to spend more freely than if the money were coming out of their own pockets. Educational opportunities, periodicals, travel amenities, and even personal computer software are among the things people might not buy for themselves, but would not hesitate to buy with company money.

Marketing Categories

As mentioned in Chapter 2, the ways you use B-T-B direct marketing usually fall into one of three broad categories: (1) lead generation, (2) sales support, (3) mail order.

Lead generation is the largest segment of business direct marketing, and it takes many forms, from general prospecting for leads to developing and qualifying leads for sales visits. In essence, lead generation implies data base building, because you're gathering responses to develop later. When you establish a new customer, you're building your back-end possibilities.

Sales support is also a broad portion of B-T-B direct marketing. It contributes to salespersons' objectives, either before or after sales calls. It lets you reach customers several times in different ways, without always requiring a salesperson's presence. The more complex your product and the lengthier the sales cycle is, the more helpful direct mail and other methods can be in reinforcing sales points, explaining benefits, and keeping prospects thinking about you.

Related to the sales support goal is awareness building. Direct mail, in particular, can be effective in establishing and fortifying your image among a small group of company decision makers and opinion leaders. If you cannot afford to buy large ads in major national business publications to keep your company name and image in front of your audience, you can select your special target market and send them several image awareness pieces.

Mail order is not as common in business as it is in consumer marketing, but that doesn't mean you can't use this form of selling. In fact, if your unit prices are not high and your products require no demonstrations, mail order can be lucrative. For the average cost of a few personal sales calls, you can reach a thousand people via direct mail and hundreds of people via telemarketing.

Business products sold by mail order include office supplies and equipment, books, seminars, PC software, periodicals, freight forwarding, advertising specialties, business forms, medical–pharmaceutical supplies, and other consumable business products. Office and computer supplies take up a large chunk of the business-to-business mail order market. One of the largest mail-order marketers is the Illinois-based Quill Corporation. Through its 376-page catalog and dozens of separate mailings, the company sells everything from pencils to computers to personalized stationery.

As with consumer mail order, you can use this sales method alone or to expand your distribution options. Many U.S. B-T-B sellers are experimenting with ways to use mail order to give themselves another way to compete. Explore mail order as an option to the rising costs of personal sales and sales through distributors.

MANAGING LEADS

Leads are a necessity for all business marketers, yet they're treated differently—sometimes indifferently—at many companies. Some organizations differentiate between inquiries and leads to reflect the degree to which an inquiry is qualified.

To be a useful and cost-effective source of new business, leads must not be merely generated—they must be managed. How complex a task that will be depends on how many leads you need to keep your company rolling, the sources of your leads, and the working relationship between your advertising and sales people.

Where do leads come from? Leads may come from space ads, direct mail, trade show exhibits, point-of-sale displays, dealers and distributors, salespeople, broadcast advertising, publicity, card-deck advertising, customer referrals, unsolicited queries, and other sources. As with consumer direct marketing, prospects or leads need to be recorded and tracked in an orderly way; software will help.

Once you record a lead, you'll want to determine its quality. Some leads generated by specific advertising may be high-quality prospects ready for the sales staff; most, however, need to be qualified. The quality of leads is the biggest bone of contention between sales and advertising departments in B-T-B firms of all sizes. Advertising people complain that not enough leads are converted to sales and that leads are not acted upon quickly. Sales people complain that advertising produces low-quality leads that are sometimes outdated by the time they reach the sales force. One way to avoid these common complaints is to qualify all leads before they go to the sales department.

Telemarketing is usually the easiest way to check out the quality of a lead and, at the same time, let the customer know promptly that you're interested in him. People who have responded to your direct mail or print advertising assume they'll receive a response, so a call will be neither unexpected nor unwelcome. Ask whether they have ever seen your product demonstrated. Ask when they think they might be making a purchase. Find out exactly how they plan to use your product. This latter question can help you cross-sell other products or supplies later on.

Qualifying and sorting leads quickly, like this, will keep you from wasting time on poor prospects. Whether you have one salesperson (you) or 20 people

		Leads		
Source:	*Gross No.*	*No. Sales*	*Percentage*	*Average Amount of Sale*
Magazine Ads	175	17	10	$1,800
Direct Mail	487	86	18	1,780
Trade Show	38	8	20	2,480
Unsolicited	4	1	25	1,850

FIGURE 14.1   Business-to-business lead tracking chart.

in the field, a key to profitable lead management is identifying the best leads early and spending the most resources on them. Furthermore, you will be able to plan the best sales approach when you know a little more about the leads and why they originated.

Continue to track leads until they result in a sale or are no longer active. Your data processing system should remind you when periodic calls need to be made to continuing prospects at various intervals. Ultimately, you should analyze your leads by source to determine their cost-effectiveness.

Figure 14.1 shows a simplified way of doing this analysis. Separate all leads according to source, then list the results of your follow-up. For the business illustrated, the chart shows that direct mail generated the most leads and a higher conversion percentage than print advertising. To find out the total gross revenue for these lead sources, add another column to the right showing total sales dollars.

Before too many conclusions can be drawn from this data, however, it is necessary to compare the results with the cost of acquiring and following up the leads. To determine your efficiency, consider the total cost of the advertising, including lists, space costs, printing, and the cost of any follow-up, including sales calls. Although leads from print ads resulted in a lower percentage of sales, the marketer would need to compare the costs of the print advertising with the costs of direct mail to see which was ultimately more profitable.

To gauge your conversion (sales) percentage accurately, you may need to track leads for six months or more, depending on your product sales cycle. This makes for lengthy list tests. Figure 14.2 shows important steps in a successful lead management program.

Offers

Another good way to help unify efforts of sales and advertising is to work together to create offers. Salespeople can tell you some of the qualities or qualifications that identify a company or person likely to buy your product. Granted, your prospect profile and your personal experience may give you similar information, but the point is to involve salespeople in the offer planning stage. Try to reach an agreement on an offer that will produce a prospect worthy of immediate personal follow-up.

• •

Lead Management

- Determine how many leads you can reasonably handle in a given period.
- Consult with sales staff in creating offers to generate leads.
- Receive and record leads.
- Sort and qualify leads and send literature requested.
- Promptly submit leads and data to sales force for follow up.
- Track leads throughout the sales process.
- Determine the percentage of leads converted to sales; sort by source.
- Calculate costs per lead generated.
- Identify most profitable, efficient lead source(s) and ways to make other sources more efficient.

• •

FIGURE 14.2　　Steps to a successful lead management program.

Sometimes, of course, you want to attract more than just the most qualified leads, to generate as many responses as you can. Even in this situation, if salespeople are involved in creating the offers, they will better understand what they will need to do to qualify the leads further, and they will be less likely to criticize the quality of leads.

Some marketers emphasize getting the most leads possible; others emphasize the importance of quality leads. By analyzing your leads and sales, you should be able to determine your most cost-effective leads. You usually get a combination of high- and low-quality leads, and you have many factors you can use to manipulate the type of leads you receive. For example, if your offers are too general, you'll increase the quantity but lower the quality. Broad, general offers, which are good for collecting stacks of consumer leads, can be a waste of time when you have an expensive industrial product and need to talk to serious buyers only. Here are some ways to increase the quality of business leads:

- Make the premium match your product. If you are trying to sell an industrial stamping machine, instead of giving away NFL caps give away calipers, which engineers will be able to use to measure the results. Pick a premium that appeals to the precise people you want to talk to.
- Use technical literature as the premium or as a low-cost front-end product.
- Choose smaller, more precise lists as a way of prequalifying prospects.
- Put the focus of your copy and graphics on the technical benefits of your product, not on premiums or other generic attention-getting devices.
- On your reply card, ask specific questions about job titles and responsibilities, and perhaps how recently readers purchased their last product similar to yours. This way prospects qualify themselves.

Trade Shows

Trade shows are an excellent source of leads and a good opportunity to mix different direct marketing techniques. Trade shows let you use the persuasive power of personal selling at a lower cost than sales calls. To multiply the benefits of a trade show, you can use direct marketing before and after a show.

Boost attendance at your hospitality suite, or get more people to visit your booth, by doing a mailing to prospects before a trade show or conference. Remember the importance of an offer. Don't just ask people to visit you; tell them what they will gain if they do. Do you have a drawing, free food, industry reports or studies, or a new type of product never before demonstrated? Send people a coupon or other action device they need to bring to your booth or suite. Direct marketers have used specially encoded diskettes, prize numbers, and other incentives to get people to visit a booth and get involved in an activity.

After a trade show, you may be able to obtain a list of everyone who attended, but your most important list will be the prospects you generated at your exhibit. Shows have new ways of letting you identify people who visit your booth and record data on them, rather than just asking everyone for a business card. Some shows give each visitor a code number, which exhibitors can use after the show to obtain business data from the show's data base. Some shows give all visitors cards with bar codes or magnetic stripes, which can be read with a scanner or similar device at each booth to get the data quickly.

You may have several different levels of prospects, based on how close they are to buying. Regardless of the size of your list of leads, each one should receive a follow-up mailing or telephone call within a week after the show. For those who don't receive calls, don't just send a bare brochure or spec sheet. Send personalized letters, along with any necessary technical or sales literature.

MEDIA SELECTION

Business-to-business direct marketing holds even more advantages for small companies than does consumer direct marketing. Most of your advantages have to do with the cost of media. Since business lists and target markets tend to be small, your direct mail CP/M will be about the same as that of your larger competitors. By contrast, in consumer direct mail, your competitors' CP/M will be much smaller than yours if they mail in high volume. When a company sends out hundreds of thousands of mailing pieces, the creative and production costs are spread out over a larger quantity. With business lists, you and your competition may be mailing to the same 3,000 prospects. In addition, since lists are smaller, there are fewer chances for direct mail testing, so you and your opponents are left to rely more on your own research and marketing savvy.

Further equalizing the competition with big business, many trade publications have limited circulations, compared to consumer magazines, and proportionately lower rates as well. A small company can often afford to advertise in the same trade journals as their larger competitors. Without going broke on a media schedule, you can have strategically placed awareness advertising.

Choosing Business Publications

To identify the right trade publications, follow the research procedures outlined in Chapter 3. Review the editorial content to see if it will attract the readers you want to reach. The more specific and narrow your field, the fewer publications from which you have to choose.

While most consumer publications are available by paid subscription only, many business journals have *controlled circulation,* which means they're sent free to people in the industry. But just because people don't pay to subscribe doesn't mean the publication is not a valuable advertising medium. In fact, some controlled-circulation periodicals deliver a more focused and relevant buying audience than paid-subscription magazines.

As mentioned earlier, you should check a publication's audited circulation figures. For many business publications, that means looking at their publishers' statements audited by BPA (Business Publications Audit of Circulation). The most important part of the statement for controlled-circulation periodicals is section 3b. This section tells you how and how frequently readers must qualify to receive subscriptions. It tells you, for example, what percentage of subscriptions originate from names on business directories, association membership lists, direct written requests from companies, or other sources. If a publication has a high percentage of readers who have *personally* written to request a subscription, that's the best audience yet; it indicates a high interest in the periodical.

Section 3b of the publisher's statement also tells you whether a publication asks readers to renew their subscription requests every one, two, or three years. Obviously a magazine that requires all readers to update their requests every year is going to be more desirable than one that only updates its lists every three years. You'd be lucky to get responses from a publication with three-year-old addresses.

BPA-audited statements also tell you the percentage of subscriptions that are sent to companies, to individuals by name and title, or to individuals by title only. If a publication is sent primarily to companies and not to individuals, it may not get as much attention when it arrives. In section 4 of the statement you'll find a geographical breakdown of circulation area by ZIP codes.

You can obtain a variety of information on publications in their media kits and from their sales representatives, but ask for the audited statements to find the unembellished figures. You should be able to negotiate some discounts on rates with business publications depending on market conditions. If you wish, ad agencies can also buy space for you in trade publications. Incidentally, magazines are called "books" by advertising sales reps and media buyers.

Bingo Cards

Reader service cards (bingo cards) are one way of providing business prospects with a simple reply device, and many magazines offer them. The value of bingo cards varies. Advertisers sometimes claim that publishers don't forward responses quickly enough. Some wait until they receive a certain number of cards before they forward the responses on to the advertisers. In contrast, some publishers say they forward leads immediately, only to have advertisers stack them up somewhere. No matter who is at fault, an old prospect is a cold prospect.

To speed up response times, magazines allow readers to send bingo card requests via facsimile machine, and some even permit requests to come in via telephone audio response system. Publishers also have offered to send sales leads to advertisers via modem for fastest turnaround.

All the electronic advancements will help you process bingo card leads faster, but for the time being, they are usually not as high-quality as leads that come to you directly via mail or telephone. Therefore, just because a magazine offers a bingo card doesn't mean you should not feature your 800 number or use a coupon. Test and compare.

Lists

In business-to-business, your house list of customers remains your strongest list resource, with your house list of leads and inquiries your second strongest. After that, you can rely on direct response lists or compiled lists. You also can compile your own list. Many small marketers do. If your target audience is a small number of companies, becoming your own compiler gives you a unique list you can update and use as many times as you like.

Before you spend your time compiling a universe of potential customers, explore the commercial lists available in your field. Compilers offer lists of executives by title and type of company. Lists are available covering most of the 10 million or so companies in the United States. Selections for compiled company lists include: Top executives by name, number of employees, number of locations, sales, geography, creditworthiness, and type of business as indicated by Standard Industrial Code (SIC). Many lists include company phone numbers. Similar to consumer versions, some compiled business lists are enhanced with results from questionnaires and overlay programs. For general prospecting, an SIC list allows you to blanket an entire business or industry nationwide or within your region.

Direct response business lists should be your first choice if you're selling through mail order. Competitors' lists may be hard to obtain, but you can find lists of people at business addresses who have responded to various mail-order offers before. To identify the best lists, use the list criteria listed in Chapter 4.

Subscribers to business publications constitute another source of lists. Some controlled-circulation publications have readers fill out detailed questionnaires every year (for BPA purposes), and thus they have a variety of relatively current selections available on their subscriber lists. If a list is updated at least annually, or has monthly hotline subscribers, it can be a good source of prospects. A qualified list broker, experienced in the business-to-business market, is your best resource for locating business lists.

No matter where you obtain your lists, accuracy is your primary concern. People in business change jobs, job titles, and companies frequently. You want to avoid mailing to people (or companies) that are no longer there. Compilers may offer refunds and guarantees based on the deliverability of their business lists. Polk, for example, will refund third-class postage for returned mail in excess of 7 percent of the total list.

One way to avoid the problem of people moving is to address your mail by title only. Mail addressed by name and title is always preferable, when it's accurate, but many business marketers get good results with mail addressed by title only. Directories and compiled lists can become outdated in a couple of months, and sometimes names are just not available, so title addressing is a satisfactory alternative.

If you compile your own list, or if you buy rather than rent, the most comprehensive and reliable way to update it is to call each company. This process is time-consuming, and you might get by with a mailed questionnaire and "address correction requested" on the envelope you send out, but the phone gives you instant results. The confirming call also lets you find out the names of other people who buy products like yours or are decision makers in the buying process.

CREATIVE

While you need to modify the creative approach slightly for business direct marketing, always remember that your messages are still aimed at people. This means you should use motivators, emotional language, deadlines, incentives, and other creative techniques we've reviewed.

Although similar to consumer advertising, business-to-business direct mail is usually shorter, more businesslike, and more direct. Copy should focus on benefits, but it doesn't need to be as lengthy as the average consumer mailer. One reason for relative brevity is that your readers are busy at work and are more likely to respond to a direct approach. Another reason is that most business direct marketing is aimed at getting a lead, not making a sale.

Whether you're writing a direct mail letter, ad, or telemarketing script, your copy should include technical attributes and benefits. You should use jargon to speak the same language as your readers or listeners and to give yourself credibility.

Developing creative direct mail or print advertising that stands out from the rest is not that difficult in the business-to-business field, because, frankly, so much of it is poorly done. Whether direct response or conventional, ads in the average trade journal vary in quality from good to awful and beyond. Read through some publications in your field, and chances are you'll find examples of the following techniques (that you should avoid):

- Cheesecake. The term is outdated, and so is the advertising technique. A woman in a bikini standing in front of a piece of industrial equipment is not going to prompt someone to return a coupon.
- Benefit-less headlines. You can read entire ads sometimes and find no reason for responding. Specifications are important, but they're not everything.
- Headlines in reverse, all-caps, or too-small type. How many of these can you find in a trade publication? Sometimes you find all three in the same ad. Even a small ad should have a dominant headline as the central focus.
- Poor artwork reproduction. It doesn't matter that half the ads in the publication have fuzzy or grainy photos; make yours sharp and your ad will stand out that much more. Make sure the originals of your photographs have a full range of dark and light tones. Avoid black-and-white photos with all medium gray values. Use crisp line art instead of photos if you're advertising in a newsprint publication that doesn't provide fine-screen photo reproduction. Often, poor-quality pictures in ads are the fault of the advertiser, however, and not the publication.
- Unnecessary, inappropriate, or tasteless plays on words. These may start out as in-house jokes or attempts to get attention, but what you want with your advertising is attention *and* responses.
- Other techniques (or lack of them) include lack of an offer, pointless pictures of company offices with employees lined up outside, use of too many typefaces, and, believe it or not, lack of a phone number.

Sales Support

The creative approach for sales support materials should include, wherever appropriate, a call for action and a response device. The exception is the sale of an expensive product that requires a salesperson to talk with a customer regularly. In that case, your sales support material may be similar to conventional brochures, ad reprints, or company capability brochures. If you're already working toward a purchase with a customer, a piece of direct mail that urges him or her to order the $150,000 product or service via mail order would be out of place.

In other instances, especially if you offer a variety of products, services, and supplies, sales support material can give potential customers ways to take action. Give customers opportunities to ask for specification sheets on various products, ask questions on technical assistance phone lines, place orders, or even get in touch with their individual sales reps.

Getting Past the Sentinels

Since you often spend more per customer or prospect in business direct mail, you can add series mailings to your creative arsenal. Often, mailers send a series of three messages, all related to a single theme and each one building on the previous mailing. Frequently, series mailings include packages, special inserts, and three-dimensional objects aimed at getting attention. The more lucrative the potential customers, the more you can afford to spend.

Doctors, for example, are often the target of expensive direct mail campaigns, and they receive golf balls, personalized desk accessories, and other items designed to grab the attention of these busy professionals.

One purpose of elaborate, series mailings is to be sure the message gets past the company mail room and the recipient's secretary or assistant. That's no small task today. Some companies, including some offices of General Motors, have announced they will not forward third-class mail beyond the mail room.

Usually the higher up the corporate ladder your target prospect is, (1) the more direct mail he or she already receives, and (2) the more likely he or she is to have a secretary who opens and carefully screens the mail. According to a survey by The Blue Chip Marketing Group of Stamford, Conn., presidents, senior-vice presidents, and chief financial officers at *Fortune* 500 companies receive an average of 175 pieces of direct mail a week and about 90 percent of it is diverted by secretaries.

To get past the gatekeepers and hit senior officers with a dramatic message, Blue Chip has mailed such items as: kites, personalized desk name blocks, stuffed footballs, model wooden train cars, and its ultimate mailing: a nine-part series that contained a miniature pool table set. The nine-part mailing, conducted for Champion International Corp., was aimed at getting the attention of 315 hard-to-reach top executives. When the mailing was completed, each executive had received a table-top pool set, including balls, cues, chalk, and a ball rack.

Blue Chip president James Hoverman says dimensional marketing (sending objects and gifts) turns an executive secretary "from an obstacle to an ally." Rather than dumping the direct mail, a secretary usually gets involved in delivering a dimensional mailing right to her boss's desk.

Dimensional mailings can be effective for getting the attention of a few important people, for breaking through the clutter of business direct mail, and for getting past the gatekeepers; however, there are other, less expensive ways to get your business mail to its intended readers. Here are other suggestions for getting beyond the corporate mail sentries:

Maintain a businesslike front.   Poor reproduction, cheap paper, and a message that's hard to grasp give a secretary good reasons for trashing your envelope and contents. Make your letters look important, even if they are mass-produced.

Try official-looking teasers.   Some people use "Personal and Confidential" on the outside of envelopes to bull their way past the secretary. If it works, the executive will probably be annoyed when your "personal" message has to do with low prices on janitorial services or executive exercise bicycles.

Teasers that make direct mail look like government forms or other personal mail fall into the same category. "Mr. Smith *only* please" is one inoffensive way I've seen advertisers try an end run around the secretary.

Get to the point.   Assume that your target executive will have the secretary open the mail. Make your offer clear and show how it's related to the business your executive is in. Most secretaries don't trash all direct mail. Mail that is professional, relevant, and correctly addressed is most likely to be delivered. Mail for personal rather than business products is not necessarily skimmed off.

Mail first-class. Here's a way to get by most mail rooms at least, but at a cost. If you mail to people at large companies with internal mail-processing facilities, first class is worth a test.

Use mail codes. Large corporations have their own internal mail codes, somewhat like company ZIP codes. If you use company mail codes, chances are your advertising will get routed as it's addressed. Some subscriber lists have mail codes, and you can always call company mail rooms to find out how to code for internal delivery. Ask about their delivery policies regarding third-class mail too.

Use a plain No. 10 envelope. The best vehicle for slipping third-class mail past the sentinels is a white No. 10 envelope with just a business logo and return address. Don't use a teaser, but do use a postage meter rather than a bulk rate permit imprint.

Aim for middle management. We'd all like to gain the interest of top officers, but if your product is usually approved and purchased by middle managers, mail to them. They're more likely to see all their direct mail and perhaps even open their own mail.

Mail tapes. A PR firm once mailed unmarked audio cassette tapes that carried a promotional message. If you received an unmarked tape, could you resist? Although they are not cheap, disposable videotapes are now available, with cartridges made primarily of cardboard. A videotape can combine the best elements of direct mail and personal selling, but at a relatively high cost.

Telemarketing

Talking is the primary skill usually associated with telemarketing, but listening is equally important. You need to practice a relaxed, professional technique for speaking on the phone, but when your customers or prospects speak, you listen. Listen carefully and you'll hear the information you need to make the sale. If you don't get enough information to work with, ask open-ended questions.

Direct mail copywriters would love to hear potential customers tell them exactly what they want and don't want. When you conduct telemarketing, that's exactly what you hear. Listen for complaints, which indicate benefits your prospect is looking for. Listen for needs you can fill, ways you can help the potential customer.

Inbound business telemarketing is not all listening, however. You need to ask for the order or ask the caller to make some type of commitment. When people call your company as a result of an ad or direct mail, they expect to be asked for some type of commitment, so do it.

In outbound telemarketing, your objectives, offer, and script, plus your listening skills, are the elements to success. Your tested script must be flexible enough to let you deal with the variety of circumstances you may come across when you call a company. Be prepared to spend time getting to the right person.

Getting past the sentinels is also a hurdle in telemarketing. Some callers say that the prospect is expecting the call. This sneaky technique might mean that the marketer wrote earlier and hinted that he'd be calling. Sometimes, when you need to get around a particularly stubborn secretary, time your calls when the secretary will be at lunch or on a break, and someone else may route your call through. You can also call after 5 P.M., when many secretaries will have gone home but many managers will still be at their desks. The telephone version of the plain white envelope is simply a straightforward, confident request to talk with the person you're calling. Getting past switchboards and call screeners makes the business side of telemarketing more expensive than the consumer side, but the higher value of a sale makes it worthwhile.

VARIATIONS FOR CONSULTANTS

Self-employed consultants who sell to businesses can use direct marketing techniques in the same way as other marketers. Maintaining the discipline to record and follow up leads is just as important, but consultants—including me—tend to gloss over recordkeeping because they think it's unnecessary. My excuse used to be, if you're working with only five or ten leads at a time, why devise a fancy system for such a small volume of data?

All three elements of direct marketing, the lists, the creative, and offers also apply to consultants, but consultants sometimes forget about the importance of an offer. An attractive, nonbinding offer is what you need to generate leads. Business consulting services are not sold by mail order or over the phone, but many consultants' direct mail and telemarketing seems to be aimed at doing just that. Why? Because the emphasis is on the service, not an offer.

To increase leads, you have to create offers that don't require prospects to sign up for your full services. Offers that sound as if they require little or no commitment will generate responses. Free printed information, closely related to your business and cleverly titled and packaged, makes a good offer. Lists of tips, particularly ways to save money, work well. Some examples are *Seventeen Ways to Save Money on Printing, Bacon's 15 Money-Saving Industrial Waste Ideas,* and *A Dozen Ways to Avoid Employee Termination Problems Before They Start.* Use direct mail or small-space ads to offer your free booklet or fact kit.

When people telephone in response to your offer, ask questions about their companies that will help you qualify them and give you the data you will need to sell them your services later. A next step might be to get the prospects to agree to a free initial consultation. Your terminology is important. Don't call it a "sales presentation."

A different offer used frequently by consultants is the free seminar. You can conduct a public program at a hotel meeting room and advertise it via direct mail or print, or you can offer to bring your program to a company, letting the company decide who will attend. Obviously, your seminar is mainly a sales presentation, but you can present the offer in a way that sounds valuable. Say you'll include ways to save money. Advertise it as a demonstration of a new product or say you'll explain a new technology. Your seminar offer must contain benefits and value for the prospects.

You can call your seminar an executive briefing, special presentation or program, or preview. If your seminar is strictly a product or sales presentation, and you're not in the training or seminar business, you should not charge for it.

Here's a good idea to help generate RSVPs for your free seminars if you can offer several half-day programs. Advertise times and dates, but add the stipulation that morning and afternoon sessions will not be available every day (or at each location if you hold programs in two areas). Ask people to call to find out which sessions will be available. This will encourage people to call and make a reservation, thus giving them a greater incentive to show up. This tactic will also work if you conduct free seminars on more than one topic. Ask prospects to call to find out which topic will be covered at which session.

Consultants usually get a large portion of their business from referrals and, judging from my own experience, largely without asking for them. Think how many more referrals you would have if you systematically asked for referrals. When you ask, you can specify the type of referrals you would like best, rather than taking what comes along. Mention referrals in your prospecting and customer service letters. Give clients forms they can use to refer someone to you or vice versa. Your house list is your most important marketing asset, and you can use it to generate referrals as well as new assignments.

POSTSCRIPTS....

Confetti Trick

Ever received direct mail filled with confetti? It certainly attracts your attention when you open the envelope and the bits of paper spill out. This technique seems to be a favorite of ad agencies, but it has a drawback, especially when used in business-to-business mail.

I've heard two different ad agency presidents tell stories about negative reactions they've received when using the confetti trick. The problem: A secretary opens the mail, spills the confetti, and gets mad because she has to pick it up. The boss never sees the confetti anyway, and often never sees the mailing because the secretary trashes it.

Don't give up. You can enclose the confetti in a cellophane envelope or use giant pieces of confetti, which won't spill out.

Double-Check Lists

Remember that when you send a series mailing and include an executive gift or novelty, that's only one-third of the direct marketing formula. Expensive mailings should be backed up with precise lists. If you spend several dollars or more per prospect, you'd better be sure that your list is immaculate, that the names are spelled correctly, and most important, that you've picked the business people who are most likely to want your product or service.

Then you will have sent an attention getter to the right people, so make sure you combine it with an attractive offer that's easy to accept.

Personalized Response Cards

If you want to personalize a mailing to a list that contains only business titles, print the title and company address on the response device and begin the letter with an appropriate generic salutation, such as *Dear Colleague* or *Dear Petroleum Executive*.

Watch Out for Titles

Limited space in computer fields often forces list compilers to abbreviate company titles, sometimes to the point of gibberish. If you're mailing to titles and not names, and the mail room at a company can't identify a title, your mailing is lost.

A bank employee with the title "loan processing officer" responded to a mail-order offer at her office but directed the shipment to her home. Later she was amused when she started receiving mail at home addressed to Ms. Ln Proc Off. Still later, her husband started getting mail to Mr. Ln Proc Off.

15 DOING BUSINESS WITH
THE POSTAL SERVICE

•••••• •••••••••••••••••••••••••••

I'm from the Government and...

While the United States Postal Service is delivering your messages to prospects and customers, it's also sorting, processing, and delivering another 170 billion pieces of mail per year. When you think of the complexity of the task, the USPS does a remarkable job.

Yet when your business depends on the advertising you send out, and it costs you a dollar in postage alone for every five to eight pieces of bulk direct mail you send, it's easy to forget about the other 170 billion pieces. Direct marketing trade journals regularly carry columns and editorials lambasting high postal rates and uneven service. Indeed, rates have been boosted about every three years for the past decade.

There is very little you can do to change postage rates, however, aside from becoming involved in direct mail political action groups and writing your representative in Congress. What you can do is try to get the most from every penny you spend in postage, and the Postal Service will show you how.

Approach the post office positively. Take advantage of postal discounts and services to save money and make your mailings more efficient. They're from the government, but they *will* help you in several ways.

WORKING WITH THE USPS

To get started, contact your local post office to find out who is responsible for working with small business bulk mailers in your area. If you live in or near a major metropolitan area, you will probably be referred to a Postal Business Center. To improve and consolidate services to small business, the USPS has set up more than 100 such centers and the number is growing. Each center is staffed by customer service representatives whose job it is to assist small business people in a variety of ways. Anyone who spends less than $200,000 per year on postage and fees is considered small.

When you call your local business center you may be assigned to a specific representative who serves your part of town. Tell her that you're starting a direct marketing program using third-class mail and that you would like to find out about postal services such as permits and bulk rate discounts. To obtain permits and other information, you don't have to drive to a business center if you do not have one in your city. You can get your permits locally. You'll need to obtain a permit for using bulk rate postage and one for business reply mail.

If you're planning to do your mail addressing, metering, and presorting yourself, the post office can tell you what you need to do to qualify for postage discounts. The higher your volume, and the smaller the geographic area you mail to, the greater your possibilities for discounts. The sorting requirements are detailed. You must sort, bundle, bag, and label mail according to postal regulations to qualify for bulk rates. You can obtain publications that explain the procedures, and you can also attend training sessions conducted by postal specialists. Some large postal facilities conduct classes weekly. The Postal Service also sells video training tapes and sponsors regional seminars on a variety of postal subjects.

A tour of a local general mail-processing facility is a valuable part of your post office education. Ask your postal representative to arrange a visit. When you see *how* mail is handled mechanically, you'll get a better understanding of the reasons for some of the regulations and some of the ways you can ensure proper handling of your mail.

For example, the Postal Service discourages you from using square envelopes. Here's why: First-class envelopes enter the mechanical sorting process on a conveyor. Each envelope travels on its edge through equipment that identifies the stamp and reads the address. The processing machines determine the position of the envelopes by their shapes. A square envelope might get fed into the sorting stream on its side and thus require special handling. For this reason, square envelopes may be subject to a nonstandard surcharge.

Establish a good working relationship with your local postal authorities, and you'll have a foundation for dealing with them if you have special requests, questions, or problems later on. If you're concerned about the delivery time for an important local third-class mailing, for instance, talk with the postmaster at the post office where you deliver your mail. Make contact well in advance and explain when you will have the mail ready and when you would like the items delivered. You won't get a guarantee, but the postmaster will probably do what he or she can to get your mail delivered on the right day.

CLASSES AND POSTAGE

Excluding Express Mail, which is in a category of its own, mail is divided into four classifications: first class, for business and personal mail; second class, for periodicals; third class, for direct mail advertising; and fourth class, for parcels. Each class has a different rate hierarchy.

In third class, which covers most direct mail, you have three options for affixing postage. Metering is the preferred method for many applications. The third-class meter imprint looks businesslike and is similar to the first-class imprint. You can also buy precanceled third-class stamps to stick on envelopes. These also make your mailing look something like first class, but they stand out because the area on the envelope around the stamp does not get canceled. To use any of the third-class options, you must pay a $75 annual bulk rate fee.

The third option is a third-class permit. To use the permit, you print the words "Bulk Rate U.S. Postage Paid" on the outside of your envelopes in the place where a stamp would normally be. This printed notice, which must also contain your permit number, is called *indicia*.

Using indicia is the least expensive way to put postage on an envelope or self-mailer. If you do the mailing yourself, it takes time to meter or put stamps on envelopes. If you have a mailing house do your mailing, you will be charged for attaching stamps or metering mail. In essence, printing the indicia is free, because it's printed at the same time the return address and any teasers are printed. On the other hand, of the three ways to use postage, it is the most obvious indication of bulk mail. A permit to use indicia requires an additional, one-time $75 fee.

Third-class mail delivery times vary greatly, depending on the time of year you mail, the part of the country where the mail originates, the accuracy of your addresses, weather, and other factors. Mailings within one metropolitan area may take about a week. National and regional mailings may take three weeks or more to reach all addresses. If you use ZIP + 4 and bar coding, you'll improve your chances for quick delivery.

For a mailing going to just one part of your state, two weeks is a good time to estimate delivery. Some pieces may be delivered sooner, but it's safer to plan mailing dates and deadlines with a buffer of extra time.

Mail delivery times in your area are something you should begin to test and track with your first bulk mailing. If you have to get something delivered within two or three days, first class is always available, but it's more expensive.

Getting Rate Discounts

To qualify for the basic third-class postal rate, you must have at least 200 identical pieces or 50 pounds at the same time. They must be sorted by ZIP code and packaged according to postal regulations. Beyond this basic rate are three more lower rate levels, depending on the sorting and density of your mail:

- 3/5 Presort. Mail must be sorted and bundled according to three-digit and five-digit ZIP codes.

- Carrier Route. If you presort your mail to the routes of the individual postal carriers you will receive the next level discount. In general, you will not qualify for this additional discount unless you are mailing to many homes within a small geographic area.

- Saturation. If you're mailing to at least 75 percent of the residences in an area, and you sort the mail for the carriers' routes in sequence according to street addresses, you receive an even higher discount.

Some additional discounts are also available:

- At some levels you will receive a small discount for mail that contains ZIP + 4 codes.
- Bar-coding your mail yourself earns you another discount.
- Although generally not applicable for small business, an additional discount can be earned if you have your mail shipped by private carrier to its destination post office.
- Nonprofit organizations have a similar but separate rate structure with substantially lower rates in most categories.

The size of your envelope will also affect your cost. To be considered for the standard "letter" rates your mailing piece must be no larger than 6⅛ × 11½ inches. Anything larger and you'll be assessed from the higher rate scale for "flats." The letter rates also cover anything under 3.3 ounces, a major difference from first-class mail, which requires substantial additional postage for anything over one ounce.

Even if you can't qualify for other discounts beyond the basic rate because of a small or geographically diverse list, you can qualify for the ZIP + 4 discount. As a service to small businesses the Postal Service will add ZIP + 4 to all the names on your list if you give them your list on diskette. They will also standardize your addresses and validate or correct your five-digit ZIP codes. Your business center will provide this service once for free and thereafter will charge a modest fee.

Bar codes, mentioned above, are the row of little lines along the front of envelopes. The codes, which contain a row of 62 little vertical bars, correspond to ZIP + 4 codes and the last two digits of street addresses, and allow mail to be sorted automatically. To earn the bar-code discount you can have a letter shop bar-code your mail or you can do it yourself with the appropriate software. (See Appendix B.)

ENDORSEMENTS, NIXIES

How much of your mail will get delivered when you send it third class? The answer to that frequent question depends on the accuracy of your list, whether or not you have used ZIP + 4 or bar coding, and, of course, on the efficiency of the Postal Service employees who handle it.

A certain percentage of all third-class mail is not delivered. These *nixies*, as they're known in DM jargon, amount to between 5 and 10 percent of the average third-class mailing, particularly rental lists. Nixies are as normal in direct mail as mosquitoes are in a marsh: While you accept their existence, you'd like to reduce their numbers.

You can just about cut your nixies in half if you have your lists enhanced with a ZIP + 4 service, or better yet, processed with the NCOA files, as mentioned in Chapter 4. Keeping your house list of customers and prospects as clean and current as possible will also help.

Normally, third-class mail that is undeliverable as addressed (UAA) is trashed. It will be dumped, whether it has an incomplete address or whether the person addressed has simply moved. To keep track of someone who has moved, you can print "Address Correction Requested" on the outside of your envelopes. With this *endorsement*, which should be printed just below your return address, the Postal Service will return your envelope or a form to you, showing the new address. The cost for each address correction, on mailers under one ounce, is the third-class single-piece postage rate. For mailers over one ounce, the rate is 35 cents.

How often you use this service depends on the condition and size of your list. With many corrections it could get expensive, but with your house list, each one represents a customer or prospect, so the cost is well worth it. Use the address correction endorsement at least once a year. The Postal Service also provides a forwarding service in third class for a higher fee.

One way to see that your third-class mail is delivered to someone is to add the words "or current resident" after the name on each label. In this case, if the addressee has moved, your mailer will be delivered to whoever is living at the address. This doesn't help you keep track of customers who have moved, and it gives your mailing an impersonal tone, but it will help get your mailer delivered to someone when you're using rental lists.

When you mail first class, the address correction service is free, but you must ask for it by having the proper endorsement on your envelope. Forwarding of first class is also free and doesn't require an envelope endorsement. If you ask for address correction, your mail will not be forwarded but returned to you with the new address. You may obtain both the forwarding and address correction services at the same time, but you pay a fee to receive the new address.

BUSINESS REPLY MAIL

Postal services that bring you leads and orders are equally as important as those for your outgoing mail. If you pay for the return postage so that your prospects or customers don't have to find their own stamps, you've removed one more hurdle to getting a response. Business reply mail is an integral part of most third-class mailings. Business reply cards are also used in FSIs, print ads, package inserts, and other applications.

To use business reply mail, you must obtain a permit and permit number. You must have the number printed on your return envelopes or postcards, and the face of your reply mail must conform to postal standards regarding the location of the address, bar code, indicia, and other elements. Ask your post office for the current specifications. They are occasionally changed.

The amount you pay for this return service depends on the type of permit you obtain. The minimum service requires an annual $75 fee. When you receive reply mail, you are charged first-class postage, plus 40 cents for each piece. You pay the postage and return fee at the time you receive the reply mail. If your reply card is larger than $4\frac{1}{4} \times 6$ inches, it will not qualify for the postcard rate, and you will be charged the first-class letter rate. (Incidentally, that's true for all postcards. Just because your mailer is a card doesn't mean it only requires postcard postage.)

To save money if you expect hundreds of reply cards or envelopes each year, you can obtain an advance deposit account for an extra $185 fee. In addition to the fee, you deposit money in advance to pay for anticipated replies. In exchange for the higher up-front costs, the Postal Service only charges you 9 cents per return, plus the first class postage, and it's deducted from your account. A further discount, to 2 cents per BRC or envelope (plus postage), is available if your reply pieces are specially coded so that the Postal Service's equipment can read and record the charges automatically. To qualify for this Business Reply Mail Accounting System (BRMAS) discount you must submit sample cards or envelopes to be tested on the processing equipment.

LETTER SHOPS

Rising postal rates, coupled with complex regulations, make it increasingly attractive for you to use a letter shop for all your mail processing. Saving the time it takes to assemble and mail letters, brochures, envelopes, and other inserts is another reason to get help. In essence you need to balance your time versus the cost of letter shop services.

The best way to decide is to contact several letter shops and obtain their prices, then compare that with the costs and time you would spend if you did it yourself. Letter shops come in such a variety of sizes that no matter how small your mailings, you can probably find someone to help you.

Here's a summary of the services you can obtain from a mailing house or letter shop:

- Collating and inserting. Letter shops take all your mailing pieces, fold them as necessary, and insert them into your envelopes. The more complex your mailing and the more pieces to be folded and inserted, the higher your costs.
- Addressing. Your names will be applied as labels or printed directly on the envelopes or self-mailers. In addition, postage will be affixed to the pieces and outer envelopes will be sealed. Shops also offer bar coding.
- Tie, bag, and deliver. Your mail is presorted to the highest level possible for postage discounts, bundled, then placed in mailbags and delivered to the appropriate postal facility.
- Use of bulk rate permit. You can use a letter shop's bulk rate permit, so you don't have to obtain your own.

A variety of other services may be available depending on the size of the mailing firm. Some letter shops specialize in small business and may offer you services such as printing personalized computer letters.

An advantage of working with a letter shop is that its personnel keep up to date on changing postal regulations, so you don't have to. An effective letter shop should have a good relationship with local postal officials and should be able to advise you about size, weight, and quantity requirements for mailing, as well as envelope and address configurations.

Some firms specialize in providing presort services for first-class mail. A typical first-class presort service will pick up your mail, sort it with mail from other customers to get the lowest postage rate, then charge you a rate that is lower than the non-presort first-class rate.

First-class presort offers you an alternative to bulk rate mailing, especially if you can only qualify for the basic third-class rate. First-class rates from presort services run approximately 5 cents more than the basic third-class rate. Thus, by increasing your CP/M by $50, you can obtain all the advantages of first-class mail.

Since you put the future of each mailing entirely in the hands of a letter shop, you should check out several firms before you select one. It's handy to have one near your office, to make deliveries easier and to permit you to drop in to check on the progress of jobs. When you're evaluating shops, visit them and check out their equipment. See if you can find shops that are big enough to handle your requirements, but small enough so that you are not considered insignificant.

HOW TO REDUCE POSTAL COSTS

Third-class presorting, similar to the service for first class, is an emerging option for small mailers. Some letter shops now commingle small mailings, which would otherwise only qualify for the basic third-class rate, to obtain higher presort discounts. Obviously letter shops charge for this service, but depending on the size and type of your mailing you can often realize per-unit savings, sometimes substantial savings.

United Presort Services, Inc. of Los Angeles began offering the service on an experimental basis several years ago. According to General Manager, Lonny Eggleston, in addition to saving customers postage, the higher level of presorting gets the mail delivered faster. For more information, ask your postal representative for the names of letter shops in your area that offer third-class presort services.

One sure way to avoid high postal rates is to use the competition. Until recently there was none, but rate increases have made it feasible for alternate delivery companies to operate. Originally, a few companies were started to deliver catalogs in limited areas. As more catalog firms and large mailers use private delivery, the companies will grow and multiply, perhaps reaching a point when they can serve small businesses economically.

• •

As a convenient reminder, here are some ways to reduce or make the most of your postal costs:

1. Use other media effectively. Test telemarketing against direct mail. Mix print advertising with your direct mail.

2. Have your house list processed with the NCOA and DFS systems. How important is this? The USPS says it processes 40 million changes of address each year. How else will you keep up?

3. Use ZIP + 4 and bar codes.

4. Clean up your list, standardizing addresses, identifying partial or incorrect addresses, and eliminating confusing business titles.

5. Focus tightly on your target market. Use selections and segmentation to narrow the outside lists you rent. Rent only the most likely and best-qualified prospect names. Use your customer profile to help identify prospects.

6. Explore possibilities for co-op mailings. Use an established local coupon-type co-op or start your own co-op with a unique format.

7. Use your house list for all it's worth. Your response rates will be higher and the nixie rate lower.

8. For occasional important mailings, consider presorted first class because of its higher delivery rate and free forwarding.

9. Try an FSI in a direct mail format. Have your self-mailer, letter, or other piece inserted in a publication.

10. Verify names and addresses by phoning.

11. Sort by carrier route when possible.

12. Have your postal scale calibrated.

13. Use a presort service for your daily, routine first-class mail.

14. Use "address correction requested" to track down valuable customers.

15. Review internal procedures to see if routine letters to suppliers, customers, and others can be consolidated or reduced.

16. Presort your newsletter. Send it as a self-mailer with indicia to save the cost of envelopes, too.

17. Substitute fax transmissions for mail to regular customers when feasible and appropriate.

18. Use promotional stuffers in routine business mailings to make every postal expenditure carry marketing material.

19. Test package inserts, card decks, and door hangers.

20. Remind customers often to notify you if they move.

• •

POSTSCRIPTS...

Postal Progress

The USPS has made significant progress in automation over the past few years and new bar-code sorting equipment may help reduce delivery times. As technology changes, so will postal rate categories, regulations, and, of course, the rates themselves. So, be sure to check with your next local Postal Business Center or post office during the planning stages of your next direct mail campaign.

GOOD INTENTIONS

Postal regulations are complex and sometimes confusing. Postmaster General Marvin Runyon has said he wants to simplify regulations and publish more how-to publications for mailers. A good first step was the revision of the *Domestic Mail Manual,* the Postal Service's massive collection of regulations and requirements. It's now available in an easier-to-read loose-leaf format with a helpful index and introductory chapter. See Appendix B for ordering information.

A less formidable and therefore easier to use how-to postal guide is available free from the Tension Envelope Co. The Kansas City–based envelope manufacturer, with regional offices around the United States, publishes the *Mail Management Manual,* the most practical, easy-to-use, and authoritative booklet on postal rates and regulations I've ever seen. The resource contains more than 40 pages of postal information and direct mail ideas and is updated regularly. Again, see Appendix B.

16 PRODUCTION

• •

Translating Ideas to Paper and Ink

Everything has been thought of before, but the problem is to think of it again.

—Goethe

Details. Direct marketing is full of them. To be successful, you not only have to use lists, offers, and creative tactics effectively, but you also have to keep track of a seemingly endless string of details. A brilliantly conceived advertising campaign can falter if you miss a magazine deadline or have a slight misunderstanding with a representative of an outside vendor.

If you're not familiar with the many little details involved in direct marketing, you will be by the end of this chapter. Direct marketing often requires you to orchestrate diverse endeavors to come up with a coordinated, successful program.

Printing is a major part of direct mail and other forms of direct marketing. To begin, we'll review some of the variables in printing and ways to save money. Then we'll use five separate checklists to review the smaller tasks that go into a successful direct marketing campaign.

PRINTING

Selecting the paper your marketing materials will be printed on is an important creative step that is sometimes left up to the printer. That's acceptable, if you don't know anything about paper selection and the printer takes the time to review the purposes of each piece in your mailing. If you work with a freelance graphic designer, he or she should suggest printing papers (and ink colors) as part of the job. With a brief understanding of some of your paper and ink options, however, you may be able to work with your printer and designer to get the best results possible.

The paper your advertising appears on communicates a message apart from the words printed on it. Heavy, watermarked paper carries a high-quality image. Paper that feels like something out of a fax machine communicates an image of a different quality. Between the two extremes is a range of subtle differences caused by the many characteristics of paper. Some of the qualities of paper you should be aware of are finish, opacity, color, caliper, and basis weight.

Most paper can be divided into two types of finishes, coated and uncoated. Uncoated paper has a flat or dull surface, which makes reading easy. Letterhead papers are uncoated and may have a textured surface. Uncoated paper, such as the paper in this book, while good for text, is not the best for the reproduction of photos and detailed artwork. Coated paper stock, which often has a high luster, shows the fine details in photographs. Ink colors are strong and brilliant on coated stock. A heavy, coated stock will convey a quality feel, but be careful using it for reply cards and coupons. Paper with a high-gloss surface is difficult to write on.

The *opacity* of paper means its ability to block light. Generally, the thicker the paper, the greater its opacity. A sure sign of a cheap printing job is ink from one side of the paper showing through to the other side.

Paper comes in a variety of colors. Colored paper is slightly more expensive than white, with the darker colors the most expensive. When printing on colored stock, you must take into consideration how the paper color will alter the color of the ink. The darker the paper, the more difficult it will be to read type printed in black, blue, or other dark-colored ink.

Caliper and *basis weight* refer to how thick a paper is and how much it weighs. The bulk or thickness of a paper does not always depend on its weight. Some new papers may be thicker than paper that is actually heavier. Since weight determines postage, thick, yet lightweight, papers can be advantageous. Many business reply cards, such as some you see in card decks, use a paper stock that doesn't weigh any more than a lightweight paper, yet is thick enough to qualify as a postcard under postal regulations. The U.S. Postal Service requires postcards to be at least .007 inches thick.

Basis weight is determined by the actual weight of 500 sheets of a paper's basic size, and different grades of paper have different basic sizes. The basic size for bond paper is 17×22 inches. Thus, a ream (500 sheets) of standard $8\frac{1}{2} \times 11$ inch, 20-pound bond paper does not weigh 20 pounds.

Ink comes in every color you can imagine. When designers select colors for a printing job, they usually use the Pantone Matching System, whose name is a trademark of Pantone, Inc. This color system, usually abbreviated PMS, contains hundreds of colors. To use the system, you need a PMS book, which contains swatches of all the colors, printed on both coated and uncoated paper. Each page of a PMS book looks something like the strips of paper, containing several paint samples, that you see in paint stores. Each PMS color is given a number so that designers can order a precise shade by specifying the number. Even if you don't select the colors yourself, a PMS book is handy to have. They're available at most graphics supply stores.

Cost Factors

One of the major contributors to the cost of printing is the number of colors you use. One-color printing is acceptable for some things, but two-color is pretty much a standard for letters, brochures, and other elements of direct mail. The cost of two-color printing will be 35 to 50 percent higher than that of one-color. In direct mail letters, you often see the signature and any hand-drawn underlining printed in blue to simulate ink from a pen. Even though the use of the second color ink is limited, you still pay as much as if you printed half the letter in blue.

Four-color printing is more than twice as expensive as two-color printing, in part because there are more steps in the process. Skillful designers can use two colors of ink in various combinations to create the effect of three, four, or more colors without having to resort to four-color printing. The four-color process is necessary, however, for reproducing full-color photos.

Experience is the best guide in judging how expensive different types of printing will be, but you should always get estimates from printers ahead of time. How do you know how much more expensive an $8\frac{1}{2}'' \times 17''$, two-color brochure on coated stock will be than an $8\frac{1}{2}'' \times 11''$ brochure with two ink colors on one side of the page and one ink color on the other? Experience tells you the smaller brochure will be substantially cheaper, but to find out how much cheaper, get an estimate.

If you're just starting to work with printers, save all the estimates you get, even the ones you don't use. Although they can get outdated, all the estimates you collect will serve as a general guide to printing costs. The next time you're planning a mailing, you can refer to your estimates for general ideas on the cost of printing various elements.

When working with a designer, you will want to determine ahead of time who will obtain the printing. If the designer furnishes the printing, he or she will seek bids, select a printer, then add from 15 to 25 percent to the price you pay. The advantage is that under this agreement, the designer works with the printer at every step of the way to be sure the job is completed as it should be. With small printing quantities, it may be worth the commission to you to have the designer find and work with the printer for you, at least for your first few jobs.

As you gain experience, you can save the markup cost by simply having your designer create the artwork for you, then taking it to different printers yourself to obtain bids. To save time, you usually get bids before the artwork is finished, but it's important to give all printers the same specifications on which to base their bids.

Ways to Save Money on Printing

Printing can often be the largest cost in a direct mail program, so it pays to shop carefully. According to Southern California graphic designer Don Markofski, you can save money on printing in a variety of ways. Markofski, who has more than 20 years' experience buying printing, offers these ideas and suggestions:

- Whether artwork bleeds off the page, the amount of ink coverage, and other technical factors all figure in the price you pay. The more specific you can be with the printer, the more accurate his or her estimate will be. "They'll tend to estimate high if you sound unsure and they think there will be changes later in the specifications," says Markofski.

- To get the lowest price, tell the printer you're shopping around and that you'll get two or three other bids. "Printers love to say, 'We'll give you the best quality you can get. We may not be the lowest price, but if you want quality we'll do it,'" says Markofski. "But if you let them know that you're shopping around," he says, "and that the quality being the same, you'll be going for the best price, you'll get a lower bid."

- Having clear, clean artwork is one way to avoid delays and misunderstandings, which can cost money. The written instructions on the artwork should be easy to understand. The printer should know ahead of time exactly how the piece should be printed. If you ask a printer to clean up or alter any artwork, there will be additional charges.

- A simple design can help keep printing costs down. If the printer doesn't have to use screens, bleeds, or other special effects, you'll save. The self-mailer featuring the silhouette of the F-18 fighter (Figures 13.5 and 13.6) is a good example of a basic, inexpensive design.

- It takes planning, but if you can run two jobs on the same printing press at the same time using the same ink colors and paper, you'll save 25 percent or more on the printing cost. This technique is called *ganging*.

  For example, say you're going to test two different offers in a mailing, so you need two different brochures. Since each brochure is going to be $8\frac{1}{2} \times 11$ inches, you could gang both at once on a press that printed on $11'' \times 17''$ paper. After the paper is printed, you simply have it cut in half to create two separate $8\frac{1}{2} \times 11$ inch brochures. After cutting, the brochures would be folded separately.

- If you create your artwork on a computer, and your printer is set up to receive the art via modem or diskette, you can also save money by not having to create camera-ready artwork. Incidentally, Markofski says the popular term *desktop publishing* is referred to by professionals as *electronic production*.

- A similar way to save money is to transfer the copy you write to your designer or typesetter via diskette or modem. You save the cost of someone having to enter your copy into a computer for typesetting.

- Understanding printing industry standards can save you money and time. For example, according to industry practice, a job may be satisfactorily completed and contain up to 10 percent more or 10 percent less than the quantity ordered. While your bill will be adjusted accordingly, that's little consolation if you're left with 10 percent fewer mailers than you have names on your list. To compensate, you can either increase your order or specify that you need a minimum amount.

  Printing estimates have limited life spans. When you obtain a written estimate from a printer, the form may specify that it's only good for 90 days. If paper or labor prices are rising, the estimates you receive will be for a shorter length of time. If you go back to the printer after the deadline, you could pay a higher price.

- Another way to save, says Markofski, is to give the printer more time. "Be honest, and if you're not in a hurry, you can often get the cost reduced," he says. "Printers are always rushing. If a printer has to take something else off the press to put your job on, you won't get a break on the price. If you tell him there's no rush, but you would like to get as good a price as possible, he'll probably save you money."

Most commercial printers, except the "instant press" variety, says Markofski, usually ask for seven to 10 working days to complete a job.

CHECKLISTS

Short of spending 20 years in the business learning the nuances and pitfalls, the best way to get control of direct marketing production is to maintain a written schedule. Many minor mistakes can be avoided if you approach the job in an organized way.

The following checklists are designed to jog your memory about creative details and to force you to structure the steps involved in producing direct response advertising. Many of the items on these lists constitute a summary of topics we've already covered. The discussion following each list explains new concepts and definitions, and suggests ways to use the items.

Editing Checklist

☐ **1.** What is the offer? Is it clear and obvious?

☐ **2.** Do the headline and first paragraph grab your attention?

☐ **3.** How does the lead in your letter begin?
  — Present the offer.
  — State the strongest benefit.
  — Use personal or inside information.
  — Use praise or fear immediately.
  — Ask a provocative question.

☐ **4.** Does your DM letter
  ☐ **(1)** Attract attention and lead the reader into the body?
  ☐ **(2)** Explain benefits clearly?
  ☐ **(3)** Overcome objections?
  ☐ **(4)** Initiate action?

☐ **5.** Are the paragraphs short (maximum seven lines for letters)?

☐ **6.** Does the copy flow well from one point to another?

☐ **7.** Is the language specific and detailed?

☐ **8.** Is it written to *one* person?

☐ **9.** What is the response requested? Is it clear?

☐   **10.** Is it easy to respond?

☐   **11.** What are your price considerations?

        __ Is the price stated more than one way?

        __ Are there price comparisons?

        __ Is there information on credit terms or credit card ordering?

☐   **12.** Is there an urgency device?

        __ Deadline

        __ Early bird reward

        __ Discount or limited sale

        __ Other

☐   **13.** What does the P.S. in your letter communicate?

        __ Unique selling proposition

        __ Deadline

        __ Second-best benefit

        __ Other

These are some of the questions you should ask yourself after you have a preliminary version of your direct response copy. Don't wait until the copy is typeset before you ask yourself whether you've used sufficient benefits, for example. You can also use this checklist to review copy written by a hired copywriter.

The design checklist that follows can be used the same way. Use it as you develop a design, or apply the questions to the work of a freelance designer.

Design Checklist

☐   **1.** Does the design contribute to selling the offer?

☐   **2.** Do the drawings and photos have captions that explain benefits?

☐   **3.** Are too many typefaces used? Does the typography contribute to or distract from the readability?

☐   **4.** Is there sufficient white space?

☐   **5.** Can you justify the use of any copy written in ALL-CAPS? (If not, put it in upper and lower case.)

☐   **6.** Does the direct mail letter *look* like a letter?

☐   **7.** Do any pages of your DM letter conclude with the end of a sentence?

☐   **8.** Does the design create an eye path that leads the reader to the offer?

☐   **9.** Is the type justified, or ragged right?

☐   **10.** Are there people in the photos?

☐   **11.** Does one headline dominate the layout and direct the reader to the text? (Does the headline contain benefits?)

☐   **12.** Do brochures and long-copy ads have subheadings to attract attention and organize the material? Do the subheads contain benefits?

PRODUCTION CHECKLIST

In previous chapters I've emphasized the importance of a work schedule. Here's a sample. The more complex the job, the more you should rely on a written time line. A typical direct response mailing may take two to three months to create, print, and mail. The more you do yourself, the more you may be able to cut down the time, because working with outside vendors always requires extra time to coordinate the work. Alternatively, some consultants can save you time. A veteran designer might be able to have a finished design in a fraction of the time you could, especially if you tackle your first direct response program yourself.

Production Schedule

Due
Date:　　　*Task:*
———　　Preliminary copy written.
———　　Preliminary (rough) design.
———　　Copy revised and approved.
———　　Comprehensive layout (comp) approved.
———　　Photos taken, artwork or illustrations selected.
———　　Colors of paper and ink selected.
———　　Paper stock selected and ordered as necessary.
———　　Dummy of finished piece(s) created, tested, and approved.
———　　Weight and postage costs determined.
———　　Conference held with letter shop on folding and inserting requirements.
———　　Time reserved with letter shop for inserting and mailing.
———　　Mechanical artwork completed.
———　　Mechanical artwork proofread and approved.
———　　Double-check addresses, phone numbers, prices.
———　　Be sure the reply card or coupon has all the necessary information.
———　　Complete artwork and instructions submitted to printer and date for completion established.
———　　Printer's blue line reviewed and approved.
———　　All inserts collected and transported to letter shop.

Understanding the various stages in production can help you expedite the work and save money. It's particularly important to know that the further into the production schedule you are, the more expensive and time-consuming it is to make changes. For instance, if you decide you need to change some of the wording in a brochure, it costs you nothing to make the changes before the type is set. The copy approval step *is* the place to make changes. Similarly, if you want to change the design, do it before the mechanical artwork is finished, and it won't cost you or delay the project.

Once a job has been turned over to the printer, changes in copy or layout will be costly and could delay your project by a week or more, depending on how extensive the changes.

The best way to understand how changes affect production is to visit a print shop, letter shop or mailing house, and even a designer's studio. As an example, you will see that once a printer has made plates for printing, any changes require going back two or more production steps.

The dummy mentioned in the list above is a full-scale model of your direct mail package. Using the same color, size, and weight paper stock and envelope you'll be printing on, your printer or designer makes up a blank model of your mail package. You do this to see that all the elements fit together in the envelope and to decide how to fold each piece. If you're going to use a window envelope, you want to be sure that the letter is folded so that the address shows through properly. The dummy also helps you when you're planning how the pieces will be mechanically inserted by your letter shop.

You also can use your dummy to determine the weight of your mailing package. When you weigh it, be sure to include the weight of a stamp and label if you're going to use those items. Although your dummy won't include the weight of the ink, unless you're close to a postage rate/weight plateau, such as one ounce for first class, it won't be a factor.

When you visit your letter shop, you'll see how the mechanical folding and inserting machines work (and sometimes don't). You'll understand why you have to heed certain specifications, such as keeping a $\frac{1}{4}''$ margin between the width of an envelope and the pieces inserted into it so that the machinery will process the job without jamming.

Your final quality check on a typical two-color printing job is a *blue line*, also called a Dylux. A blue line is a final proof of your job, reproduced in one color (blue) but with gradations of blue indicating the different colors of the job. At this stage, your main goal is to see that the printer has interpreted the instructions properly and that all type and illustration elements are arranged correctly on the page. Avoid making copy or design changes at this stage, because they'll be costly.

The production schedule assumes that you use a printer to print your materials, then a separate letter shop to collate, insert, and mail the packages. Some letter shops, however, can do all the work themselves.

Mailing and Testing Checklists

Mailing Lists:

☐ Confirm list orders with broker.
☐ Review specific selects (list segments).
☐ Broker verifies tape/diskette format.
    -or-
☐ Verify address format and label type.
    __ Self-adhesive (Avery or pressure sensitive)
    __ Paper (Cheshire)
☐ Coordinate printing production schedule with broker.

☐   When list order arrives, check labels, tape dump.
☐   Prepare house list labels or computer medium.
☐   Salt house list.
☐   Check postage deposit accounts for adequate balances.

Letter Shop:

☐   Review specific, written instructions.
☐   Provide completed, stuffed example.
☐   Check quantities of materials, such as envelopes, at letter shop.
☐   Perform merge/purge, list hygiene.
☐   Label envelopes or reply coupons.
☐   Add bar coding.
☐   Add laser or ink-jet imprinting on letters, coupons, or envelopes.
☐   Folding and insert.
☐   Seal; meter or affix stamps.
☐   Sort and place in mailbags.
☐   Deliver to post office.
☐   Provide check for postage.
☐   Obtain copy of Postal Service receipt for mailing from letter shop. The paperwork will differ, depending on whether you use your own bulk rate permit or the letter shop's.

Testing:

☐   Identify what to test.
      — Offer
      — Lists
      — Periodicals
      — Creative
      — Other
☐   Request A-B split from periodical(s).
☐   Double-check accuracy of periodical insertion orders.
☐   Order list test panels from brokers or managers.
☐   Prepare cost analysis, determine break-even level.
☐   Assign codes to tally results.
☐   Prepare tally sheets or computer programs to record results.
☐   Organize office procedures for recording, analyzing results.

When your computer tape or mailing labels arrive, check to see what you've got. With labels, you can randomly check names and addresses. If the list was ordered according to geography, business type, business title, or other identifiable selections, you should be able to glance through the list to see if it looks correct. For instance, if you've ordered a business list and you see nothing but residential names and addresses, you know a mistake has been made.

Mailing labels usually come in one of two forms. Cheshire labels are simply names and addresses printed on computer paper. They need to be cut, glued, and affixed. Avery labels are the peel-and-stick variety.

If you receive a tape, it will come with a limited printout (*dump*) used mainly to identify the proper format. It's a good idea to check a batch of names and addresses either before or during your imprinting run, again to make the same address checks as mentioned above for labels.

I recommend salting your house list with several names and addresses of your own. This way you'll be able to judge *when* the mailers arrive and see exactly how they are processed and sent by your mailing house. You should constantly monitor your mailing house (and the U.S. Postal Service) this way. The decoy names let you monitor third-class delivery times.

Before a mailing, be sure to check your deposit accounts with the post office. If you don't have enough money deposited to cover business reply mail, for example, the Postal Service may hold up delivery of your orders.

When you deliver printing, tapes, labels, and other materials to your letter shop, include specific written instructions and a sample of your mailing pieces inserted in the envelope. While I was working at Orange County Federal, our letter shop once used standard No. 10 envelopes with labels on the outside for a job that was supposed to have been inserted in window envelopes with the labels on the response cards showing through the window. As a result, the people who wanted to respond had to write their name and address in the open space on the reply card where a label should have been. The DM letter in the envelope referred to the reply card, with the member's "name and address already on it." Mistakes are good teachers sometimes, but this is one lesson you can learn the easy way. Make sure communications with your letter shop are clear and in writing.

Another item to check is the quantity of your printed materials the letter shop has. If you're mailing to a list of 10,000, you will deliver 10,000 envelopes, brochures, letters, and reply cards to the mailing house. Simple. But after you have done a few mailings, you may have excess supplies, such as envelopes or BRCs, stored at the mailing house, and it may be difficult for you to know exactly how many items the letter shop has. You'll often wind up with something left over after each mailing.

The point is to review periodically, in person if possible, the quantities of your materials the letter shop has. The problem you want to avoid is the letter shop calling you halfway through a run to say they ran short of something. When that happens, who is at fault? Did the printer deliver enough envelopes? Should the letter shop have had enough left over? If you keep good records and review quantities before each mailing, you can head off this common problem. When you see the large quantities of printed materials that the average letter shop processes, it's not surprising that some occasionally get misplaced.

Among the other things to decide in advance are how the addresses will be put on your envelopes, letters, or cards. You can have them printed on labels or printed directly on the mailing pieces with an impact printer or via laser or ink-jet process. You also decide ahead of time which type of postage you will use. The letter shop will want to be paid in advance for stamps or metered postage. If you use indicia, you'll need a check for the Postal Service ready to be delivered along with the mailing.

Before a test mailing goes out is the time to prepare for tabulations and analysis. You should know in advance how many responses you need to break even or to consider the program a success.

Production Costs

How much will a direct mail job or campaign cost? The mailing lists, printing, and postage are the most expensive, but other costs remain. If you want to estimate how much a job will cost, here are the categories of expenses you might incur, depending on how much or how little you do yourself. The division of labor might be slightly different for your jobs, but the tasks should be the same. Your letter shop, for instance, could be set up to do the data processing work, or you might have that done separately.

Cost Estimate Checklist

Creative:

Layout, design (Designer)

Copywriting (Copywriter)

Mechanical artwork (Graphic artist, typesetter)

Photos, illustrations (Photographer, illustrator)

List Managers, Brokers, Compilers:

Rental charges

Selections

Tape charges, deposits

Printers:

Printing

Paper

Bindery (For additional services such as gluing, binding, cutting; often included in printing charges)

Data Processing Service Bureau:

Merge/purge

List hygiene

Suppression

NCOA, DSF, ZIP + 4, Carrier route

Letter Shop:

Printing

Labeling

Bar coding

Imprinting labels or addresses

Personalizing letters

Folding, inserting

Sealing, metering, affixing stamps

Sorting, bagging, delivering to post office

U.S. Postal Service:

Postage, return postage

Deposits, fees

POSTSCRIPT....

Rental Decoys

If you're doing a mailing to a large area, you'll want to have decoy names and addresses in strategic cities. If you can't provide these yourself, yes, there's a service that does this for you too. Your envelopes are returned to you unopened, as soon as they're received. For the name of such a service, see Appendix B.

17 CUSTOMER SERVICE

Keeping 'em Coming Back for More

All the pretty words and pictures in the world won't make a satisfied customer. Satisfied customers are made—one at a time—through exceptional levels of quality and service.

—Harry and David® catalog

What happens after your direct marketing programs get results? It's up to you.

After years of emphasis on excellence in customer service through books, magazines, training seminars, awards, and government programs, service in the United States is still mediocre. While some companies excel at serving customers, others have had to improve to become mediocre.

So many organizations give adequate-at-best service that customers' expectations are low. People expect a certain level of ambivalence.

When I was doing research for this book, I called a large public company. The only phone number I could find was the customer service line, so I dialed it, then waited through three separate recordings on the voice mail system, each of which varied in voice tone quality and professionalism. When I finally reached a human being, I explained that I was calling for the corporate marketing department. There was a pause on the line and I thought the person was looking up an extension number. She said, "What is the problem?"

Perhaps customer service reps are used to having people call with complaints or problems, but assuming that every call is prompted by a problem presents a sorry impression. Unfortunately everyone is familiar with the "what's *your* problem" attitude.

The average level of service today gives you an enormous opportunity. Since people expect nominal service, it doesn't take much to be above average. With just a little care and interest in doing a good job, your company can soar above the competition.

Accentuating positive customer service will yield dividends for your company in many ways, and it's easy to implement; much is based on common sense. Ship orders promptly. Treat customers as human beings, the way you would want to be treated. Stand behind your warranties. Keep your customers informed about delays or problems. Don't keep people waiting, either on the phone or in person.

Succeeding at customer service requires not only the physical actions but a personal commitment. You can't win customers with the mechanical actions alone. It takes sincerity. Recognize that customer service is a responsibility of everyone in your organization.

While there are many positive reasons for adopting excellent customer service (among them the personal satisfaction you'll feel), good service can also help you avoid several perils of direct marketing. Here's what you can prevent:

- Negative referrals. People tend to tell others more frequently when they have a bad experience with a company than when they have a good one. Negative word-of-mouth communication is almost impossible to counter effectively with advertising. Good service avoids image problems before they arise.
- Official complaints. By following the dictates of good service policies and appropriate regulations, you don't have protracted involvements with regulatory agencies. Customers who are treated fairly don't complain to the FTC, the district attorney, or consumer journalists.
- Inordinate customer turnover. It's more expensive and time-consuming to attract a new customer than it is to keep an existing one. With excessive turnover you are forced to spend more money on advertising to replace your missing customers. You lose back-end opportunities because you spend too much time on front-end marketing.
- Customers changing their minds. Prompt, efficient responses to customer orders and inquiries do not encourage customers to change their minds. On the other hand, if merchandise is late, customers may go elsewhere or simply decide they don't want to buy. If an interested prospect doesn't hear from you soon after asking for product information, he or she may buy from another company that responded quickly.

Open, *two-way* communication is a principal element in good customer service. In addition to the communications you initiate, you should encourage customers to talk to you, to tell you what they think. In fact, your customers are the people you should consult when you're planning and documenting your customer service policies.

You should seek regular feedback from your customers. Here's where brief customer questionnaires can help. A survey will tell you what you're doing right, but more importantly it will help you identify potential problem areas before they seriously affect your business. Surveys about services create goodwill too, because people will be pleased you asked for their opinion. Randomly calling customers to find out if they are satisfied with your products and services is another way to gauge customer satisfaction. Your call will probably be a pleasant surprise for the people you contact.

INBOUND TELEMARKETING

Unless you're solely in the mail-order business, you may not consider answering telephone inquiries as a form of telemarketing, but it is. Even if you don't have operators sitting in front of computer screens taking orders, you still practice inbound telemarketing. Every time someone at your office picks up the phone, he or she becomes a telemarketing representative.

Whether you sell to businesses or consumers, whether you are a retailer or mail-order marketer, you need to set up practices and procedures that ensure that everyone who calls you gets first-class treatment. Your telephone plan should include (1) guides for courteous use of the phone, (2) simple order-fulfilling procedures, (3) background information to help employees answer questions about your products and services, (4) techniques for qualifying callers, and (5) suggestions and prompts for cross selling.

Written telemarketing material is not meant to impose an inflexible structure on inbound calls, but having it in writing is essential. When the phone rings, if you are busy doing something else, a written outline can help you refocus your thinking quickly.

Courtesy is mandatory and should always include using a customer's name. The person who answers the phone should identify himself. If customers must be put on hold, they should be told the reason and asked their permission. Telephone ordering procedures need to be structured to the extent that the employee obtains all the pertinent product and payment information.

Employees who answer customer calls should know the details of current advertising: what merchandise you're advertising and the details of your direct marketing offers. When I was a credit union marketing director, I made sure that every department, even those with little public contact, received advance copies of our advertising along with a memo explaining what types of questions and requests might be coming in.

In some businesses you will need initially to qualify callers to see what level of follow-up they should receive. A person who's collecting data for a library does not get placed on the same follow-up list as someone who's going to make a buying decision in two weeks.

Toll-Free Numbers

Offering a toll-free number encourages your customers and prospects to call you, and many telecommunications companies have cost-effective service for small businesses. In many parts of the country, you can obtain 800 number service and limit the area for which you provide toll-free calling. In other words, you can identify certain parts of your state, region, or city and provide a toll-free number just for customers in those areas.

Today, 800-number services are available through local Bell companies and through national long-distance firms, so you usually have a choice of vendors. Often you can have 800 service without having to change your phone number. Here's an example of some of the options and services that may be available to you. These are provided for customers of Pacific Bell who use "Custom 800" service:

- You may take your number with you if you move. For example, real estate agents working for one firm and using their own 800 number can take it with them if they move to another firm. (Clients will still call the same 800 number they're used to and still get the same sales agent.)

- The area served can be as small as the territory covered by one three-digit phone number prefix, or you may specify several different areas.
- Printed reports from Pacific Bell, sorted by phone number, will tell you the prefixes your calls come from. They will also identify the area codes and prefixes for people who tried to call you toll-free but could not because they were outside your specified 800-number area.
- You can have calls routed to different offices at different times of the day. For example, if you have two offices that are staffed at different hours, you could have all 800 calls routed to one office during normal business hours and calls after hours routed to another office.

Services and costs vary substantially, so it's in your interest to check with different companies in your area. Firms levy setup charges and will charge extra for written usage reports in addition to the charges for each call. One question to ask your 800–number provider is how the toll charges are billed. Some firms charge a flat rate per call, which may be more expensive for you than doing business with a company that bases the toll fees on the distance each call travels.

Cross Selling

To cross over from one product or service to another is natural in the course of serving someone or taking an order. If a caller orders a skirt and you have a belt that matches it on special sale, it's just natural to tell her about it. I like to refer to cross selling as cross *telling*. In many instances all it takes to get an additional sale is to *tell* a customer about a product or service. Telephone orders or inquiries are perfect opportunities for cross selling, but remember that the same techniques can be applied in person.

Sometimes, people avoid cross selling because they think customers will be irritated. The opposite is usually the case. Telling customers about additional and appropriate products shows you have an interest in them. If you suggest a product on sale, customers will appreciate the information. In fact, if they found out later that you had items on sale that you didn't mention, they might be disappointed. Furthermore, your customers do business with you because they like your products or service. They will probably want additional products and services of similar quality.

Cross telling is the easiest, least threatening sales and marketing technique, and it has one of the highest sales completion percentages. Here are five fundamentals of cross telling:

1. Know Your Products. In order to tell customers about appropriate products, employees must know what the products are. In financial institutions, when someone opens a checking account, a good customer service representative knows that an automated teller card is a related service that many people will want. Some products inherently need something else to make them complete, such as batteries for electronic toys, ink for stamp pads, diskettes for computers.

2. Know your customers. If service employees know customers personally, they're in the best position to make cross-selling suggestions. The smaller your business, the more likely this will be. At the minimum, however, service personnel should have a good idea of your customer profile. The more they know about customers, the better they will be able to make service or product suggestions.

3. Ask questions and listen for cues or clues. When a customer complains that he ran out of a product at a crucial time, that's a cue to suggest he buy in larger quantities. Many of the things a customer says in conversation can be a clue to a specific product or service need, even a need the customer doesn't fully realize himself.

4. Evaluate customers' needs and select appropriate products. When a service person knows the customer and hears some cues or clues, it should suggest certain cross-telling tactics. With a little experience in working with customers, the product or service evaluations will become almost automatic.

5. Make the suggestion. If it's treated simply as a *suggestion*, it will be easy for the employee to volunteer it, and easy for the customer to accept.

WRITTEN COMMUNICATIONS

Some customer communications can be handled more efficiently with a letter than on the phone. The larger your customer base and the smaller your staff, the more you must rely on letters and printed messages for various customer service functions.

Whenever possible, personal letters should accompany literature sent in response to an inquiry. The business letters companies often send form a sharp contrast with direct mail letters. Where direct mail letters are personal, friendly, and filled with benefits, follow-up letters are often terse, impersonal, and lacking any persuasive punch. After a company spent thousands of dollars on a direct mail campaign to generate sales leads, why would they send out a follow-up letter like the following?

Dear friend:

Here is the information you requested relative to our new Model VI. Thanks for your interest in our firm.

Sincerely,
FLAPDOODLE ENTERPRISES

Follow-up letters should be *better* than your direct mail letters, because each one is sent to an interested prospect. Letters should be personalized and aimed at the specific needs of each company or individual. The letters should be brief, but they should point out some of the most important benefits shown in the accompanying literature. Follow-up letters can also make cross-selling suggestions about accessories or supplies.

Even with the advantages of word processing, there are some times when it's just not feasible to send everyone a personalized letter. Mass-produced customer notices are a necessary evil, especially in mail order, but there are steps you can take to make even form letters become goodwill ambassadors.

If you can't personalize the notice, at least use personal pronouns, as in direct mail, to talk directly to the reader. Make the message clear and easy to understand. Explain any jargon. If you're asking the customer to do something, explain it in terms of his interests, not yours. For instance, to get someone to finish an incomplete application, rather than saying, "It is our company policy that all forms must be filled out in full," you could say, "We'll process your application faster, and you'll get an answer sooner, if you fill out the bottom section of this form."

Form letters and notices should be signed by someone, even if it's a reproduction of the signature. At the least, the name of the person who wrote the note should be on the bottom. Sometimes, people hesitate to put their names on form notices because they don't want customers calling *them* with questions. The simple solution is to include the name and phone number of the person customers should call if they do have questions. And customers often have questions. To make your form notices sound friendly and personal, use the style techniques discussed in Chapter 8.

One type of form notice, which can be highly profitable for many businesses, is the order reminder notice. You should remind customers when it's time for scheduled equipment maintenance or health check-ups. Tell them when their insurance, service contracts, or other continuing agreements are up for renewal. If you sell supplies, remind customers that they ordered their annual refills almost a year ago. Be creative. Develop service or buying intervals that make sense for customers. Offer to remind them when various parts or supplies need replacing.

FTC Mail Order Rule

One series of written customer notices you must use, if you're in mail-order marketing, are those necessary to comply with the FTC's Mail Order Rule. If a customer orders and pays for merchandise and you are not able to ship it within 30 days, you must send a delay notice, or *option notice* in FTC terminology, which tells the customer that you are experiencing delays in shipping.

If you expect to be able to make the shipment within another 30 days, state the revised shipping date. You must give the customer the option of agreeing to the delay (by doing nothing) or of canceling the order (by contacting you).

According to the FTC Mail Order Rule, if you cannot provide a revised shipping date, you must explain that to your customer and say that the order will be *automatically canceled* unless (1) you ship the merchandise within 30 days of the original shipping date and you do not, before shipping, receive a customer's notice to cancel, or (2) you receive your customer's consent to the delay.

Other notices and actions are required if you experience further delays. When a customer requests a refund, it must be mailed first-class, within seven days. If a customer paid for the merchandise by credit card, the refund must be made within one billing cycle after the order is canceled. You may not issue a credit voucher instead of a cash refund.

The FTC rule says that when you advertise merchandise, you must have a "reasonable basis" for expecting to ship within the time you state in your ads. If you think shipping times are going to exceed 30 days, you can state the time in your ad, such as, "Please allow 6 to 8 weeks for delivery." Without a statement of shipping times, you are automatically bound by the 30-day requirements.

For complete details and sample notices, the FTC has a guide to the Mail Order Rule (see Appendix B). The regulations also apply to all telemarketers.

NEWSLETTERS

A free newsletter is a relatively inexpensive way to maintain contact with customers, and for that reason alone many companies create their own house publications. A newsletter, however, can and should do more than just keep your name in front of customers.

A free newsletter can help build rapport between you and your customers; it can establish and improve your image; it can give customers opportunities to order or give you feedback; and it can communicate important news about your organization. To be effective, a newsletter should do all of these things. To do only one or two of them reduces the credibility or diminishes the value of the publication.

Like all of your marketing materials, your newsletter should have specific goals. To be effective, your publication should inform, entertain, attract interest, maintain company image, sell and cross sell.

The usual purpose of a newsletter is to maintain a relationship with customers. To do that and keep customers reading, your newsletter should be lively or casual and easy to read. Naturally, newsletters for business need to be a bit more formal. Interesting-sounding headlines and a mixture of artwork and stories make an attractive layout.

While most stories should be related to your business or individual customers, you can use advice columns and inside industry information. If your newsletter goes to homes, rather than businesses, consumer awareness articles are appropriate. Articles that demonstrate your technical knowledge and give useful ideas help build your professional reputation. You can indirectly position your firm as an industry leader. Technical articles also attract readers and provide a balance to the rest of the newsletter, which promotes your company.

Articles about individual customers will attract readers, as human interest stories in newspapers do, and will cement your relationship with the subjects of the articles.

The other *news* portion of your newsletter should contain any important information customers need to do business with you. Changes in hours, services, policies, and staff that affect customers should be explained.

Newsletters don't have to be a non–income-producing expense. By offering products for sale, you can at least make a newsletter pay for itself. Every edition should give customers a chance to place an order or ask for more information. Making part of the newsletter a perforated reply card is one easy way. Have special offers mentioned only in the newsletter. Run a "news" article about some remnant stock you have that you're selling off at reduced prices. You also can include your own print ads in the newsletter if you want to separate promotion from news. You don't want your newsletter to be full of ads; you would then have a catalog, and customers would perceive it as such.

The writing style of the newsletter should match your industry, your customers, and you. Company newsletters range from folksy and corny to starched and professional.

If you're a self-employed professional, writing to individual clients or patients rather than company representatives, you should still maintain the balance of news and promotion. Build your image, but also give your readers low-commitment and high-commitment offers they can respond to.

To help you formulate a balanced editorial policy for your newsletter, here are some article ideas:

- How a company (or individual) used your product to solve a common industry problem
- New products, services available
- Changes in your hours or phone numbers
- Mini-profile of one of your customer service people
- Accessories customers can use to customize or expand the use of your products
- Letters from customers
- Question and answer column about product uses or technical or industry problems
- A new use for one of your products
- Special sales, close-outs
- Customer feedback corner, asking customers to tell you what they think about you and your products
- Information response card to let customers request information about your other products or services
- New regulations in your industry
- Profile of one of your customers

To break out of the pack by offering customers something different, some firms mail audio newsletters on cassette tape. The costs for mailing and production may be higher than for a standard newsletter, but an audio tape allows you to reach customers with a dramatic presentation of words, sounds, and music. La Quinta Inns, a motel chain, sends audio cassettes in talk-show format to members of its frequent visitors club. If you use an audio format, remember to maintain your balance of information, entertainment, and promotion/advertising. Be sure to mention your toll-free telephone number so customers can respond to your offers. You might even include a business reply card with each cassette to give customers another way to respond.

HONORING CREDIT CARDS

A final consideration in setting up a direct marketing program is the need to honor bank credit cards. If you wish to do a portion of your consumer sales over the phone, credit card acceptance is mandatory. The more consumer- and mail-order–oriented your business, the more you should consider using credit cards.

To get started, contact your own commercial banker. Banks and some savings and loan associations can provide you with everything you need to accept and process MasterCard and VISA credit card transactions. You should contact your bank first, because that's where you're likely to get the best deal, especially if you've done business with the bank for a long time; however, you should also shop around to compare services and prices.

The main advantage of honoring credit cards, in addition to providing customer convenience, is the opportunity to reduce your losses from bad checks. A certain percentage of the checks you receive will be returned for insufficient funds, and sometimes you will never collect the money. On the other hand, if you follow established procedures for processing credit card transactions, you are protected against loss.

The credit card slips you generate and deposit in your bank account are treated much like checks. How quickly your bank gives you credit for the funds is a matter of bank policy and is sometimes open to negotiation. Unlike checks, your deposited charge card slips will not bounce. If a customer has run over his credit limit or uses a stolen card, your bank will absorb the loss, provided you have followed processing rules.

The major cost of a credit card program comes from the percentage of your gross receipts which the bank charges for processing. Fees range from 2 to 5 percent, and since bank charges vary, it will benefit you to check several financial institutions.

Most banks will not only process your charge slips, but will provide the equipment and training you need to start honoring credit cards.

CONCLUSION

As direct marketing costs rise, catering to the needs of existing customers becomes increasingly important. Remember, it's the goal of data base marketing not just to make a sale, but to establish a lasting relationship with a customer.

As your relationship with your customers expands, your advertising becomes less expensive and more effective, because you advertise additional offers to people who already know and trust you. Like a credit union's members, your long-term customers will become your most important asset.

POSTSCRIPTS....

Mail-Order Service

If you're in the mail-order merchandise business, you have additional incentives to give great service. First, many of your competitors have excellent service. The top companies in the business set the standard for mail order. Second, in mail order, service is the reason people choose to buy from you. People use mail order because it so easy to order directly from their home or office. If they don't get prompt, courteous service, mail order has lost its advantage.

99 Percent Attitude

When hiring people for customer service jobs, look for a positive attitude first, technical skills second. It's easier to teach your employees how your products work than it is to change attitudes.

A WHEN TO HIRE PROFESSIONALS

When to Hire Outside Help, Where to Find It, and How Much to Pay

Armed with this book, you can conduct direct marketing with little outside help, except a printer.

Chances are though, that at times you may want to get help from selected experts. Chapters 4 and 6 review the advantages of working with a list broker, who may double as a direct marketing advisor. The quantity and sophistication of your direct mail, and the number of employee-hours you have available to do stuffing and mailing, will dictate whether or not you use a mailing house or letter shop. Beyond those choices, there is a variety of other specialists on call. When should you ask for help?

As a small business grows, the owner will reach a point when he or she no longer has time to do all the marketing and still manage the business. That's when it's time to consider outside help.

The more successful your marketing, the more it will hasten the time when you need additional help. You can select a high- level creative specialist to come up with the campaigns and copy to keep your business growing. Alternatively, if you have established a successful formula for your marketing, you may want to find someone simply to execute it for you. In that case, consider in-house help in addition to freelancers.

Poor results may be another signal to consult outside help. If you're pinpointing your potential customers but don't seem to be getting the responses you'd like, your offers and creative work may need a pro to give them more life. If you think your lists are at fault, then you need a list specialist. If you don't know what's wrong, a consultant may be the answer.

Ultimately, the decision to seek outside help is founded either on your need for expertise in a specific area or simply on your need for people to do tasks in order to free you up to attend to other areas of your business. You have to decide what is the best, most effective use of your time.

What Help Is Available?

Following are some of the outside specialists and organizations available:

Copywriters Independent direct response writers work for themselves, and many agency copywriters do moonlight work.

Designers Design studios come in all sizes. Consider the one- or two-person shops first. Designers usually offer to do the design, layout, typesetting, and full mechanical artwork.

Consultants Among the ranks of direct marketing consultants are former employees of marketing agencies, DP service bureaus, list brokers, and direct mail merchandisers. Their services may include everything from constructing marketing plans to primary research to copywriting and media selection.

Direct Marketing Agencies You're more likely to find specific direct marketing agencies in larger cities.

DP Service Bureaus Computer service companies vary in size and capabilities.

Telemarketing Firms Telemarketing consultants can help you set up your own program, and larger firms will do the calling for you.

TV Stations Some local television stations will produce your commercials for you, often at lower cost than you would pay to hire a private production company. The same is true for radio stations.

Where to Find Them

Locating a good copywriter or graphic designer is about like trying to find a doctor or lawyer. Your choices include getting a referral from someone you know, getting a name through a referral service or association, and picking a name out of a directory. When you're searching for a direct marketing professional, you have additional advantages, such as being able to scrutinize samples of the person's work.

When looking for a copywriter, designer, or consultant, first ask any business people you know who might be able to refer you to someone they have worked with before. List brokers and printers can also refer you to consultants and direct marketing creative people. In addition, writers can refer you to designers, designers can refer you to writers and printers, and so on.

Have you seen some advertising that you thought was effective and that reflected creative techniques you would like to have working for you? Contact the advertisers to find out the names of the creative people they work with.

Direct marketing clubs, which are scattered all over the U.S., are a good source of referrals. If you have a club in your area, attend a meeting. Introduce yourself to the president. Say that you're doing your own direct marketing and that you're interested in getting some help from a copywriter or telemarketer.

You can also find outside help from directories. The *Direct Marketing Market Place*, available at some libraries, lists the names of direct response writers, designers, and other specialists. Many specialty firms and freelancers advertise in the trade publications listed in Appendix B, and many of the larger direct marketing clubs publish service directories. *Target Marketing* magazine publishes an annual directory of creative services.

Who to Select... What to Pay

Looking at the portfolios or *books* of creative people is one way to judge their work. When you make an appointment to talk with them, they should bring plenty of samples. For copywriters, ask for photocopies of some of their samples so that you can read them carefully later. Don't pay attention to the fancy graphics when you're picking a writer, although writers have a tendency to pick attractive, as well as well-written, samples for their books.

To pick a designer for direct mail, I'd rather review the samples in the envelopes as they're delivered rather than elaborately mounted in a book. Designers like to show you things that look nice, but what you want are designs that sell. Of course, you should ask all outside specialists for the results of their campaign examples. The answers you get will vary in the amount of specific details they contain and in their accuracy.

One way to judge an outside specialist you're talking to is by the number of questions he asks. Are his questions designed to help him understand your business? Does he show interest and expertise by asking about your specific direct marketing goals, or is he simply an order taker who will do what you ask, but little more? A good consultant or freelance creative person should ask you questions all the time you're working together. You want someone who learns more about your business so that he can make useful, money-saving suggestions.

No matter where you live, you should have an assortment of freelance writers from which to choose, but you should only talk with writers who have extensive direct response experience. With the help of this book, you might be able to turn a conventional copywriter's work into direct response copy, but why should you have to? Work with someone who knows how to get responses. It's not as critical to find a designer who specializes in direct response, which is good, because they seem to be harder to find. Don't hire someone who just designs annual reports and magazines. You can tell by looking through a designer's portfolio whether most of the work is simply attractive or is designed to get responses and sell.

Experience or expertise in your particular field may be a concern when you're looking for a writer or consultant. If you're looking for someone to write copy for a mainstream business service, or to advise you on direct mail marketing for general merchandise, you probably don't need a specialist per se. If you're in a heavily regulated industry or a high-tech field, you may need someone who is familiar with the intricacies of your business. In many cases "specialists" don't charge higher fees for their expertise in your industry.

Don't expect any outside specialist to guarantee the percentage response you will get. If you use a consultant to plan an entire advertising program for you, however, you should discuss the levels of response you need to make a profit.

The prices you agree on with designers or writers will include reasonable revisions. A copywriter will not charge you extra to rewrite portions of his copy, unless the changes are necessary because you provide new information or change your offer. Designers will make changes too, but remember that the time to make major changes is at the beginning of the design process.

How much should you pay a consultant or freelancer? Rates quoted may be by the hour or by the job. At first, it's probably better for you to obtain quotes for the specific job you have in mind. When you ask for quotes, be as specific as you can about the job. Tell the freelancer exactly what you expect. Ask him or her to be equally precise in explaining what the fee will include. If you both decide ahead of time on the size of the mailing pieces or the ad you're going to use, your price quote can be more exact.

Here's an example. Say you want someone to write a typical direct mail package with an outer envelope, two- to four-page letter, brochure, and coupon or other reply device. Copywriter fees will range from $1,500 to $4,000, depending on the experience of the copywriter. Understand that these are average fees for professional direct response writers. The top people in the industry get $15,000 and more for a direct mail package and beginners with little experience might charge only $1,000 or less. For an 11" × 17" or smaller self-mailer you might expect a fee of $1,500 to $2,000. For print ads, prices range from $350 to about $1,500, depending on the writer's experience and the size of the ad.

The prices charged by designers vary as much as the copywriters'. With most self-employed creative types, the amount of work they have sometimes affects their estimates. If I'm swamped, for example, I may up my fee a little, thinking that if I *do* get the job, the extra money will pay for my overtime.

Some designers may divide their charges between the creative design side (that is, doing the layout and the comp) and the mechanical work of creating the finished artwork.

For the typical direct mail package described in the example, design charges for a two-color job range from $1,000 to $3,500. That does not include the mechanical artwork, the cost for which approximately doubles the above costs. Again, this average is for mid-range professionals. The cost for the design *and* mechanical for an 11" × 17" self-mailer ranges from $750 to $2,000.

Some designers may quote you a fixed price for a comp (design) and an hourly rate ($25 to $65 per hour) for doing the mechanical artwork. The complexity of the artwork and the amount of copy can greatly influence the cost of design and mechanicals. A simple job would be in the lower range of the prices quoted; a more complex job, in the upper range. When you obtain an estimate from a designer, be sure to determine what the estimate covers. Photography, illustrations, and typesetting are usually extra.

Designers, who like to work with people they know, will recommend photographers to you. If you insist on finding your own photographer, or if you're doing your own design and need photos, your local newspaper is a source of talent. Many newspaper photographers do freelance work on the side, and they charge far less than do commercial photographers specializing in advertising. There will be a difference in quality. Newspaper photographers photograph life. Ad photographers picture life as someone would like it to be.

Talk to local commercial photographers to get their rates. They usually charge a shooting fee and may have a half-day minimum charge, with extra costs for the film and prints. Newspaper freelancers charge about the same way, but where a commercial photographer's half-day rate may be $500 or more, a newspaper photographer's might be $100 to $200.

Direct marketing consultants may charge by the hour at rates ranging from $75 to $150. Depending on a consultant's specialty, he or she may suggest bringing in other people as well, such as a designer or service bureau. If you're looking for special help with research, telemarketing, mail-order fulfillment, or some other individual aspect of direct marketing, look for a consultant with experience in that area. Not every direct marketing consultant is an expert in all aspects of this broad field. Some consultants may act as direct marketing agencies, providing you with planning and implementation of campaigns.

What can you expect from a consultant? He or she should ask to see samples of your past direct mail materials and ads. The consultant will review your customer profile, your business plan, advertising budget; see how your implementation has matched your goals; review specific results from ads and direct mail; and determine your CP/Ms to compare them to industry figures.

You can hire someone to troubleshoot your marketing in this way, or you can do all of these things yourself first, *then* decide if you need outside help.

Direct marketing agencies are not nearly as plentiful as general advertising agencies, although ad agencies are increasingly adding direct response staff. Agencies like to do everything for you. If you just need some help with creativity or lists, you would be better off seeking the individual specialists you need rather than paying agency fees, which are not necessarily designed to attract small businesses.

Telemarketing firms vary in size and sophistication. Automated firms have banks of phones staffed by telemarketing sales representatives who don't even need to dial a phone to make a call. A computer automatically reads phone numbers off a list, dials, and connects the call to any representative who is free. This saves time, increasing the number of calls per hour. At smaller firms, the callers dial the phones themselves.

If you have a complex or technical product, telemarketing representatives at outside firms may not be qualified to make calls for you without an inordinate amount of training. In this case you should consider in-house telemarketing.

If you think telemarketing is suited to your product or service, you can test it by hiring a telemarketing firm for a small job. As mentioned before, business-to-business telemarketing is usually more time-consuming and therefore will be more costly when you hire an outside firm.

Minimum charges, or minimum numbers of calls, will vary with the size of the telemarketing firm. While automated calling services are more suited to lists of 8,000 to 10,000 and above, other, nonautomated firms may agree to make 500 or fewer calls.

Talk with representatives of several firms before you make a decision. Ask to see their offices and equipment. Ask for the names of some clients you can contact for a reference. Ask how they verify calls. Some firms call back a certain number of customers to verify sales.

Telemarketing firms charge by the hour. The typical charge per person, per hour, ranges from $25 to $35 for a simple consumer-oriented sales program and $55 and up for complex consumer or business-to-business campaigns. In addition, firms may have extra charges for training employees about your product or service, developing a telemarketing script, and producing special reports on the marketing results.

When you work with any self-employed specialists, you may be asked for some money up front. Don't be offended. When you work with a designer who will also supply the printing on a direct mail package, for instance, you have a multi-thousand dollar transaction that may cover six weeks or more. It's not unreasonable for the designer to ask you for a down payment, so to speak, because he or she may have to pay some outside costs in advance. It's typical for outside experts to ask for incremental payments. This works in your favor too. You agree ahead of time that certain stages of the work will be completed by a certain time. As a stage is completed, you pay for that step along the way.

To summarize, follow these suggestions when working with outside specialists:

- Clearly identify what you want the specialist to do. Provide as much detail and specification as possible. This also allows you to get estimates you can compare easily.
- Agree between you exactly what the charges will be, what they cover, and when they're due. It's best to have this in writing. Letters of agreement are common, formal contracts rare.
- Ask for references and check them.
- Ask to see work samples. Ask questions about previous jobs.
- Initially, don't commit yourself to working with someone or some firm beyond one project. If things work out, you can maintain the relationship.
- When you give an assignment, put deadlines in writing.
- Don't select solely on the basis of the lowest price. Balance the costs with the talent and knowledge the professional displays.

B RESOURCES

● ●

PUBLICATIONS

Books and Directories:

The Arthur Young Business Plan Guide

By Eric Siegel, Loren Schultz, Brian Ford, and David Carney
John Wiley & Sons, Inc., 1987
It all starts with your business plan and this guide tells you how.

Communication Graphics

By Wendell C. Crow
Prentice Hall, 1986
Contains details and background on graphics, printing, and basic design principles.

Successful Direct Marketing Methods, 5th Edition

By Bob Stone
NTC Business Books, 1993
The industry's standard reference/text.

Write Like the Pros

By Mark S. Bacon
John Wiley & Sons, Inc., 1988
Applies the response-getting techniques of copywriters to all your routine business communications.

These books give further details on specific subjects:

Mailing List Strategies

By Rose Harper
McGraw-Hill, 1986

Catalog Marketing

By Katie Muldoon
American Management Association, 1988

The Complete Guide to Marketing and the Law

By Robert J. Posch, Jr.
Prentice Hall, 1990

Standard Rate and Data Service (SRDS)

3004 Glenview Road
Wilmette, IL 60091
(708) 256-6067
SRDS publishes the bibles of the marketing/advertising industry. Directories include: *Direct Mail Lists Rates and Data, Consumer Magazine and Agri-media Rates and Data, Newspaper Rates and Data,* and *Spot Radio Rates and Data.* A single copy of the direct mail list book is $152 and six bi-monthly issues are $345.

Gale Directory of Publications and Broadcast Media

Gale Research, Inc.
Published annually.

Writer's Market

Writer's Digest Books
Guide to periodicals is published annually.

National Directory of Mailing Lists

Oxbridge Communications, Inc.
(800) 955-0231
Published annually with four quarterly supplements. Also available on diskettes or CD-ROM.

Direct Marketing Market Place (DMMP)

Reed Reference Publishing
121 Chanlon Road
New Providence, NJ 07974
(800) 323-6772
Contains listings of service firms and suppliers, creative services and direct marketing agencies, meetings and events, and awards and contests. Cost is $157 for annual edition.

Mail Management Manual:

A Digest of Postal Rates and Regulations

Tension Envelope Corp.
819 E. 19th St.
Kansas City, MO 64108-1781
This free booklet clarifies the often-confusing postal regulations and requirements and contains an up-to-date list of rates and classes of mail. A must for small business mailers.

Periodicals

Direct Marketing Magazine

Hoke Communications, Inc.
224 Seventh St.
Garden City, NY 11530-5771
Each issue of this monthly magazine contains a variety of useful articles, a section listing video and audio tapes of direct marketing training programs you can order, plus listings of DM clubs and creative services.

DM News

19 W. 21st Street
New York, NY 10010
Free weekly tabloid with industry news and many helpful how-to columns. Read Lee Epstein's authoritative column on the Postal Service.

Target Marketing

North American Publishing
401 N. Broad St.
Philadelphia, PA 19108
Monthly magazine with news and features. Read Ray Jutkins's column for good creative ideas.

Telemarketing

Technology Marketing Corp.
One Technology Plaza
Norwalk, CT 06854

TeleProfessional

209 W. Fifth St. Suite N
Waterloo, IA 50701-5420

Business Marketing

Crain Communications
220 E. 42nd Street
New York, NY 10017

Fund Raising Management

Hoke Communications
224 Seventh St.
Garden City, NY 11530-5771

Who's Mailing What!

P.O. Box 8180
Stamford, CT 06905
Monthly newsletter also publishes an annual directory of freelancers and what they charge.

What's Working in DM and Fulfillment

4550 Montgomery Ave. #700
Bethesda, MD 20814
Newsletter covers industry trends.

Government Publications

Federal Trade Commission.   The FTC publishes an array of books and booklets containing regulations and advice for business. Listed below are the sources cited in this book and a few others that relate to direct mail and direct marketing. For copies, contact the FTC, 6th and Pennsylvania Ave. NW, Washington, D.C. 20580 (202) 326-3175. The FTC also has regional offices in Atlanta, Boston, Cleveland, Dallas, Denver, Los Angeles, San Francisco, New York, and Seattle.

Booklets:

   How to Advertise Consumer Credit: Complying with the Law

   A Businessperson's Guide to Federal Warranty Law

   A Business Guide to the Federal Trade Commission's Mail Order Rule

   Guides Concerning Use of Endorsements and Testimonials in Advertising

   Guides for Advertising Allowances and Other Merchandising Payments and Services

   Guide Concerning the Use of the Word "Free" and Similar Representations

   Guides Against Deceptive Pricing

   Guides Against Bait Advertising

   Guides Against Deceptive Advertising of Guarantees

United States Postal Service.   The definitive explanation of postal services and policies is contained in the *Domestic Mail Manual.*
The loose-leaf format publication is updated twice a year and is available for $56 from your local Postal Business Center or you can write to:

Superintendent of Documents
Government Printing Office
710 N. Capitol St. NE
Washington, D.C. 20402-9371

An easier-to-read reference is *Memo to Mailers,* a free monthly newsletter that carries how-to articles, listings of postal rates and classes, and news on the Postal Service's work to automate mail sorting. For a subscription write:

Memo to Mailers
P.O. Box 999
Springfield, VA 22150-9830
or call (800) 238-3150.

Another useful USPS publication is *Third Class Mail Preparation.*
Ask your postal representative for publication 49.

If you plan to market out of the United States, two paperback books published by the USPS and Braddock Communications of Alexandria, VA will be helpful:

Direct Marketing Guide to Canada
International Direct Marketing Guide

Ask for these books at your Postal Business Center or contact the USPS international product management office at (202) 268-2263.

Small Business Administration. The SBA offers a variety of publications to help you start or manage a business. A few of the dozens of titles include, *Simple Break-Even Analysis for Small Stores*, *Pricing Your Product and Services Profitably*, and *Market Overseas with U.S. Government Help*. For information about these and other titles, ask for the Small Business Directory (Form 115A). Write to:

SBA Publications
P.O. Box 30
Denver, CO 80201-0030

Copyright Office. To obtain greatest copyright protection of your advertising you may want to register it with the U.S. Copyright Office. Ask for Form TX and instructions. In order to copyright material in your name that was written by a freelancer, ask the writer to sign an agreement giving you all rights to the material in exchange for the copywriting fee.

Register of Copyrights
Library of Congress
Washington, DC 20559
(202) 707-3000

ORGANIZATIONS

Local direct marketing clubs or associations are great sources of help and information. Clubs are located in many major cities in the United States and around the world. Many publish directories of local direct marketing professionals, freelancers, and service companies. Many also sponsor educational seminars or conferences. Clubs are listed in *Direct Marketing Magazine*, *DMMP*, and the USPS *International Direct Marketing Guide*. You can also contact the national association, listed below.

Direct Marketing Association
6 East 43rd Street
New York, NY 10017-4646
(212) 768-7277

The national association provides educational, legislative, research, and other services to member companies.

SOFTWARE

Below are the names and addresses of software firms mentioned in the text plus a few others. In addition, *Direct Marketing Magazine* occasionally publishes reviews of direct marketing software and *DM News* carries a frequent column by David Raab reviewing new software.

Dydacomp Development Corp.
150 River Road Suite N1
Montville, NJ 07045
(800) 858-3666
Publishers of *Mail Order Manager*.

The Haven Corporation
802 Madison St.
Evanston, IL 60202
(800) 860-0098
Publishers of The Mail Order Wizard, a full-function mail order/direct mail software program.

U.S. West Marketing Resources Group, Inc.
3190 S. Vaughn Way
Aurora, CO 80014
(303) 784-1800
The company markets Sales Edge, a direct mail and data base program for small service and retail firms. The base price is $395 and includes telephone consultation. Ongoing marketing sup-
port and other services are available.

Hallogram Publishing
1532 S. Dawson St.
Aurora, CO 80012
(303) 752-2086
Sells Mighty Mail, a low-cost multifunction mailing list
management program.

Peoplesmith Software
50 Cole Parkway Suite 34
Scituate Harbor, MA 02066
(617) 545-7300
Offers DynaKey, Datalift, and other ingenious list enhancement programs.

Mailer's Software
970 Calle Negocio
San Clemente, CA 92673
(800) 800-6245
This company's catalog, published several times a year, is a valuable marketing resource. It includes not only ZIP code–based software but information on a variety of other computer programs, bar coding, mailing lists, and services such as NCOA processing. Get on this mailing list!

Duns Marketing Service
3 Sylvan Way
Parsippany, NJ 07054-3896
(201) 605-6000
Among its many offerings for the direct marketing industry is Duns Direct Access, a PC-based
list service.

American Business Information
5711 S. 86th Cir.
P.O. Box 27347
Omaha, NE 68127
(402) 593-4500
Suppliers of Business Lists-On-Disc.

BusinessWeek Leadfinder
P.O. Box 518
Montvale, NJ 07645-0518
(800) 545-0411
BusinessWeek Leadfinder is a low-cost diskette-based business data base program compiled by
Database America Companies that lets you select and download prospect lists. Sorts are available
by geography, type of business, and other categories. Prices start at $149.

NCOA Diskette Coding Center
National Customer Support Center
U.S. Postal Service
6060 Primacy Parkway Suite 101
Memphis, TN 38188-0001
This is the address to obtain information on low-cost NCOA list processing for small business.
The USPS forwards your diskettes to FDC, Inc. for processing. For more information call FDC
at (612) 623-3130 or the USPS National Address Information Center (800) 238-3150.

SERVICE FIRMS

List Compilers. Many of the large compilers have regional sales offices in major cities. See your yellow pages for local list companies and local representatives of the national firms. Below are the headquarters of some large firms:

R.L. Polk & Co.
6400 Monroe Blvd.
Taylor, MI 48180

Duns Marketing Services
Div. of Dun & Bradstreet Corp.
3 Sylvan Way
Parsippany, NJ 07054

TRW Target Marketing Services
901 N. International Parkway #191
Richardson, TX 75081

Gale Research Inc.
P.O. Box 33477
Detroit, MI 48232

Database America Companies
100 Paragon Drive
Montvale, NJ 07645-0419

Telemarketing Companies. Firms are listed regularly in *DM News, Direct Marketing Magazine,* and *DMMP.* Also consult your local phone book.

Telematch
6883 Commercial Drive
Springfield, VA 22159
This firm will add phone numbers to the names and addresses on your mailing list.

List Brokers. Brokers are listed in SRDS's *Direct Mail Lists and Data, DMMP,* direct marketing periodicals, and local phone books.

Decoy Service. U.S. Monitor Service
86 Maple Ave.
New York, NY 10956-5092
Salt your house list with this firm's addresses scattered all over the United States and they'll return all mailings that use your list.

LEGAL/REGULATORY UPDATES

Do's and Don'ts of Advertising Copy is a loose-leaf update service covering state and local laws governing advertising. For subscription information contact:

Council of Better Business Bureaus, Inc.
4200 Wilson Boulevard # 800
Arlington, VA 22203
(703) 276-0100

Advertising Compliance Service is a twice-monthly publication providing information on advertising regulations, government and industry restrictions. For prices and information contact:

Greenwood Publishing Group
88 Post Road West
P.O. Box 5007
Westport, CT 06881
(203) 226-3571

REFERENCES

Chapter 1

1. Bob Stone, *Successful Direct Marketing Methods*, fourth edition, Lincolnwood, IL, NTC Business Books, 1988.
2. U.S. Council of Economic Advisers, *Economic Indicators*, Washington, DC, U.S. Government Printing Office, December 1990.
3. "Scan & Win" *Direct Marketing Magazine*, November 1988, p. 95.
4. "Direct Sells ... Or Else" *Adweek*, March 24, 1986, p.34.

Chapter 6

1. *DM News*, November 19, 1990.

Chapter 7

1. Panel Publishers, Inc., a Wolters Kluwer Co. Greenvale, NY.
2. The Economist, New York, NY. Copy written by Ken Scheck.
3. American Heart Association, Orange County Chapter, Ervine CA.
4. The Kiplinger California Letter, Washington, DC.
5. Foundation for Research & Education in Drug Abuse, Inc. Santa Monica, CA.
6. *Bulldog Reporter, an Insider's Report on PR and Media Relations*, Berkeley, CA.
7. Everett & Lloyd, Inc., Los Angeles, CA.
8. TRW Federal Credit Union, Redondo Beach, CA.
9. *Sunset Magazine*, Sunset Publishing Co. Inc., Palo Alto, CA.
10. *Communications Concepts, the Best Ideas in Print for Professional Communicators*, Washington, DC. © Communications Concepts, Inc., 1991. Publisher of newsletters on writing, editing, and publication management topics. P.O. Box 1608, Springfield, VA 22151-0608.
11. AT&T, New York, NY.
12. The Danbury Mint, Norwalk, CT.
13. Michigan Bulb Co., Grand Rapids, MI.

Chapter 9

1. Comfortably Yours®(Catalog), 1990, Maywood, NJ.
2. Owner/President Management School, Harvard Business School, Boston, MA.
3. Foley-Belsaw Institute, Kansas City, MO.

Chapter 10

1. Charles R. McManis, *Unfair Trade Practices*, Second Edition, West Publishing Co., St. Paul, Minn., 1988, p. 362.
2. McManis, p. 390.
3. Earl W. Kintner, *Primer on the Law of Deceptive Practices*, Macmillan, New York, 1978, p. 253.
4. FTC, *Guide Concerning Use of the Word "Free" and Similar Representations*, 1971.
5. Robert J. Posch, Jr. "Copy Headliner Compliance", *Direct Marketing Magazine*, April 1985, p. 143. Reprinted with permission of *Direct Marketing Magazine* (224 Seventh St., Garden City NY 11530-5771 516/764-6700).
6. Drew Kaplan, DAK, Inc. Conoga Park, Calif. 1990.
7. Posch, p. 140.
8. John Lichtenberger, *Advertising Compliance Law: Handbook for Marketing Professionals and Their Counsel*, Quorem Books, New York, 1986. p. 40.

INDEX